# The Common Lisp Condition System

## Beyond Exception Handling with Control Flow Mechanisms

Michał "phoe" Herda

Apress®

*The Common Lisp Condition System: Beyond Exception Handling with Control Flow Mechanisms*

Michał "phoe" Herda
Krakow, Poland

ISBN-13 (pbk): 978-1-4842-6133-0          ISBN-13 (electronic): 978-1-4842-6134-7
https://doi.org/10.1007/978-1-4842-6134-7

Managing Director, Apress Media LLC: Welmoed Spahr
Acquisitions Editor: Steve Anglin
Development Editor: Matthew Moodie
Coordinating Editor: Mark Powers

Cover designed by eStudioCalamar

Cover image by Ricardo Gomez on Unsplash (www.unsplash.com)

Distributed to the book trade worldwide by Apress Media, LLC, 1 New York Plaza, New York, NY 10004, U.S.A. Phone 1-800-SPRINGER, fax (201) 348-4505, e-mail orders-ny@springer-sbm.com, or visit www.springeronline.com. Apress Media, LLC is a California LLC and the sole member (owner) is Springer Science + Business Media Finance Inc (SSBM Finance Inc). SSBM Finance Inc is a **Delaware** corporation.

For information on translations, please e-mail booktranslations@springernature.com; for reprint, paperback, or audio rights, please e-mail bookpermissions@springernature.com.

Apress titles may be purchased in bulk for academic, corporate, or promotional use. eBook versions and licenses are also available for most titles. For more information, reference our Print and eBook Bulk Sales web page at http://www.apress.com/bulk-sales.

Any source code or other supplementary material referenced by the author in this book is available to readers on GitHub via the book's product page, located at www.apress.com/9781484261330. For more detailed information, please visit http://www.apress.com/source-code.

Printed on acid-free paper

# Table of Contents

# About the Author

**Michał "phoe" Herda** is a professional programmer who has contributed to multiple parts of the Common Lisp ecosystem: CL implementations, existing and widely used CL utilities, documentation, and some of the new library ideas that he slowly pushes forward and works on. This book is his first literary work — an attempt to create the tutorial on the condition system which had been missing even all these years after ANSI Common Lisp was standardized.

# About the Technical Reviewers

**Adlai Chandrasekhar** is busy detangling the moral implications of having suffered the cruelly unusual punishment of performing quality control procedures on rocket targeting electronics that did not offer a condition system, despite the operators having studied Common Lisp before enlistment.

**Dave Cooper** is CTO at Genworks International and enjoys spending his time maintaining, extending, and supporting the Genworks GDL Knowledge-Based Engineering System and the Gendl Project which comprises its open source core (all based on Common Lisp language).

**John Cowan's** friends describe him as knowing at least something about almost everything, his enemies as knowing far too much about far too much.

**Vsevolod Domkin**, a.k.a. vseloved, is a Lisp aficionado and professional Common Lisp developer for more than 10 years, who is also a writer (author of the book *Programming Algorithms*) and occasional teacher of the courses on system programming, algorithms, and natural language processing.

**Michael Fiano** is a Common Lisp developer with 12 years of experience, who has made many contributions to the Common Lisp ecosystem, including pngload, and various game development software such as Virality Engine.

**Marco Heisig** is a passionate Lisp hacker, free software advocate, and researcher in the fields of high-performance computing, numerical mathematics, and compiler technology.

**Jerome Onwunalu** is a researcher in the fields of mathematical optimization and fluid flow modeling and is currently using Common Lisp for the development of a large-scale integrated software application.

**Georgiy Tugai** is a professional compiler developer who, having reviewed this book, now bemoans even more often the lack of a proper condition system, or object system for that matter, in the more mainstream languages he uses at work.

# Introduction

This book is intended to be a tutorial for the Common Lisp condition system, teaching its functioning and presenting a range of example uses. It is aimed at beginning and intermediate Lisp programmers, as well as intermediate programmers of other programming languages. This book provides detailed information specifically about the CL condition system and its control flow mechanisms, so it is envisioned as a supplement to already existing material for studying Common Lisp (CL) as a language. The book also contains a description of an example ANSI-conforming implementation of the condition system.

## What is a condition system? Introduction by Kent M. Pitman

There have been many attempts to declare the Lisp family of languages dead, and yet it continues on in many forms. There are many explanations for this, but an obvious one is that it still contains ideas and features that aren't fully appreciated outside the Lisp community, and so it continues as both a refuge and an idea factory.

Gradually, other languages see the light and these important features migrate to other languages. For example, the Lisp community used to be unusual for standing steadfastly by automatic memory management and garbage collection when many said it couldn't be trusted to be efficient or responsive. In the modern world, however, many languages now presume that automatic memory management is normal and natural, as if this had never been a controversy. So times change.

But proper condition handling is something which other languages still have not figured out that they need. Java's `try/catch` and Python's `try/except` have indeed shown that these languages appreciate the importance of representing exceptional situations as objects. However, in adopting these concepts, they have left out restarts—a key piece of the puzzle.

When you raise an exception in Python, or throw one in Java, you are still just performing an immediate and blind transfer of control to the innermost available handler. This leaves out the rich experience that Common Lisp offers to perform actual reasoning about where to return to.

The Common Lisp condition system disconnects the ability to return to a particular place in the program from the necessity to do so and adds the ability to "look before you leap." In other languages, if you create a possible place to return to, that is what will get used. There is no ability to say "If a certain kind of error happens, this might be a good place to return to, but I don't have a strong opinion ahead of time on whether or not it definitely will be the right place."

The Common Lisp condition system distinguishes among three different activities: describing a problem, describing a possible solution, and selecting the right solution for a given problem. In other languages, describing a possible solution is the same as selecting that solution, so the set of things you can describe is necessarily less expansive.

This matters, because in other languages such as Python or Java, by the time your program first notices a problem, it already will have "recovered" from it. The "except" or "catch" part of your "try" statement will have received control. There will have been no intervening time. To invoke the error handling process *is* to transfer control. By the time any further application code is running, a stack unwind already will have happened. The dynamic context of the problem will be gone, and with it, any potential intervening options to resume operation at other points on the stack between the raising of the condition and the handling of an error. Any such opportunities to resume operation will have lost their chance to exist.

"Well, too bad," these languages would say. "If they wanted a chance, they could have handled the error." But the thing is a lot of the business of signaling and handling conditions is about the fact that you only have partial knowledge. The more uncertain information you are forced to supply, the more your system will make bad decisions. For best results, you want to be able to defer decisions until all information is available. Simple-minded exception systems are great if you know exactly how you want to handle things ahead of time. But if you don't know, then what are you to do? Common Lisp provides much better mechanisms for navigating this uncertain space than other languages do.

So in Common Lisp you can say "I got an argument of the wrong type. Moreover, I know what I would do with an argument of the right type, I just don't happen to have one or know how to make one." Or you can say "Not only do I know what to do if I'm given an argument of the right type (even at runtime), but I even know how to store such a value so they won't hit this error over and over again." In other languages, if the program doesn't know this correctly typed value, even if you (the user) do know it at runtime, you're simply stuck.

In Common Lisp, you can specify the restart mechanism separately from the mechanism of choosing among possible restarts. Having this ability means that an outer part of the program can make the choice, or the choice can fall through to a human user to make. Of course, the human user might get tired of answering, but in such a case, they can wrap the program with *advice* that will save them from the need to answer. This is a much more flexible division of responsibility than other languages offer.

# Daydreaming

As programmers, let us daydream for a moment about an ideal system for handling special situations in our code.

Some of us already know the exception handling systems of popular programming languages, such as C++ or Java. When an exception is thrown, it "bubbles up," immediately travelling to the caller of the offending code, or the caller's caller, and so on. Not only is the state of the program destroyed during the process of attempting to find a handler for that exception, but also, if no handler is available, the program will be in no state to continue, since all of its stack will have been unwound (lost). The program will crash with no means of recovering, only in certain scenarios leaving a core dump in its wake.

We could do better than that.

Let us imagine a system where stack unwinding is a choice, not a diktat—a system where, when an exceptional situation is detected, the stack is wound further instead of being immediately unwound. Such a system, at the time of signaling an error, would inspect the program state for all handlers that are applicable to that situation. It would then execute them and let them choose either to repair the program state or to execute some code. Finally, it would transfer control to a known place in the program, and continue execution from there.

Such a system could even use that mechanism for situations which are not traditional errors, but which would nonetheless benefit from being treated in such a way. A program could, at some point during its execution, announce that a given condition has just happened, as well as listing the callbacks suitable for that particular situation.

These callbacks might have been declared completely outside the given piece of code. They might have been passed into it dynamically, also from outside, as applicable to the wider context in which the given code is run. The program could then call all of these callbacks in succession. Or, it could perform additional logic to check if a callback applies to a given situation, and only then call it. Or, it could attempt to call a particular class of callbacks first, before resorting to a less preferable method of recovery.

Our imagined system would also be closer to perfect if an error situation, once it ran out of means of being handled, would not crash the program. Instead, an internal debugger would pop up and allow the programmer to inspect the full state of the program when the error happened, offering them some predefined means of handling the error. It could also allow them to issue arbitrary commands for inspecting, recovering, or even modifying the program's state.

Ideally, we could express such a system in the self-same programming language for which we design it. Even more ideally, we could construct such a system from scratch in that programming language and seamlessly integrate it into the rest of that language, ensuring that its operation will be able to fit well with any particular domain for which a program is meant to work.

The good thing about such a daydream is that you can experience it even outside the world of your daydreams.

This reality is called the Common Lisp condition system. It is the main focus of this book.

# Preface

The Common Lisp condition system has its early roots in PL/I, a programming language designed by IBM in the 1960s. It was promptly adopted in Multics, an operating system from the same time period, as its main programming language. PL/I had an initial condition mechanism whose traits were, among others: separation of condition *signaling* from condition *handling* (in detail: separation of *handler invocation* from *stack unwinding*), the ability to resume an erring computation, the ability to associate a block of data with a signaled condition, and the provision of default handlers for otherwise unhandled conditions. These four ideas ended up inspiring extensions made in the MIT dialect of Lisp Machine Lisp; from there, they have given rise to the contemporary Common Lisp facilities of, respectively, *handlers*, *restarts*, *condition types*, and the *debugger*.

The first book to describe Common Lisp as a dialect was *Common Lisp the Language, First Edition* (also called "CLtL1"), by Guy L. Steele, Scott E. Fahlman, Richard P. Gabriel, David A. Moon, and Daniel L. Weinreb. From there, the standardization work continued, and took two slightly differing branches: one of them came from private work of Guy L. Steele, who described the ongoing standardization work by the X3J13 committee in the book *Common Lisp the Language, Second Edition* (also called "CLtL2"). The other branch, and the final version of the language, was defined in the ANSI document ANSI INCITS 226-1994 and standardized in 1994, giving birth to ANSI Common Lisp as we know it nowadays. (Modern Common Lisp implementations that purport to conform to the ANSI specification also include many CLtL2-only features as language extensions.)

With such a background, the Common Lisp condition system is organized differently than the exception handling mechanisms in other programming languages, such as C++, Java, or Python. Despite being built of ordinary control mechanisms that are also present in other languages, the Common Lisp condition system includes concepts which are glaringly missing from those others. It is as if the exception systems in other languages are in a rush to exit the context of the error immediately and transfer control to a point higher on the call stack, where less contextual information and fewer control options are available.

This difference often creates misunderstanding and confusion about how the CL condition system functions and what are its possible and actual use cases. Knowledge about the internal functionality and utility of all aspects of the condition system is not widely spread. This lack of knowledge, too often, dissuades CL programmers from utilizing the condition system, even in situations where using it would provide clear overall benefit.

The hope of improving this situation is the *raison d'être* of the book whose introduction you are reading right now. *The Common Lisp Condition System* is one more attempt to explain the functionality and utility of Common Lisp conditions, handlers, and restarts, using an approach that is different from former work on the topic. We gratefully acknowledge the many previous authors who have, over the years, used various approaches to explain the Common Lisp condition system to novice and intermediate CL programmers. An incomplete list includes Kent M. Pitman, Peter Seibel, Chaitanya Gupta, Justin Grant, Timmy Jose, Jacek Złydach, and Robin Schroer as well as the collaborative effort behind the Lisp Cookbook; nonetheless, this book takes a fresh and novel approach which we feel is needed and wanted and which will bring a new level of understanding and appreciation to both old-timers and newcomers alike.

Instead of describing the condition system from an outside perspective, we implement the basics of the handler and restart subsystems piecewise from scratch. We take this approach to demonstrate how such subsystems can be bootstrapped from certain key basic language features including dynamic variables and a few simple data structures. We then rewrite these examples to use standard CL functionality to draw parallels between our implementation and the CL-provided tools. In addition, we elaborate on all aspects of the condition system which are defined by the standard, including the lesser-used and not commonly understood ones. At the end, we also propose a few portable extensions to the condition system which augment the tools defined by the ANSI CL standard.

TCLCS is intended to be read in order. Some topics are simplified or given very brief treatment in the earlier chapters, only to be defined, detailed, and expanded upon later in the book. Therefore, it would be unwise to attempt to use this entire book as a reference for the condition system and CL control flow operators. Happily, we have provided such a reference, replete with examples, as an appendix.

In addition, TCLCS is meant to present the basic flow of working with CL as an interactive programming language. We frequently test expressions in the read-eval-print loop (REPL) before defining them as concrete functions. Conversely, we sometimes test concrete functions in the REPL immediately after defining them as well. We also make use of Common Lisp's ability to redefine functions at runtime in order to define function "stubs" that help us test our programs.

The code shown in the first part of this book is published as a Git repository. The code in the second part is adapted from the Portable Condition System repository. The code listings contained in this book are rendered in black-and-white; if the reader prefers syntax highlighting/colorizing, then the code available at the aforementioned links can be viewed and edited in a preferred tool such as Gnu Emacs which performs such highlighting automatically.

TCLCS assumes that you know the basics of the C programming language and some basics of Common Lisp. If you're familiar with neither of these languages, but do know some fundamentals of computer programming, you may still be able to glean the meanings of most of the operations from the text. In case of questions, feel free to throw them at the author via email.

The book is divided into two parts. The first part will construct the basic components of the condition system from scratch, starting from the concept of dynamic variables that makes the condition system possible and then going through the handler and restart subsystems, assertion operators, and other details of a condition system. We will use a storytelling approach in the book to describe the scenarios in which a condition system may prove useful and then write our code.

The second part of the book will use the concepts from the first part to implement an ANSI-compliant condition system from scratch. Reading the first part of the book is not strictly necessary to understand the second; however, the concepts established in the first part should prove useful for someone who has not worked with a condition system before.

# Hall of Fame

*The Common Lisp Condition System* is a work of the Common Lisp community. Without many people who contributed changes, reviews, ideas, and former work, this book would never have come into existence or enjoyed such level of polishing and review.

Thanks to Lonjil, John Cowan, Michael Reis, Aleksandr Treyger, Elias Mårtenson, Adam Piekarczyk, Nisar Ahmad, Robert Strandh, Daniel Kochmański, Michael Fiano, cage, Bike, Nicolas Hafner, Hayley Patton, Grue, Gnuxie, Tom Peoples, Marco Heisig, Georgiy Tugai, Selwyn Simsek, Shubhamkar Ayare, Philipp Marek, Vsevolod Dyomkin, vindarel, François-René Rideau, Jerome Onwunalu, sarna, Travis Sunderland, Jacek

Podkański, Dave Cooper, orbifx, Kent M. Pitman, Peter von Etter, Florian Margaine, and Paul F. Dietz for various remarks, suggestions, reviews, and fixes to the text of this book and to the code of `trivial-custom-debugger` and the Portable Condition System.

Thanks to Kent M. Pitman, Peter Seibel, Paul Graham, David Lamkins, Robin Schroer, Chaitanya Gupta, Justin Grant, Timmy Jose, and Jacek Złydach as well as the Lisp Cookbook contributors for their collective work on evolving, defining, teaching, and writing about the Common Lisp condition system.

Thanks to Vsevolod Dyomkin, Daniel Kochmański, and Georgiy Tugai for providing input about practical examples of using the condition system beyond exception handling.

Thanks to Marco Heisig, Michael Raskin, and Gilbert Baumann for their help with the example implementation of dynamic variables in the C programming language.

Thanks to David A. Moon, Kent M. Pitman, and Bernard S. Greenberg for providing information about the history of the Common Lisp condition system and its predecessors.

Thanks to Alexander Artemenko, Paul M. Rodriguez, ein Strauch, and Chris Bøg for financial support on Patreon and GitHub Sponsors. (If you like what I write, feel free to tip me there yourself.)

Thanks to Nina Palińska for all kinds of personal support during the process of working on the text.

Thanks to you—the reader—for deciding to take a peek at the contents of this book.

# CHAPTER 1

# Basic concepts

Before diving into the depths of the Common Lisp condition system, we will first introduce three programming concepts that collectively form the foundation of the condition system: *dynamic variables, performing non-local transfers of control, and lexical closures*. Understanding these lower-level techniques is important to understanding the functioning of the CL condition system as a higher-level mechanism; therefore, readers who are already proficient with these techniques may consider skipping the relevant sections and continue from the next chapter of the book.

Other programming languages tend to implement some of these concepts in various ways. For completeness, however, this book explains each of these concepts from the very beginning, since utilizing all three of them in combination to form a complete condition system is unique to CL as a language.

## 1.1 Dynamic variables

We will begin with the very feature of CL that makes the handler and restart subsystems possible and in fact easy to implement: dynamic variables. Instead of defining the term "dynamic variable" directly, we will try to convey its meaning through examples instead and only provide the definitions afterward.

## 1.1.1 Dynamic variables in C

Let's start with an example in C—the *lingua franca* of our profession, in a way.

```
int x = 5;

int foo() {
  return x;
}

foo(); // -> 5
```

© Michał "phoe" Herda 2020
M. "phoe" Herda, *The Common Lisp Condition System*, https://doi.org/10.1007/978-1-4842-6134-7_1

In the preceding example, we have a global variable named x, with the function foo returning the value of that variable. The result of calling foo() will be the integer 5.

```
int x = 5;

int bar() {
  return x;
}

int foo() {
  return bar();
}

foo(); // -> 5
```

In the preceding example, we have a global variable named x, with the function bar returning the value of that variable and the function foo calling the function bar. Compared to the previous example, we have added a level of indirection. But the result is still the same: calling foo() still gives us 5.

```
int x = 5;

int bar() {
  return x;
}

int foo() {
  int x = 42;
  return bar();
}

foo(); // -> 5
bar(); // -> 5
```

The preceding example adds one more change: a new variable binding for x is introduced in the body of foo, with a value of 42. That variable is *lexically scoped*, though, meaning that it is only effective within the body of the block in which it is declared. The variable x is not used within the block of function foo; the definition int x = 42; is effectively unused.

```
dynamic_var(int, dynamic_x, 5);

int bar() {
  return dynamic_x;
}

int foo() {
  dynamic_bind(int, dynamic_x, 42) {
    return bar();
  }
}

bar(); // -> 5
foo(); // -> 42
bar(); // -> 5
```

The preceding example adds one more twist: our global variable is now defined via dynamic_var. This means that the scope of this variable is no longer lexical, but *dynamic*; the scope of the variable is not affected by curly braces (or a lack thereof), but by the runtime *environment* in which that variable is accessed.

This modification is enough to cause foo() to return 42, even though calling bar() alone still returns 5!

(The operators dynamic_var and dynamic_bind are not a part of the C standard; in fact, C has no intrinsic notion at all of dynamic variables. We describe a means of adding these operators to the C language in an appendix to this book.)

At runtime, each new binding of a dynamic variable creates a new *environment*, in which the name of that variable (in this case, dynamic_x) is bound to a value (in this case, 5 for the global binding and 42 for the binding in foo()). These environments are always accessed in order, from the last defined one to the first defined one; looking up the value of a dynamic variable consists of going through the environments until we find the first environment (i.e., the most recent one chronologically) that has the binding for that dynamic variable. The value of that binding is then accessed.

(One can notice that x, in this example, has been renamed to dynamic_x. Such a distinction in naming is important. Dynamic variables have different semantics from standard variables and should therefore be visually distinguished from normal, lexically scoped variables.)

If one knows the stack data structure, then one can think of the set of environments as a stack. Variable bindings are pushed onto this stack such that the most recent one is on top. If the system later has need to search that stack for a given variable binding, then it looks from top to bottom (i.e., starting with the most recent) for the first instance of that variable binding. Therefore, in a program without any dynamic variables, the stack of environments is empty:

```
        (nothing here)

------------b-o-t-t-o-m-------------
```

(It therefore would result in an error to attempt to access a dynamic variable named dynamic_x; it is unbound, meaning there is no value whatsoever associated with it!)

But, if we wanted to illustrate the top-level environment from the earlier example with dynamic_x, it would look like this:

```
        --------------------
        |   dynamic_x: 5    |
------------b-o-t-t-o-m-------------
```

There is only one (global) dynamic environment that contains the binding of the variable dynamic_x. If we called the function bar(), which returns the dynamic value of dynamic_x, then the system would access that environment, and it would return 5.

The situation changes, however, if we call foo(), because of the dynamic_bind(int, dynamic_x, 42) binding found there. dynamic_x has been declared dynamic at the top level, which "infects" all future binding of that variable; it means that it becomes a dynamic variable, and its value therefore becomes stored on the environment stack when foo() is called. The situation inside foo(), after *rebinding* the dynamic variable but before calling bar(), looks like this:

```
        --------------------
        |   dynamic_x: 42   |
        --------------------
        |   dynamic_x: 5    |
------------b-o-t-t-o-m-------------
```

When bar() gets called, it returns the value of dynamic_x. The system looks it up in the environment stack, starting from the top. The first environment that contains a binding for dynamic_x is the one with the value 42, which bar() then returns to foo() and which foo() then returns to the original caller.

This stack-like lookup mechanism means that, with this simple change in declaration, calling `bar()` still gives us 5, but calling `foo()` gives us 42 instead of 5!

It also means, indirectly, that dynamic variables give us a way to affect the environment of functions that we execute *dynamically*. "*Dynamically*," in this sense, means "depending on *where* a given function was run from." If we run it from the top level or from a `main()` function that itself has no dynamic bindings, then only the global dynamic bindings shall be in effect; if it gets called from another scope in the code, then it will be called with whatever dynamic bindings this particular scope may have defined *on top of* all the dynamic bindings that have been defined in previous dynamic environments.

The difference between lexical variables and dynamic variables can be summarized in one more way: *a lexical variable cannot be seen outside its textual scope*, while *a dynamic variable cannot be seen outside its runtime scope*. When a dynamic scope ends, the *environment* defined in it is discarded: after runtime control leaves `foo()`, the dynamic environment defined in `foo()` is removed from the environment stack, leaving us in a situation similar to the previous one:

```
--------------------
|   dynamic_x: 5   |
------------b-o-t-t-o-m--------------
```

This dynamic scoping means that if we were to try to call `bar()` again immediately after calling `foo()`, then the dynamic environment created inside `foo()` would not affect the subsequent execution of `bar()`. When `foo()` finishes, it cleans up the dynamic environment that it created, and therefore `bar()` sees, and can access, only the global environment which is remaining.

This operating principle means that the dynamic environment is preserved even in situations with more deeply nested function calls. If we have a function `foo` that calls `bar` that calls `baz` that calls `quux`, and we define a `dynamic_var(int, dynamic_x, 42)` at the top of `foo()`'s body, and then we try to access `dynamic_x` inside `quux`, then the access is going to work. Of course, `bar` and `baz` can introduce their own `dynamic_binds` of `dynamic_x` that are then going to affect the value that `quux` will find; all that is necessary for a dynamic variable access to work *always* is at least one binding for that particular variable, which—in our example implementation in C—is guaranteed to exist.

Nothing prevents us from using multiple dynamic variables either. For simplicity, we will use an environment model in which a single environment frame always holds only one variable-value binding. Let us assume that we have three variables, `dynamic_x` (which is later rebound), `dynamic_y`, and `dynamic_z`. At one point in execution of the program, the environment stack is going to look like the following:

```
      ------------------------------
      | dynamic_z: [2.0, 1.0, 3.0] |
      ------------------------------
      |     dynamic_x: 1238765     |
      ------------------------------
      |     dynamic_y: "Hello"     |
      ------------------------------
      |       dynamic_x: 42        |
------------------b-o-t-t-o-m--------------------
```

Accessing a `dynamic char*` `dynamic_y` will return `"Hello"`, accessing a `dynamic int` `dynamic_x` will return `1238765` (it was rebound once, and the previous value of `42` is ignored), and accessing a `dynamic float` `dynamic_z[3]` will return the vector `[2.0, 1.0, 3.0]`. Note that I mentioned "accessing," which means not just getting the values but *setting* them too. It is possible, for example, to execute the following body of code that sets the values of these variables:

```
{
  dynamic_x = 2000;
  dynamic_y = "World";
  dynamic_z[1] = 123.456;
}
```

The resulting environment is going to look like this:

```
      ---------------------------------
      | dynamic_z: [2.0, 123.456, 3.0] |
      ---------------------------------
      |       dynamic_x: 2000          |
      ---------------------------------
      |       dynamic_y: "World"       |
      ---------------------------------
      |        dynamic_x: 42           |
----------------b-o-t-t-o-m--------------------
```

It is noteworthy that the last environment, containing the original binding for `dynamic_x`, was not affected by the operation of setting. When the system tried to set the value of dynamic_x, it searched for the first environment where dynamic_x was bound from top to bottom and modified that environment only.

One consequence of this principle is that only the most recent binding for each dynamic variable is visible to running code; running code cannot access any environments or bindings defined previously. This approach is useful in case we expect that some code might modify the value of a dynamic variable; for instance, if we want to protect the current value of dynamic_x from modification, then we can define a new binding in the form of dynamic_bind(int, dynamic_x, dynamic_x)—a binding which is then going to be affected by any subsequent dynamic_x = ... setters.

To sum up, there are three parts of syntax related to dynamic variables:

- Defining a variable to be dynamic

- Creating new dynamic bindings

- Accessing (reading and/or writing) the most recent dynamic binding

The only sad thing about dynamic variables in C is that the preceding code that uses dynamic_var and dynamic_bind variables will not compile by default. As mentioned earlier, that code is invalid, due to C having no notion of dynamic variables whatsoever. Therefore, even though these code examples (hopefully!) illustrate the concept of dynamic variables, they will not work out of the box with any known C compiler on planet Earth. However, such notion can be added to C by means of programming the C *preprocessor*, using the technique that we will describe now.

## 1.1.1.1 Implementing dynamic variables in C

All fibbing aside though, it is in fact possible to implement dynamic variables in C and other languages that do not have them in their standard. The technique involves the following steps: save the original value of a variable in a temporary stack-allocated variable, set the variable with the new value, execute user code, and then restore the variable with its original value.

This technique is sometimes used in practice to implement dynamic variables (e.g., in Emacs C code), and it replaces the explicit, separate stack of environments with an *implicit* stack, embedded within the temporary variables that are allocated by the program.

Example:

```
int x = 5;

int bar() {
  return x;
}

int foo() {
  int temp_x = x;  // Save the original value of X
  x = 42;          // Set the new value to X
  int ret = bar(); // Execute user code and save its return value
  x = temp_x;      // Restore the original value of X
  return ret;      // Return the user code's return value
}

foo(); // -> 42
bar(); // -> 5
```

We are binding the dynamic variable by means of creating new lexical variables and temporarily storing the old dynamic values there. The original lexical variable gets overwritten with a new value and then restored when control is leaving that runtime scope.

This approach is messy and prone to errors due to the amount of assignments required; it is, however, possible to hide them by writing macros for the C preprocessor. The reader can consult an appendix to this book for an example implementation of `dynamic_var` and `dynamic_bind` that uses a variant of the preceding technique.

## 1.1.2  Dynamic variables in Common Lisp

In contrast to C, certain languages, notably Common Lisp, do have built-in support for dynamic variables. We will be restricting our discussion to Common Lisp (CL) for the rest of the book. CL is an ANSI-standardized dialect of the Lisp programming language that supports various programming paradigms, including procedural, functional, object-oriented, and declarative paradigms. CL has dynamic scoping as part of its ANSI standard, and it should be possible to execute all of the examples here in any standard-conforming CL implementation. This happy fact frees us from the need to depend on any particular CL implementation or compiler.

Let us begin with a simple example showing how Lisp variables work in general. Contrary to C, it is possible in Lisp to define a function that has access to lexical variables which themselves are defined outside that function definition, substantially reducing the need for global variables in a program (at least non-dynamic ones).

```
(let ((x 5))
  (defun foo ()
    x))

(foo) ; -> 5
```

In the preceding example, we have a lexical variable named x, with the function foo returning the value of that variable. Exactly as in the related C example, the result of calling foo will be 5.

```
(let ((x 5))
  (defun bar ()
    x)
  (defun foo ()
    (bar)))

(foo) ; -> 5
```

After adding a level of indirection to accessing the variable, this example still behaves the same way as in C.

```
(let ((x 5))
  (defun bar ()
    x)
  (defun foo ()
    (let ((x 42))
      (bar)))
  (defun quux ()
    (let ((x 42))
      x)))

(foo) ; -> 5
(quux) ; -> 42
```

If we experiment with introducing new lexically scoped variables in Lisp, the result will still be consistent with what C produces: calling (foo) gives us 5 (the variable definition (let ((x 42)) ...) inside the body of foo going effectively unused), and calling (quux) gives us the shadowing value 42.

```
(defvar *x* 5)

(defun bar ()
  *x*)

(defun foo ()
  (let ((*x* 42))
    (bar)))

(foo) ; -> 42
(bar) ; -> 5
```

The preceding example changes two things. First, the name of our variable is now modified from x to *x*—the "earmuff notation" which in CL is the conventional notation for dynamic variables. Second, the variable we define is now global, as specified via defvar.

(It is possible to neglect the earmuff notation and do things like (defvar x 5), since the earmuffs themselves are just a part of the symbol's name and their use is not mandated by any official standard. Earmuffs were introduced as a convention for separating global dynamic variables clearly from other symbols, since unintentionally rebinding a dynamic variable might—and most often will—affect code that executes deeper in the stack in unexpected, undesired ways.)

The environment stack works in the same way as in the C example: calling (bar) gives us the original, top-level value 5, but calling (foo) will give us the rebound value 42.

In Common Lisp, it is additionally possible to refer to a dynamic variable *locally*, instead of using a variable that is globally special. If we were to do that, then the following would be an incorrect way of doing that:

```
;;; (defvar *y* 5) ; commented out, not evaluated

(defun bar ()
  *y*) ; this will not work

(defun foo ()
  (let ((*y* 42))
    (declare (special *y*))
    (bar)))
```

Inside foo, we locally declare the variable *y* to be *special*, which is Common Lisp's notation for declaring that *y* denotes a dynamic variable in this context. However, we have not done the same in the body of bar.

Because of that omission, the compiler is free to treat *y* inside the body of bar as an undefined variable and to produce a warning:

```
; in: DEFUN BAR
;      (BLOCK BAR *Y*)
;
; caught WARNING:
;   undefined variable: COMMON-LISP-USER::*Y*
```

(Note that we no longer use the symbol *x* as the variable name, since the previous example proclaimed it to name a global dynamic variable. If we wanted to "undo" that fact and be able to proclaim *x* as dynamic locally, we would need to (unintern '*x*) in order to remove the symbol *x*, along with that global proclamation, from the package in which we are currently operating. Removing the symbol will not affect the Lisp system negatively; it will be re-created the next time we use it, as soon as the reader subsystem reads it.)

The correct version is:

```
;;; (defvar *y* 5) ; commented out, not evaluated

(defun bar ()
  (declare (special *y*))
  *y*)
(defun foo ()
  (let ((*y* 42))
    (declare (special *y*))
    (bar)))

(foo) ; -> 42
```

Similarly, calling (bar) directly (e.g., from the top level) is an error, since the variable *y* does not have a global dynamic binding.

An environment stack with multiple dynamic variables (named *x*, *y*, and *z* in Lisp) may look like the following:

```
        ---------------------------------
        |     *z*: #(2.0 1.0 3.0)     |
        ---------------------------------
        |       *x*: 1238765          |
        ---------------------------------
        |       *y*: "Hello"          |
        ---------------------------------
        |         *x*: 42             |
-----------------b-o-t-t-o-m---------------------
```

11

We may set the values of the three by using setf, the universal Common Lisp assignment operator:

```
(locally (declare (special *x* *y* *z*))
  (setf *x* 2000)
  (setf *y* "World")
  (setf (aref *z* 1) 123.456))
```

and thereby produce the following environment:

```
---------------------------------
|   *z*: #(2.0 123.456 3.0)      |
---------------------------------
|            *x*: 2000           |
---------------------------------
|           *y*: "World"         |
---------------------------------
|            *x*: 42             |
---------------b-o-t-t-o-m--------------------
```

To summarize, the actual syntax for working with dynamic variables is threefold. We need a means of:

- Declaring that a symbol denotes a dynamic variable

- Creating new dynamic bindings between a symbol and a value

- Setting the topmost visible binding

In Common Lisp, the first is achieved via declare special (if we want to work with a variable proclaimed locally dynamic) or via defvar (which *proclaims* the variable to be globally special); the second is achieved via let, among other operators; the third is achievable with Common Lisp's general setting mechanism, named setf which can set the value of any place designator.

While defvar will not change the value of a variable if it's already set, the alternative defparameter will indeed change the value if it's already set. For clarity, we will stick with defvar in this tutorial; a curious reader may consult the related chapter in *Practical Common Lisp* for more details.

# 1.1.3  Alternatives in other languages

## 1.1.3.1  Scheme

Instead of dynamic variables, Scheme uses a first-class object called a *parameter*, which can be held in a global or local variable or in a data structure. Parameter objects are created and initialized with the `make-parameter` procedure. The global dynamic environment is updated to associate the parameter object to the value passed to `make-parameter`.

A parameter object behaves like a procedure which accepts zero or one argument. If called with zero arguments, it returns the value; if called with one argument, the value is mutated. (Some Schemes do not support the one-argument case.)

The `parametrize` has the same syntax as `let`, except where `let` takes a local variable, `parameterize` takes an expression whose value is a parameter object. Each specified parameter object is bound to the associated value for the dynamic extent of the `parameterize` form. As in `let`, the order of evaluation is unspecified, and the new bindings are only visible in the body of the `parameterize` special form.

If all parameters are assigned permanently to global variables, parameter objects are equal in power to dynamic variables. However, related parameters can be stored in a list or vector and passed around before being individually parameterized, which is not possible with dynamic variables.

## 1.1.3.2  Design patterns

The fact that CL has dynamic variables trivializes certain constructions that are decidedly non-trivial in other programming languages and therefore require *design patterns* to achieve the same goal.

In other programming languages, such as Java, C#, C++, or Rust, modifying an object's behavior is often done through an *interface*. An *interface object* defines a set of functions that must be *implemented* by another object called the *implementation object* of the interface. An interface is simply a layer of behavioral abstraction, and implementations of such an interface (objects or classes fulfilling the interface requirements) are behavioral specializations. These abstract objects (interfaces in Java and C#, abstract classes in C++, and traits in Rust) often follow the *dependency injection* pattern, which is frequently used in that family of programming languages.

Some languages, most prominently Java, make heavy use of a design pattern known as *context and dependency injection.* It is a pattern in which some dependencies of an object are provided from outside, as opposed to being hard-coded internally; the information regarding which dependencies to provide to which objects may additionally depend upon a context object, which must also be provided from outside.

Still other programming languages, mostly the ones oriented toward functional programming, use a concept known as the *environment monad* (also known as the *reader monad*), an object which holds a shared environment as a part of its internal state, allowing subsequent computations to read that state and return new instances of the monad which contain new values of the environment.

In Common Lisp, it is not necessary to instantiate or refer to any separate context object nor enclose the environment in an object, because contextual information is available by means of dynamic variables, which can be accessed and rebound as appropriate. New means of passing contextual information can be provided by defining new dynamic variables, and utilizing this new information channel does not require creating or altering any existing abstractions. While this mechanism could be considered to be a form of dependency injection, it does not require support from a language framework of any sort (such as Java EE's CDI); rather, it is built into the standard language.

## 1.2  Non-local transfers of control

The mechanism of dynamic binding is used to dynamically provide different pieces of *data* at different points within the program execution. That "data" may also include references to pieces of code that one can execute; this capability is one of the needed components for building a working condition system. A further necessity is that these additional pieces of code must be able to alter the *control flow* of a running program.

The control flow of the program is understood as an order in which the individual instructions within a program are executed. In many programming languages which permit linear or structured programming paradigms, that order is linear.

One way to express the linear-flow programming style in CL is with the `progn` operator, which evaluates its subforms in order, returning the values returned by the last subform. (It is common to encounter a so-called *implicit progn* in the bodies of many other CL operators as well, meaning that the subforms within such a body will be evaluated as if they were wrapped in a progn.) For example, evaluating the following form will print five lines to the standard output and then return the value 42:

```
CL-USER> (progn
           (format t ";; Foo~%")
           (format t ";; Bar~%")
           (format t ";; Baz~%")
           (format t ";; Quux~%")
           (format t ";; Frob~%")
           42)
;; Foo
;; Bar
;; Baz
;; Quux
;; Frob
42
```

This linear-flow programming paradigm may be customized by separating some code forms into logical blocks. These blocks, depending on the programming language, may be named *routines subroutines*, *procedures*, *methods*, or *functions*. (In Common Lisp, we use the term "function"; the term "method" is reserved for the object-oriented facilities of Lisp, which we will introduce later in the book.) In a structured programming paradigm, a standard flow of control may be understood as a tree data structure, where the standard control flow uses inorder tree traversal.

```
CL-USER> (defun print-some-stuff ()
           (format t ";; Bar~%")
           (format t ";; Baz~%")
           (format t ";; Quux~%"))
PRINT-SOME-STUFF

CL-USER> (progn
           (format t ";; Foo~%")
           (print-some-stuff)
           (format t ";; Frob~%")
           42)
;; Foo
;; Bar
;; Baz
;; Quux
;; Frob
42
```

In such a context, a *non-local transfer of control* (or *non-local exit*) is an instance where the execution flow of the program no longer follows this standard tree traversal. The execution departs from standard flow and picks up again at a different, well-established point of the program. This may cause some operations within the program to be reordered, skipped, and/or repeated; as an additional effect of such a jump, a part of the program's execution state may also be undone before the actual transfer of control happens.

## 1.2.1 TAGBODY and GO

Perhaps the most (in)famous idea of implementing a non-local exit is the *go-to* instruction, which is meant to cause the control flow to jump immediately to another point in the program. Its infamy comes from the fact that the control flow of code that uses go-to instructions is typically hard to visualize, compute, and understand; go-to is, nonetheless, still the most prevalent means of transferring control in the world. Every modern processor utilizes the hardware equivalent of a go-to, called a *jump instruction*, possibly thousands or millions of times every second. It can be said that this construct is the foundation upon which all other means of transferring control may—and, in many people's opinions, *should*—be built.

CL provides the possibility to use the go-to style of transferring control by means of a pair of special operators, named tagbody and go. The tagbody operator establishes a *lexical scope* similar to the one defined by progn, in which execution progresses linearly. However, it also makes it possible to specify *go tags*: special locations in the code to which it is possible to transfer control by using the go special operator.

By using tagbody and go, it's possible, for example, to skip some operations within a block of code.

```
CL-USER> (tagbody
           (format t ";; Foo~%")
           (go :there)
           (format t ";; Bar~%")
           (format t ";; Baz~%")
           (format t ";; Quux~%")
         :there
           (format t ";; Frob~%"))
;; Foo
;; Frob
NIL
```

Using these operators, it is also possible to translate a certain famous BASIC program (perhaps the most famous one, even!) into Lisp.

```
10 PRINT "HELLO WORLD!";
20 GOTO 10;
RUN;

CL-USER> (tagbody
          10 (format t ";; Hello, world!~%")
          20 (go 10))
;; Hello, world!
;; Hello, world!
;; Hello, world!
;; Hello, world!
;; Hello, world!
;; Hello, world!
;; Hello, world!
;; Hello, world!
;; ...
```

The transfers of control with go may be conditional—it is possible to specify whether or not the jump will occur, based on whether or not a certain expression is true or false. A practical example is using tagbody with go to achieve *iteration*, in which we evaluate a body of code in a loop while assigning new values to some iteration variables, only finishing when some expression no longer holds true:

```
CL-USER> (let ((x 0))
          (tagbody
           :loop
             (unless (< x 5) (go :exit))
             (setf x (+ x 1))
             (format t ";; ~A~%" x)
             (go :loop)
           :exit))
;; 1
;; 2
;; 3
;; 4
;; 5
NIL
```

(The above format call uses the value of the argument passed to it, x, to populate the ~A format *directive* in the format *control string* ";; ~A~%". The resultant string will end up having the ~A replaced with that value, printed in an aesthetic way. The directive ~% prints a newline into the string. The reader should be advised that this book will use more advanced format control strings throughout the rest of the text; hence if they are unfamiliar with format, they may at some point want to skim the chapter "A Few FORMAT Recipes" of *Practical Common Lisp* by Peter Seibel.)

The preceding example is equivalent to a higher-level loop form—(loop for x from 1 to 5 do (format t ";; ~A~%" x)). In fact, the loop macro usually expands into code which uses tagbody and go internally in order to perform actual, low-level iteration. (For clarity, we use the explicit (setf x (+ x 1)) instead of the more idiomatic equivalents (setf x (1+ x)) or (incf x).)

## 1.2.2  BLOCK and RETURN-FROM/RETURN

The operators tagbody and go offer an environment where it is possible to perform arbitrary linear-flow programming and communicate with the outside world via side effects. However, in some cases, a different means of transferring control is desirable, in which we may want a particular value to be returned from a given block of code immediately. This form of transfer of control is especially common within nested iteration forms, in which we might want to "break out" of a given loop, stopping its further iteration. The CL special operators implementing this control-passing style are named block and return-from.

The operator block establishes a *block*, which is a body of code from which one can return a value. These blocks are named, which makes it possible to distinguish multiple nested blocks at compilation time and to be able to choose from which block to return a value.

```
CL-USER> (block foo
           (+ 100
             (block bar
               (return-from foo 42))))
42

CL-USER> (block foo
           (+ 100
             (block bar
               (return-from bar 42))))
142
```

All defined functions automatically establish blocks named after themselves, which allows the programmer to return-from them.

```
CL-USER> (defun foo (x)
           (when (= 24 x)
             (return-from foo 42))
           :try-again)
FOO

CL-USER> (foo 0)
:TRY-AGAIN

CL-USER> (foo 24)
42
```

return is shorthand for return-from nil; certain CL operators, especially the ones related to iteration, automatically establish nil-named blocks, enabling the programmer to use the return operator inside them.

```
CL-USER> (block nil
           (tagbody
            :loop
              (return 42)
              (go :loop)))
42
```

Using a return-from (or a shorthand return), it is therefore possible, for example, to escape an ongoing loop, even an otherwise infinite one. Since tagbody normally returns nil, in practice tagbody is often combined with a block from which one may return-from in order effectively to return a non-nil value from the tagbody. We may use this technique to perform iterations that do not contain side effects and instead communicate with the outside world purely via the returned value.

```
CL-USER> (block :return
           (let ((result '())
                 (x 0))
             (tagbody
              :loop
                (unless (< x 5) (go :exit))
                (setf x (+ x 1))
                (push x result)
                (go :loop)
```

```
          :exit
            (return-from :return
              (nreverse result)))))
(1 2 3 4 5)
```

(The preceding style of programming, in which the imperative parts are well-contained behind interfaces free of any side effects, is sometimes called "mostly functional" style and can be observed often in typical Lisp code.)

## 1.2.3  CATCH and THROW

The operators `tagbody` and `block` allow establishing the means of transferring control within lexical scope, which is useful for code written as a single block of code, but it makes it non-trivial to transfer control between function boundaries. (We will elaborate on the aforementioned non-triviality in the next subchapter.) In addition, it is very hard to dynamically (meaning, in dynamic scope, or at runtime) specify points of transferring control or to dynamically specify where we want to transfer control to. Common Lisp has a solution to these two problems in form of special operators `catch` and `throw`. They are different from the throw/catch operators commonly found in languages such as C++ or Java, since they are not directly related to any kind of exceptions, errors, or even the condition system in general.

In Lisp, `throw` and `catch` are analogous to `go` and `tagbody` or `return-from` and `block`—the operators that allow non-local transfers of control within lexical scope. The first difference from that analogy is that `catch` and `throw` work in *dynamic* scope, not in lexical one. By using them, it is therefore possible to break the function boundary that was hard to cross via the previous control flow operators.

```
CL-USER> (defun foo ()
           (throw :somewhere 42))
FOO

CL-USER> (defun bar ()
           (catch :somewhere
             (foo)))
BAR

CL-USER> (bar)
42
```

Second, the catch tags are *evaluated*, which means that it is possible to pass them as arguments.

```
CL-USER> (defun foo (catch-tag)
           (throw catch-tag 42))
FOO

CL-USER> (defun bar ()
            (catch :somewhere
              (foo :somewhere)))
BAR

CL-USER> (bar)
42
```

To sum up the differences, they are threefold:

- `throw` and `catch` work in dynamic scope, not in lexical one.

- The tags used by `catch` and `throw` are evaluated.

- `throw` requires two arguments: the `catch` tag and a value that is then returned from the `catch` form, whereas the value argument to `return-from` and `return` is optional and defaults to `nil`.

# 1.3  Lexical closures

The third and final building block of our condition system consists of *lexical closures*. A closure is a function which accesses some state that is bound outside its body. Such state might be a lexical variable, a function, or some other elements of the lexical environment existing at the point of creating such a function; it is said that such a function *closes over* that data.

A typical simple pattern using a closure is a "`let` over `lambda`": an anonymous function which closes over a variable. In the following example, we bind a new lexical variable named x which is then closed over by a `lambda`. The resulting closure becomes the value of the global variable *counter*.

```
CL-USER> (defvar *counter*
           (let ((x 0))
             (lambda () (incf x) x)))
*COUNTER*
```

This closure can then be called in the same manner as any other function. When it is called, its lambda function modifies and returns the value of x over which it has closed.

```
CL-USER> (funcall *counter*)
1

CL-USER> (funcall *counter*)
2

CL-USER> (funcall *counter*)
3
```

From this behavior, we can induce that this lambda function has access to a certain *implicit state*. Where the lexical variable x has otherwise gone out of scope, we can still access that variable via calling the closure which itself still has access to it—and indeed, we cannot access the variable in any other portable way.

Variables are not the only category of data that can be closed over. A function can also close over another lexically defined function:

```
CL-USER> (defvar *answer*
           (flet ((foo () 42))
             (lambda () (funcall #'foo))))
*ANSWER*

CL-USER> (funcall *answer*)
42
```

And, perhaps surprisingly, it can even close over a tagbody tag or a block name:

```
CL-USER> (defun call-a-function (function)
           (funcall function))
CALL-A-FUNCTION

CL-USER> (block foo
           (call-a-function (lambda () (return-from foo 42))))
42

CL-USER> (tagbody
             (call-a-function (lambda () (go :true)))
           :false
             (print :true)
             (go :exit)
           :true
```

```
      (print :true)
      (go :exit)
   :exit)
```

```
:TRUE
NIL
```

We construct functions that close over the `block` name and the `tagbody` tag and then pass these functions as arguments to the function `call-a-function`. By using this technique, we are giving ourselves the power to perform transfers of control over boundaries of lexical scope. While any `go` and `return-from` operators must be used within the lexical scope of their respective matching `tagbody` and `block` operators, any closure which closes over a `tagbody` tag or a `block` name may nonetheless be passed as an argument to other functions, crossing said boundary. This technique shows up extensively in most implementations of the condition system, including the one implemented by us in the last part of the book.

It is not easy to perform the equivalent of this in other programming languages. To emulate this technique in a programming language which does not support calling `go` or `return-from` from outside its immediate lexical scope, the programmer would need, for example, to set up unique exception classes within the outer scope, to which to throw the exception. The outer scope would also need to catch the exception and return the value associated with that exception explicitly and rethrow it if required.

(Due to the dynamic nature of `catch` and `throw`, it is not required to close over `catch` tags in order to be able to `throw` to them. The tags are evaluated in both `catch` and `throw`, which makes it possible to pass those tags as arguments to functions which establish new `catch` bindings and which utilize `throw`.)

# CHAPTER 2

# Introducing the condition system

In the previous chapter, we described three programming concepts which we will now start to utilize to describe and build the components of our condition system. We will apply these concepts to a simple code example that we will extend over time, some of which we'll tell in the form of the story of characters named Tom, Kate, and Mark.

Let's meet Tom.

## 2.1 A simple system of hooks

Once upon a time, there was a sociable young lad named Tom. Tom liked to meet his friends, classmates, sometimes his family, and healthcare providers in person, but one fine spring season, there was a nasty worldwide pathogen going around and folks were keeping physical distance from each other. So Tom chose to do his socializing and health consultations by telephone and via the online computer game Counter-Strike. Let's visit Tom during this time.

Here we are with Tom. Tom tends to call various people often and for various purposes. He tends to do various things before calling them, such as launching the Counter-Strike game on his computer when calling some of his schoolmates who also play that game, flipping a coin before calling his parents to see if he should actually call them, maybe calling his girlfriend two times in a row, and so on. He does not always want to perform all of these everyday tasks, though; sometimes, for example, on holidays, he wants to call all of them (except his ex-girlfriend) and wish them happy holidays.

© Michał "phoe" Herda 2020
M. "phoe" Herda, *The Common Lisp Condition System*, https://doi.org/10.1007/978-1-4842-6134-7_2

From a programming point of view, we could express this problem in the following way. We have a group of people that we could express as a list of objects. Let's describe each person as a set of Lisp keywords that describe the relationship of a given person to Tom.

```
(defvar *phonebook*
  '((:mom :parent)
    (:dad :parent)
    (:alice :classmate :csgo :homework)
    (:bob :classmate :homework)
    (:catherine :classmate :ex)
    (:dorothy :classmate :girlfriend :csgo)
    (:eric :classmate :homework)
    (:dentist)))
```

(For brevity, we will refer to Counter-Strike: Global Offensive in our code as csgo.)

Let us assume that each time Tom wants to make calls, he goes through the whole phonebook. Programmatically, we could express this procedure as:

```
(defun call-person (person)
  (format t ";; Calling ~A.~%" (first person)))

(defun call-people ()
  (dolist (person *phonebook*)
    (call-person person)))
```

An example execution of that function looks like the following:

```
CL-USER> (call-people)
;; Calling MOM.
;; Calling DAD.
;; Calling ALICE.
;; Calling BOB.
;; Calling CATHERINE.
;; Calling DOROTHY.
;; Calling ERIC.
;; Calling DENTIST.
NIL
```

Plainly, this method of calling everyone works. However, we also want to account for situations in which he wants to do something else before calling certain people. What kind of "something"? That depends on Tom's current situation, and we are unable to define each situation ahead of time clearly enough to encode all the possibilities into the call-people function itself. We'd like to give that responsibility to the caller of call-people. To empower the caller to add this extra information when it invokes call-people, we can use a technique called hooking.

## 2.1.1  Hook #1: Launching Counter-Strike

Let us use an example where we recall that Tom is a Counter-Strike player. Just in case someone else wants to have a quick match, he wants to launch Counter-Strike before calling any :csgo people. In code, it could be expressed as a hook function that will be executed for each person that Tom is about to call. That function will check whether the person is a Counter-Strike player or not and will execute some code based on the result of that check.

This approach needs us to define a variable that tells us whether or not Tom has already launched Counter-Strike. Once Tom is about to call a CSGO player, he will launch Counter-Strike, and that variable will be set to true.

```
(defvar *csgo-launched-p* nil)
```

This approach will work well, but only once: we also need some means of turning Counter-Strike back off. In our model, Counter-Strike will always be turned off in the beginning, so we will set *csgo-launched-p* to nil in the beginning of the function call-people.

```
(defun call-people ()
  (setf *csgo-launched-p* nil)
  (dolist (person *phonebook*)
    (call-person person)))
```

Now we can focus on the hook itself. For example, such a hook could be represented in code as:

```
(lambda (person)
  (when (member :csgo person)
    (unless *csgo-launched-p*
      (format t ";; Launching Counter Strike for ~A.~%" (first person))
      (setf *csgo-launched-p* t))))
```

We would like the call site of the function (call-people) to remain unchanged; the function must still be called with zero arguments. Therefore, we need to pass the data about the currently present hooks into that function through other means—in our case, we will do it via a dynamic variable.

Let us define the special variable *hooks* with a default value of an empty list, representing the default case of no special situations.

```
(defvar *hooks* '())
```

We will use *hooks* in the following way: if we bind the hook we have created earlier to the value of *hooks* around the call of (call-people), it means that we want to launch Counter-Strike before calling any people who play Counter-Strike.

```
(let ((*hooks*
        (list
          (lambda (person)
            (when (member :csgo person)
              (unless *csgo-launched-p*
                (format t ";; Launching Counter Strike for ~A.~%" (first person))
                (setf *csgo-launched-p* t)))))))
  (call-people))
```

Obviously, calling it like that has no effect at the moment, since call-people does not yet refer to the value of *hooks* in any way. Let us change that and re-implement the function to take our *hooks* into account:

```
(defun call-people ()
  (setf *csgo-launched-p* nil)
  (dolist (person *phonebook*)
    (dolist (hook *hooks*)
      (funcall hook person))
    (call-person person)))
```

Let us now go ahead try to evaluate the previous form:

```
CL-USER> (let ((*hooks*
                (list
                  (lambda (person)
                    (when (member :csgo person)
                      (unless *csgo-launched-p*
```

```
                   (format t ";; Launching Counter Strike for ~A.~%" (first person))
                   (setf *csgo-launched-p* t)))))))
             (call-people))
;; Calling MOM.
;; Calling DAD.
;; Launching Counter Strike for ALICE.
;; Calling ALICE.
;; Calling BOB.
;; Calling CATHERINE.
;; Calling DOROTHY.
;; Calling ERIC.
;; Calling DENTIST.
NIL
```

We can see that before we called the first person marked with :csgo, we had launched Counter-Strike—exactly the behavior we wanted. Doing it with a lambda expression can become unwieldy, however; the body of each function is present in each invocation of (call-people). In order to avoid verbosity, we can define the function with a name and then use that name to refer to the function in the list of hooks.

```
(defun ensure-csgo-launched (person)
  (when (member :csgo person)
    (unless *csgo-launched-p*
      (format t ";; Launching Counter Strike for ~A.~%" (first person))
      (setf *csgo-launched-p* t))))

CL-USER> (let ((*hooks* (list #'ensure-csgo-launched)))
           (call-people))
;; Calling MOM.
;; Calling DAD.
;; Launching Counter Strike for ALICE.
;; Calling ALICE.
;; Calling BOB.
;; Calling CATHERINE.
;; Calling DOROTHY.
;; Calling ERIC.
;; Calling DENTIST.
NIL
```

## 2.1.1.1 Equivalent examples

One may note at this point that the preceding example could be achieved without using dynamic variables. One way to do so would be to write all of the preceding code in fully local lexical style by using *closures*. In the following example, the local function ensure-csgo-launched *closes over* the local lexical variable csgo-launched-p and call-people over phonebook.

```
(let ((csgo-launched-p nil)
      (phonebook '((:mom :parent)
                   (:dad :parent)
                   (:alice :classmate :csgo :homework)
                   (:bob :classmate :homework)
                   (:catherine :classmate :ex)
                   (:dorothy :classmate :girlfriend :csgo)
                   (:eric :classmate :homework)
                   (:dentist))))
  (labels ((ensure-csgo-launched (person)
             (when (member :csgo person)
               (unless csgo-launched-p
                 (format t ";; Launching Counter Strike for ~A.~%" (first person))
                 (setf csgo-launched-p t))))
           (call-person (person)
             (format t ";; Calling ~A.~%" (first person)))
           (call-people (hooks)
             (setf csgo-launched-p nil)
             (dolist (person phonebook)
               (dolist (hook hooks)
                 (funcall hook person))
               (call-person person))))
    (call-people (list #'ensure-csgo-launched))))
```

One issue with the preceding code is that the functions are only available locally; they are gone once they go out of scope. A solution for that is to define global functions with defun instead of using labels to define local ones:

```
(let ((csgo-launched-p nil)
      (phonebook '((:mom :parent)
                   (:dad :parent)
                   (:alice :classmate :csgo :homework)
                   (:bob :classmate :homework)
```

```
                    (:catherine :classmate :ex)
                    (:dorothy :classmate :girlfriend :csgo)
                    (:eric :classmate :homework)
                    (:dentist))))
  (defun ensure-csgo-launched (person)
    (when (member :csgo person)
      (unless csgo-launched-p
        (format t ";; Launching Counter Strike for ~A.~%" (first person))
        (setf csgo-launched-p t))))
  (defun call-person (person)
    (format t ";; Calling ~A.~%" (first person)))
  (defun call-people (hooks)
    (setf csgo-launched-p nil)
    (dolist (person phonebook)
      (dolist (hook hooks)
        (funcall hook person))
      (call-person person))))
```

```
(call-people (list #'ensure-csgo-launched))
```

One more issue with such code is that it is tightly coupled and therefore hard to extend. The phonebook is a local lexical variable, which means that it is impossible to access it from outside its scope—for example, we cannot add another function which accesses the phonebook without adding it to, and reevaluating, the whole preceding form.

We may mitigate this issue using one more technique: while we will define a global dynamic variable, we will not access or rebind it anywhere in our code, treating it as a global and ignoring its dynamic nature. We will instead pass data explicitly via function arguments.

```
(defvar *csgo-launched-p* nil)
```

```
(defvar *phonebook*
  '((:mom :parent)
    (:dad :parent)
    (:alice :classmate :csgo :homework)
    (:bob :classmate :homework)
    (:catherine :classmate :ex)
    (:dorothy :classmate :girlfriend :csgo)
    (:eric :classmate :homework)
    (:dentist)))
```

```
(defun ensure-csgo-launched (person csgo-launched-p)
  (when (member :csgo person)
    (unless csgo-launched-p
      (format t ";; Launching Counter Strike for ~A.~%" (first person))
      t)))

(defun call-person (person)
  (format t ";; Calling ~A.~%" (first person)))

(defun call-people (hooks phonebook csgo-launched-p)
  (setf csgo-launched-p nil)
  (dolist (person phonebook)
    (dolist (hook hooks)
      (setf csgo-launched-p (funcall hook person csgo-launched-p)))
    (call-person person)))

(call-people (list #'ensure-csgo-launched) *phonebook* *csgo-launched-p*)
```

This approach works, but it has greatly complicated our code and made it burdensome to maintain. First of all, our functions now need to accept new arguments that are explicitly passed to them. In addition, our code is still highly coupled: our hooks are now called with the csgo-launched-p variable passed in by call-people, and that same variable in call-people is set by the return value of the hook function. This new interdependence, in turn, means that our hook system has become effectively impossible to extend—adding a new hook that depends on some external state requires us to modify the function that calls the hooks, which defeats the whole purpose of having hooks in the first place.

In this programming style, what we previously could achieve via adding a new dynamic variable now requires modifying multiple functions and their lambda lists in order to pass the new parameters around, exactly the problem that dynamic variables are meant to solve. Dynamic variables provide one more channel for providing state to code that executes within some dynamic context.

In summary, everything that can be done using dynamic variables can also in principle be done with either creating closures or adding yet another function argument; whether it is worth it to solve it that way is left as a question for the reader.

# 2.1.2  Hook #2: Only call Counter-Strike players

In the next example, in addition to launching Counter-Strike before calling the first CSGO-playing person, we would like *only* to call Counter-Strike-playing people and not call any other ones. We will need some logic that will *prevent* a person from being called, in other words, logic that will prevent execution of the (call-person person) form inside the body of call-people. We will also want the prevention to occur only on a per-person basis; we do not want to cease calling people altogether if we happen to encounter one person that we do not want to call.

First of all, we will modify the function call-people once more, this time to add logic that prevents a person from being called. We will use a pair of operators named throw and catch for capturing that logic. Our next modification of the function call-people will look like this:

```
(defun call-people ()
  (setf *csgo-launched-p* nil)
  (dolist (person *phonebook*)
    (catch :do-not-call
      (dolist (hook *hooks*)
        (funcall hook person))
      (call-person person))))
```

We have additionally wrapped the forms within the dolist (person *phonebook*) in a catch form, with the *catch tag* being the symbol :do-not-call. Every throw form that throws a value to the catch tag :do-not-call within the dynamic scope of this block will transfer control to the end of that block. In our example, it means that if the hook called by (funcall hook person) throws anything to the catch tag :do-not-call, then execution of any remaining hooks stops, and the (call-person person) form is not executed.

This modification allows us to add a second hook. For people who are *not* playing Counter-Strike, we would like to avoid making any call at all.

```
(defun skip-non-csgo-people (person)
  (unless (member :csgo person)
    (format t ";; Nope, not calling ~A.~%" (first person))
    (throw :do-not-call nil)))

CL-USER> (let ((*hooks* (list #'ensure-csgo-launched
                              #'skip-non-csgo-people)))
           (call-people))
```

```
;; Nope, not calling MOM.
;; Nope, not calling DAD.
;; Launching Counter Strike for ALICE.
;; Calling ALICE.
;; Nope, not calling BOB.
;; Nope, not calling CATHERINE.
;; Calling DOROTHY.
;; Nope, not calling ERIC.
;; Nope, not calling DENTIST.
NIL
```

If the second hook throws anything at the :do-not-call catch tag, it prevents the person from being called. The first hook on the list still takes care of launching Counter-Strike for the first player that we call.

The preceding code provides us with one more means of controlling the execution of the program. We can now choose to unwind the stack and transfer control (and data) to any point of the dynamic scope of our program that has a matching catch tag, putting us on mostly even terms with the ability to throw exception objects exhibited by some other languages, such as C++ and Java.

## 2.1.3  Hook #3: Only call parents… maybe

Let us go for a third example: Tom wants to call only his parents, and he only *maybe* wants to call them. That is, for each of them, he flips a coin and only calls them if he gets heads.

```
(defun maybe-call-parent (person)
  (when (member :parent person)
    (when (zerop (random 2))
      (format t ";; Nah, not calling ~A this time.~%" (first person))
      (throw :do-not-call nil))))

(defun skip-non-parents (person)
  (unless (member :parent person)
    (throw :do-not-call nil)))
```

(In order to reduce output verbosity, we decide not to print any information from within the body of skip-non-parents. From now on, we will only produce output that states whether we have called a given parent or not.)

```
CL-USER> (let ((*hooks* (list #'maybe-call-parent
                              #'skip-non-parents)))
           (call-people))
;; Nah, not calling MOM this time.
;; Calling DAD.
NIL

;;;;;;;;;;;; Or...
;; Calling MOM.
;; Calling DAD.
NIL

;;;;;;;;;;;; Or...
;; .........
```

In the preceding example, the output is randomized; it is possible to call both parents, or either, or neither, based on the output of the random call that is embedded in the body of maybe-call-parent.

## 2.1.4  Hook #4: Holiday wishes

In another situation, perhaps Tom wants to call everyone (excluding his ex) and wish them happy holidays.

```
(defun skip-ex (person)
  (when (member :ex person)
    (throw :do-not-call nil)))

(defun wish-happy-holidays (person)
  (format t ";; Gonna wish ~A happy holidays!~%" (first person)))

CL-USER> (let ((*hooks* (list #'skip-ex
                              #'wish-happy-holidays)))
           (call-people))
;; Gonna wish MOM happy holidays!
;; Calling MOM.
;; Gonna wish DAD happy holidays!
;; Calling DAD.
;; Gonna wish ALICE happy holidays!
;; Calling ALICE.
;; Gonna wish BOB happy holidays!
;; Calling BOB.
```

```
;; Gonna wish DOROTHY happy holidays!
;; Calling DOROTHY.
;; Gonna wish ERIC happy holidays!
;; Calling ERIC.
;; Gonna wish DENTIST happy holidays!
;; Calling DENTIST.
NIL
```

In the second hook in the preceding form, there are no conditional checks, meaning that we want to use this hook for all persons that we call.

A somewhat trained eye may then notice that we have an unconditional hook that should execute for every person, and yet it is not executed for Catherine—Tom's ex. The function (call-people) walks the list of hooks in order, which is an important property, because the first hook throws at the :do-not-call catch tag, which transfers control out of the dolist that walks the hook list, preventing the second hook function from being executed. If we were to reverse the order of the two hooks, we would not get the intended behavior.

# 2.1.5  Accumulating hooks

One important matter is the accumulation of hook functions. In more elaborate code, we might want to have multiple layers of bindings that add more and more hook functions onto the list, but do not override any previously established hooks. In practice, this result can be achieved by *appending* new hooks on top of the previously established ones. For example, this previous form:

```
(let ((*hooks* (list #'skip-ex
                     #'wish-happy-holidays)))
  (call-people))
```

could be rewritten in the following way, if we first decided that we want Tom to wish everyone happy holidays *and only then remembered* that he should not call his ex and added that on top of the previous hooks:

```
CL-USER> (let ((*hooks* (list #'wish-happy-holidays)))
           (let ((*hooks* (append (list #'skip-ex) *hooks*)))
             (call-people)))
;; Gonna wish MOM happy holidays!
;; Calling MOM.
;; Gonna wish DAD happy holidays!
;; Calling DAD.
```

```
;; Gonna wish ALICE happy holidays!
;; Calling ALICE.
;; Gonna wish BOB happy holidays!
;; Calling BOB.
;; Gonna wish DOROTHY happy holidays!
;; Calling DOROTHY.
;; Gonna wish ERIC happy holidays!
;; Calling ERIC.
;; Gonna wish DENTIST happy holidays!
;; Calling DENTIST.
NIL
```

(This approach ensures that the hook function skip-ex will be called before wish-happy-holidays, since the resulting list prepends skip-ex before the previous hooks: if we were to swap the order of arguments to the append call, we could change this behavior as required.)

## 2.1.6  Hook #5: Calling Tom's girlfriend again

Let us suppose that we are okay with the current behavior and would like to add one more thing: after calling Tom's girlfriend, he would like to call her again, since one time is not enough for them. As simple as such a situation sounds, it is currently unrepresentable in our code; the list of hooks that we have created is executed inside (call-people) *before* calling each person, whereas we require a method to execute hooks *after* calling each.

Let us therefore modify our code to take that into account. Instead of using a singular variable *hooks*, let us use twin variables *before-hooks* and *after-hooks*.

```
(defvar *before-hooks* '())

(defvar *after-hooks* '())

(defun call-people ()
  (setf *csgo-launched-p* nil)
  (dolist (person *phonebook*)
    (catch :do-not-call
      (dolist (hook *before-hooks*)
        (funcall hook person))
      (call-person person)
      (dolist (hook *after-hooks*)
        (funcall hook person)))))
```

This approach will allow us to execute code after a given person is called:

```
(defun call-girlfriend-again (person)
  (when (member :girlfriend person)
    (format t ";; Gonna call ~A again.~%" (first person))
    (call-person person)))

CL-USER> (let ((*after-hooks* (list #'call-girlfriend-again)))
           (call-people))
;; Calling MOM.
;; Calling DAD.
;; Calling ALICE.
;; Calling BOB.
;; Calling CATHERINE.
;; Calling DOROTHY.
;; Gonna call DOROTHY again.
;; Calling DOROTHY.
;; Calling ERIC.
;; Calling DENTIST.
NIL
```

It will also let us compose before- and after-hooks:

```
CL-USER> (let ((*before-hooks* (list #'ensure-csgo-launched))
               (*after-hooks* (list #'call-girlfriend-again)))
           (call-people))
;; Calling MOM.
;; Calling DAD.
;; Launching Counter Strike for ALICE.
;; Calling ALICE.
;; Calling BOB.
;; Calling CATHERINE.
;; Calling DOROTHY.
;; Gonna call DOROTHY again.
;; Calling DOROTHY.
;; Calling ERIC.
;; Calling DENTIST.
NIL
```

# 2.1.7 Multiple types of hooks

One issue that is evident with the preceding approaches is that defining a new point of hooking requires us to define a new variable. So far, we have defined *before-hooks* and *after-hooks*. The multiple-variable approach will become clumsy when we, for example, complicate the logic inside call-person and allow hooks to be called during the call. Such an approach will require us to handle multiple variables, which quickly may become unwieldy.

We will propose a somewhat different mechanism, which re-introduces the singular variable *hooks* for storing *all* hooks that we create. This mechanism will require us to have some way of discriminating the individual groups of hooks that, in our previous approach, would belong to different variables. To achieve that, we will arrange for each value in *hooks* to be a list of two values: the first will be a symbol that denotes the *kind* of hook, and the second will be the hook function itself (same as up till now).

This arrangement will allow us to invoke hooks based on their *kind*. For instance, if we have some hooks of kind before-call and some others of kind after-call, we would like the form (call-hooks 'before-call) to call only the former ones and not the latter ones.

We can remove the old *before-hooks* and *after-hooks* variables, define the new *hooks* variable, and implement the function call-hooks that iterates over the list of all hooks and calls only the ones of the kind relevant to us.

```
(makunbound '*before-hooks*)

(makunbound '*after-hooks*)

(defvar *hooks* '())

(defun call-hooks (kind &rest arguments)
  (dolist (hook *hooks*)
    (destructuring-bind (hook-kind hook-function) hook
      (when (eq kind hook-kind)
        (apply hook-function arguments)))))
```

(In the preceding example, destructuring-bind performs *destructuring* on the hook variable. It verifies that the content of each hook is a two-element list and then binds the variable hook-kind to that list's first element and hook-function to its second. You could think of it as a macro for limited pattern matching in CL that can work with basic list structures.)

Now we can redefine `call-people` to take this new function into account.

```
(defun call-people ()
  (setf *csgo-launched-p* nil)
  (dolist (person *phonebook*)
    (catch :do-not-call
      (call-hooks 'before-call person)
      (call-person person)
      (call-hooks 'after-call person))))
```

We now need to adjust the way in which our dynamic environment is created around (`call-people`). For brevity, we will use *backquote notation* to build our list this time. (A brief tutorial on this notation is available in our appendix covering the basics of macro writing.)

```
CL-USER> (let ((*hooks* `((before-call ,#'ensure-csgo-launched)
                          (after-call ,#'call-girlfriend-again))))
           (call-people))
;; Calling MOM.
;; Calling DAD.
;; Launching Counter Strike for ALICE.
;; Calling ALICE.
;; Calling BOB.
;; Calling CATHERINE.
;; Calling DOROTHY.
;; Gonna call DOROTHY again.
;; Calling DOROTHY.
;; Calling ERIC.
;; Calling DENTIST.
NIL
```

This approach allows us to define multiple hooks on a single variable. Let us, at once, skip calling Tom's ex, ensure that Counter-Strike is launched, wish everyone happy holidays, and ensure that we call Tom's girlfriend again.

```
CL-USER> (let ((*hooks* `((before-call ,#'skip-ex)
                          (before-call ,#'ensure-csgo-launched)
                          (before-call ,#'wish-happy-holidays)
                          (after-call ,#'call-girlfriend-again))))
           (call-people))
```

```
;; Gonna wish MOM happy holidays!
;; Calling MOM.
;; Gonna wish DAD happy holidays!
;; Calling DAD.
;; Launching Counter Strike for ALICE.
;; Gonna wish ALICE happy holidays!
;; Calling ALICE.
;; Gonna wish BOB happy holidays!
;; Calling BOB.
;; Gonna wish DOROTHY happy holidays!
;; Calling DOROTHY.
;; Gonna call DOROTHY again.
;; Calling DOROTHY.
;; Gonna wish ERIC happy holidays!
;; Calling ERIC.
;; Gonna wish DENTIST happy holidays!
;; Calling DENTIST.
NIL
```

Note, however, that the backquote notation in the preceding two examples is not strictly necessary. The style of notation which we use uses the #' reader macro, which returns function objects that are suitable for passing to funcall or apply. However, it is also possible to pass *symbols* to funcall and apply whenever they name a global function. In our case, we do have named global functions, so we can use symbols and quote the whole expression instead; it will still work. The first symbol in each sublist of *hooks* will then denote the hook type and the second the function that we want to call.

```
CL-USER> (let ((*hooks* '((before-call skip-ex)
                          (before-call ensure-csgo-launched)
                          (before-call wish-happy-holidays)
                          (after-call call-girlfriend-again))))
           (call-people))
;; Gonna wish MOM happy holidays!
;; Calling MOM.
;; Gonna wish DAD happy holidays!
;; Calling DAD.
;; Launching Counter Strike for ALICE.
;; Gonna wish ALICE happy holidays!
;; Calling ALICE.
```

```
;; Gonna wish BOB happy holidays!
;; Calling BOB.
;; Gonna wish DOROTHY happy holidays!
;; Calling DOROTHY.
;; Gonna call DOROTHY again.
;; Calling DOROTHY.
;; Gonna wish ERIC happy holidays!
;; Calling ERIC.
;; Gonna wish DENTIST happy holidays!
;; Calling DENTIST.
NIL
```

If we want to expand this example further, we can define new hook sites inside the body of (call-people). For instance, we could define hooks that are meant to be run before we start calling anyone (such hooks may, e.g., inspect the list of people that we are about to call) and after we finish calling altogether (such hooks may, e.g., inspect the list of people that have actually been called). Perhaps we might want to stop calling altogether at some point: if, for example, Tom's mother tells him that he needs to show up in the living room this instant, then he should cease all further calling (even if she had been the first person he was to call!) and go straight to the living room instead to receive his fate. Implementing such functionality can require us to bind additional kinds of hooks in the body of (call-people) to collect the people that we have actually called or to insert additional catch forms in different places to short-circuit the algorithm further. Such additional complication is left as an exercise for the reader.

## 2.1.8  Summary: The hook subsystem

To summarize, starting with dynamic variables and simple code, we have implemented a system of hooks, which are places that allow the user to *extend the behavior of an existing system* with their own code at predefined points. All of the particular hooks are called in the inverse order to that in which they were bound; the "newest" ones are called first, the "oldest" ones last.

In fact, there exists another system of dynamically scoped hooks, into which we can readily translate the preceding example. And that system happens to be a part of the ANSI CL standard. Let's go ahead and explore that standard system in the next section.

# 2.2  A simple system of condition handlers

As we said in the earlier section, the Lisp condition system has the same basis as the system we created in the section previous to it: a dynamically scoped hook system. It is a more elaborate system than the one we constructed there, but the principles of its functioning boil down essentially to the same thing. To demonstrate this similarity, this chapter will re-implement all of the examples we have shown so far, but via the condition system instead of our homegrown code.

The Common Lisp HyperSpec states:

---

A situation is the evaluation of an expression in a specific context. A condition is an object that represents a specific situation that has been detected. (...) Signaling is the process by which a condition can alter the flow of control in a program by raising the condition which can then be handled.

---

In this context, a *situation* is not really a technical term: it conveys its usual meaning of a state of affairs or a set of circumstances. We may, however, re-word the preceding statement in order to bring it into the context of our former work with hooks. *Handlers* contain the actual code for hooks. The action of invoking the hooks is called *signaling*. *Conditions* are the objects that may trigger some of the hooks when they are signaled, allowing handlers to access arbitrary *data* that is a part of the given condition that was signaled.

Let us start from the same initial codebase, where we start off calling everyone on the list and where we already have the code required for checking whether Counter-Strike was launched.

```
(defvar *phonebook*
  '((:mom :parent)
    (:dad :parent)
    (:alice :classmate :csgo :homework)
    (:bob :classmate :homework)
    (:catherine :classmate :ex)
    (:dorothy :classmate :girlfriend :csgo)
    (:eric :classmate :homework)
    (:dentist)))
```

```
(defun call-person (person)
  (format t ";; Calling ~A.~%" (first person)))

(defvar *csgo-launched-p* nil)

(defun call-people ()
  (setf *csgo-launched-p* nil)
  (dolist (person *phonebook*)
    (call-person person)))
```

Calling this code produces the expected result:

```
CL-USER> (call-people)
;; Calling MOM.
;; Calling DAD.
;; Calling ALICE.
;; Calling BOB.
;; Calling CATHERINE.
;; Calling DOROTHY.
;; Calling ERIC.
;; Calling DENTIST.
NIL
```

Previously, our hook system called each hook with the person that was about to be called. In the Common Lisp condition system, there is one more layer of indirection: *condition types.* In order to run our hooks using the condition system, we need to create an instance of a *condition*, equip it with arbitrary data that we want to pass to the handlers, and call the function signal on that condition.

(There is an analogy between condition types and hook kinds which we have constructed earlier. Instead of creating hook kinds, which are symbols, we define new condition types, which denote *Lisp types.* Operations on Lisp types are more complex, since Lisp types are an implementation of mathematical sets; therefore, operating on those allows for more complexity, compared to matching symbols by equality. An example of this extended capability will be demonstrated later in the book, just like the case of dealing with multiple condition types.)

For now, we want to define one condition type: for the situation where we are about to call someone.

```
(define-condition before-call ()
  ((%person :reader person :initarg :person)))
```

This creates a condition type named before-call. We will want to pass the person that we are about to call to the code, so we create a single *slot* on that condition type. The internal name of that slot is %person—the percent sign is a notational convention which indicates that the symbol is *internal* and should not be depended on by client code. (In addition, it allows us to later export the person symbol naming the reader function without, at the same time, exporting the %person symbol naming the slot itself. If the two were one and the same symbol, it would have been unable to separate these two concerns.)

We can read the value of that slot via the reader function named person, and we can set the initial value of that slot by using the initialization argument :person, like this:

```
(defun call-people ()
  (setf *csgo-launched-p* nil)
  (dolist (person *phonebook*)
    (signal 'before-call :person person)
    (call-person person)))
```

This modification ensures that a before-call condition is going to be signaled before calling each person from Tom's phonebook.

Now that we have that additional layer of indirection, we need to slightly modify our hook function. Each hook function that will be called will accept a single argument that is the condition object; in order to fetch the person from it, we will need to call the person function on the condition object.

```
(lambda (condition)
  (let ((person (person condition)))
    (when (member :csgo person)
      (unless *csgo-launched-p*
        (format t ";; Launching Counter Strike for ~A.~%" (first person))
        (setf *csgo-launched-p* t)))))
```

The only remaining issue is to associate this function with the signaled condition. We can use the standard Lisp macro handler-bind to achieve that. The act of associating a given condition type with its associated function is called *binding* a *handler*.

(Technically speaking, a Common Lisp condition handler is a pair of two elements: a condition type that the handler should wait for and the actual code that gets executed. In contrast to our homegrown hook system described in the previous chapter, not all handlers are executed in turn; only handlers that successfully match the condition's type are run for a given condition object.)

```
CL-USER> (handler-bind
            ((before-call
               (lambda (condition)
                 (let ((person (person condition)))
                   (when (member :csgo person)
                     (unless *csgo-launched-p*
                       (format t ";; Launching Counter Strike for ~A.~%" (first person))
                       (setf *csgo-launched-p* t)))))))
           (call-people))
;; Calling MOM.
;; Calling DAD.
;; Launching Counter Strike for ALICE.
;; Calling ALICE.
;; Calling BOB.
;; Calling CATHERINE.
;; Calling DOROTHY.
;; Calling ERIC.
;; Calling DENTIST.
NIL
```

In order to avoid verbosity, again, we can define that hook function with a name:

```
(defun ensure-csgo-launched (condition)
  (let ((person (person condition)))
    (when (member :csgo person)
      (unless *csgo-launched-p*
        (format t ";; Launching Counter Strike for ~A.~%" (first person))
        (setf *csgo-launched-p* t)))))

CL-USER> (handler-bind ((before-call #'ensure-csgo-launched))
           (call-people))
;; Calling MOM.
;; Calling DAD.
;; Launching Counter Strike for ALICE.
;; Calling ALICE.
;; Calling BOB.
;; Calling CATHERINE.
;; Calling DOROTHY.
;; Calling ERIC.
;; Calling DENTIST.
NIL
```

Our next modification was short-circuiting and not calling some people; we need to modify (call-people) for that.

```
(defun call-people ()
  (setf *csgo-launched-p* nil)
  (dolist (person *phonebook*)
    (catch :do-not-call
      (signal 'before-call :person person)
      (call-person person))))
```

Now, let's define the handler for skipping people and attempt skipping them:

```
(defun skip-non-csgo-people (condition)
  (let ((person (person condition)))
    (unless (member :csgo person)
      (format t ";; Nope, not calling ~A.~%" (first person))
      (throw :do-not-call nil))))

CL-USER> (handler-bind ((before-call #'ensure-csgo-launched)
                        (before-call #'skip-non-csgo-people))
           (call-people))
;; Nope, not calling MOM.
;; Nope, not calling DAD.
;; Launching Counter Strike for ALICE.
;; Calling ALICE.
;; Nope, not calling BOB.
;; Nope, not calling CATHERINE.
;; Calling DOROTHY.
;; Nope, not calling ERIC.
;; Nope, not calling DENTIST.
NIL
```

The syntax for handler-bind requires us to specify the condition type for each handler, which is why we duplicate the condition type before-call. For every condition of type before-call that is signaled, ensure-csgo-launched will be called first, and skip-non-csgo-people will be called second.

Next comes the example of calling parents only, and only calling them sometimes:

```
(defun maybe-call-parent (condition)
  (let ((person (person condition)))
    (when (member :parent person)
      (when (= 0 (random 2))
```

```
          (format t ";; Nah, not calling ~A this time.~%" (first person))
          (throw :do-not-call nil)))))

(defun skip-non-parents (condition)
  (let ((person (person condition)))
    (unless (member :parent person)
      (throw :do-not-call nil))))

CL-USER> (handler-bind ((before-call #'maybe-call-parent)
                        (before-call #'skip-non-parents))
           (call-people))
;; Nah, not calling MOM this time.
;; Calling DAD.
NIL

;;;;;;;;;;; Or...
;; Calling MOM.
;; Calling DAD.
NIL

;;;;;;;;;;; Or...
;; .........
```

Wishing happy holidays to everyone who is not Tom's ex?

```
(defun skip-ex (condition)
  (let ((person (person condition)))
    (when (member :ex person)
      (throw :do-not-call nil))))

(defun wish-happy-holidays (condition)
  (let ((person (person condition)))
    (format t ";; Gonna wish ~A happy holidays!~%" (first person))))

CL-USER> (handler-bind ((before-call #'skip-ex)
                        (before-call #'wish-happy-holidays))
           (call-people))
;; Gonna wish MOM happy holidays!
;; Calling MOM.
;; Gonna wish DAD happy holidays!
;; Calling DAD.
;; Gonna wish ALICE happy holidays!
;; Calling ALICE.
```

```
;; Gonna wish BOB happy holidays!
;; Calling BOB.
;; Gonna wish DOROTHY happy holidays!
;; Calling DOROTHY.
;; Gonna wish ERIC happy holidays!
;; Calling ERIC.
;; Gonna wish DENTIST happy holidays!
;; Calling DENTIST.
NIL
```

Adding different handlers at different moments?

```
CL-USER> (handler-bind ((before-call #'wish-happy-holidays))
           (handler-bind ((before-call #'skip-ex))
             (call-people)))
;; Gonna wish MOM happy holidays!
;; Calling MOM.
;; Gonna wish DAD happy holidays!
;; Calling DAD.
;; Gonna wish ALICE happy holidays!
;; Calling ALICE.
;; Gonna wish BOB happy holidays!
;; Calling BOB.
;; Gonna wish DOROTHY happy holidays!
;; Calling DOROTHY.
;; Gonna wish ERIC happy holidays!
;; Calling ERIC.
;; Gonna wish DENTIST happy holidays!
;; Calling DENTIST.
NIL
```

(The preceding form differs from the hook-based implementation in one detail: the handler mechanism has one property called *clustering* that the hook system does not have. We will elaborate on that later in the book.)

Doing different things before calling people and different things after calling people?

```
(define-condition after-call ()
  ((%person :reader person :initarg :person)))

(defun call-people ()
  (setf *csgo-launched-p* nil)
  (dolist (person *phonebook*)
```

```
  (catch :do-not-call
    (signal 'before-call :person person)
    (call-person person)
    (signal 'after-call :person person))))

(defun call-girlfriend-again (condition)
  (let ((person (person condition)))
    (when (member :girlfriend person)
      (format t ";; Gonna call ~A again.~%" (first person))
      (call-person person))))

CL-USER> (handler-bind ((before-call #'ensure-csgo-launched)
                        (after-call #'call-girlfriend-again))
           (call-people))
;; Calling MOM.
;; Calling DAD.
;; Launching Counter Strike for ALICE.
;; Calling ALICE.
;; Calling BOB.
;; Calling CATHERINE.
;; Calling DOROTHY.
;; Gonna call DOROTHY again.
;; Calling DOROTHY.
;; Calling ERIC.
;; Calling DENTIST.
NIL
```

So we can see that the hook system defined in the previous chapter maps perfectly into the Lisp condition system, to the extent for which we have used it so far. Further extending the function call-people is analogous to extending it in our hook system, except instead of iterating through the different hook variables, we signal distinct condition types.

## 2.2.1 Exception handling

So far, we have implemented the situation where Tom is in full control of what is going on; he is the caller, and other people are the callees. But, other people have the possibility to call us as well; let us try to program that situation.

Let us assume that every person on Tom's phonebook is able to call him; they can make Tom's phone ring. Generally, he will want to answer phone calls from everyone—except from his ex. We do not want to think what happens if Tom answers a call from her—we must simply assume that this is an erroneous situation from which Tom cannot recover.

## 2.2.1.1 First iteration: No handling

Programmatically, we could describe the naïve, always answering code in the following way:

```
(defun receive-phone-call (person)
  (format t ";; Answering a call from ~A.~%" (first person))
  (when (member :ex person)
    (format t ";; About to commit a grave mistake...~%")
    (we do not want to be here)))
```

We purposefully do not define the (we do not want to be here) form, leaving it as it is to denote the unwanted and undefined behavior that we never want to have happen. If control ever were to reach that form, then Tom's program would have failed him, and that would have been due to a mistake on the programmer's side; therefore, we need to ensure that this form will never be reached under any circumstances.

To achieve this assurance, we can use a similar method to the one employed in the previous chapter. Using throw and catch, we have performed a *non-local transfer of control*; in other words, we have escaped from a part of code inside call-people before it led to an erroneous situation.

The Common Lisp condition system has accounted for such a situation. There is a *subtype* of all conditions named serious-condition which is signaled in such situations. Contrary to the usual, non-serious conditions, serious conditions in CL are defined so that they **must** be handled in some way.

So far, we have not discussed condition subtypes. This is a part of the Common Lisp condition system that is more powerful than the hook kinds which we implemented earlier. While hook kinds only provide lookup by means of symbol equality (e.g., calling all hooks with kind before-call will only invoke hooks whose kind is *equal* to the symbol before-call), the Common Lisp condition system allows for a *hierarchy* of condition types, in which one condition type is allowed to *subtype* one or more other condition types.

These condition types can then be utilized to trigger handlers with *distinct* condition types; for instance, a handler for the system-defined condition type error is going to be triggered whenever an error of any kind is signaled, no matter if it is, for example, an undefined-function error, a program-error, a plain error, or any other condition type which itself is a subtype of error. Further, we may define a handler on serious-condition, which is going to handle all errors as well—since the condition type error is a subtype of serious-condition.

The inheritance model of Common Lisp condition types allows a condition type to be a subtype of *more than one condition*; for instance, it is common to define custom error types which are themselves subtypes both of error and of a different condition type that is specific to a certain class of problems in which we find ourselves.

This means that the inheritance model of conditions (which is, actually, the inheritance model of *Common Lisp Object System* in general) solves the diamond problem that occurs with multiple inheritance. (Since the diamond problem is a non-trivial issue, details about it or multiple inheritance in general are out of scope of this book.)

## 2.2.1.2  Second iteration: Signaling a condition

We could extend the preceding example to illustrate the workings of inheritance in condition types:

```
(define-condition grave-mistake (error)
  ((%reason :reader reason :initarg :reason)))

(defun receive-phone-call (person)
  (format t ";; Answering a call from ~A.~%" (first person))
  (when (member :ex person)
    (format t ";; About to commit a grave mistake...~%")
    (signal 'grave-mistake :reason :about-to-call-your-ex)
    (we do not want to be here)))
```

We have defined the condition grave-mistake to be an error. This means, among other things, that handlers that expect an error will now be notified when a grave-mistake is signaled within their scope, and their code will be run. This enables us to write two code examples that safely defuse the situation: one that binds a handler to all error conditions and another, more specialized, which binds a handler to grave-mistake conditions only. Specializing in this way allows the programmer to query the condition objects for properties that only grave-mistakes have, for instance, the reason that each grave-mistake condition has.

```
(defun defuse-error (condition)
  (declare (ignore condition))
  (format t ";; Nope nope nope, not answering!~%")
  (throw :do-not-answer nil))

(defun defuse-grave-mistake (condition)
  (let ((reason (reason condition)))
    (format t ";; Nope nope nope, not answering - reason was, ~A!~%" reason))
  (throw :do-not-answer nil))

CL-USER> (handler-bind ((error #'defuse-error))
           (dolist (person *phonebook*)
             (catch :do-not-answer
               (receive-phone-call person))))
;; Answering a call from MOM.
;; Answering a call from DAD.
;; Answering a call from ALICE.
;; Answering a call from BOB.
;; Answering a call from CATHERINE.
;; About to commit a grave mistake...
;; Nope nope nope, not answering!
;; Answering a call from DOROTHY.
;; Answering a call from ERIC.
;; Answering a call from DENTIST.
NIL

CL-USER> (handler-bind ((grave-mistake #'defuse-grave-mistake))
           (dolist (person *phonebook*)
             (catch :do-not-answer
               (receive-phone-call person))))
;; Answering a call from MOM.
;; Answering a call from DAD.
;; Answering a call from ALICE.
;; Answering a call from BOB.
;; Answering a call from CATHERINE.
;; About to commit a grave mistake...
;; Nope nope nope, not answering - reason was, ABOUT-TO-CALL-YOUR-EX!
;; Answering a call from DOROTHY.
;; Answering a call from ERIC.
;; Answering a call from DENTIST.
NIL
```

So far, so good. However, handling these kinds of errors is left solely to the handlers, and so the receive-phone-call function is itself dangerous. Let us imagine what happens if Tom ever forgets to handle that condition and simply answers calls from everyone, in turn, from his phonebook.

```
CL-USER> (dolist (person *phonebook*)
           (catch :do-not-answer
             (receive-phone-call person)))
;; Answering a call from MOM.
;; Answering a call from DAD.
;; Answering a call from ALICE.
;; Answering a call from BOB.
;; Answering a call from CATHERINE.
;; About to commit a grave mistake...
;;
;;
;;
;; Phone call answered.
;;
;;
;;
;; Grave mistake successfully committed.
;;
;;
;;
;; ...so, what do we do now?
```

We have passed control to a form that should not have executed under any circumstances. We had an erroneous situation in our program, and we have nonetheless allowed the program to proceed. At this point, *the behavior of the program is undefined,* and so are the results of it. We no longer know what is the state of Tom or what the call has been like. We may never know it. Or we may, after which we would wish we never got to know it.

## 2.2.1.3 Third iteration: Entering the debugger

This is why signal is not powerful enough to handle erroneous situations. There is a function that is more powerful than that, though—powerful enough to invoke the ultimate means of saving us from the problem. That function is named error, and using it in place of signal is enough to prevent the ultimate from happening.

```
(defun receive-phone-call (person)
  (format t ";; Answering a call from ~A.~%" (first person))
  (when (member :ex person)
    (format t ";; About to commit a grave mistake...~%")
    (error 'grave-mistake :reason :about-to-call-your-ex)
    (we will never get here)))
```

The function error works by first signaling the condition in question. This allows the external handlers to function just like they would with standard signal: they can intercept the control flow and route it out on their own terms. However, if no handlers decide to transfer control outside and therefore signal returns, error then calls the ultimate means of saving Tom from making regrettable life choices: it calls invoke-debugger with the condition object as its argument.

The function invoke-debugger, and the Lisp debugger, will be described in later chapters. For now, all we need to know about it is that it is the equivalent of a turtle falling on its back and wiggling its limbs hopelessly in the air; the program has exhausted all chances of handling an error gracefully and, therefore, has no choice but to handle it disgracefully. It is a point of no return; code that follows immediately after an invoke-debugger call (and, therefore, immediately after an error call) cannot be reached by the program.

The debugger is an *interactive* condition handler; it is called to prevent crashing the system by giving the programmer an interface to handle conditions manually. Once it is invoked, execution of the program is effectively paused, and Lisp requires programmer attention in order to resume the program. This means that there is no way to return programmatically from the debugger whatsoever.

It is not a pleasant situation to be in by any means, but at least it is a defined one—for all imaginable cases, we would rather want Tom to think "now I need to call a Lisp technician to fix that program for me" than think "why in the heavens have I even answered this call from her".

(It is possible to disable the interactive debugger in most Lisp implementations. In such case, the Lisp system will simply crash and leave a backtrace and other information to be analyzed during post-mortem debugging. Such situations or debugging techniques are not considered in this book.)

For now, let us consider the debugger as a place of controlled programmer failure. We can assume that the debugger will prevent us from doing unwise things, such as adding 42 to "42" or having Tom answer a call from someone he should not answer a call from. Nonetheless, it is a programmer failure—and so we will discuss one more tool that helps us defend against errors in places where we expect them to happen.

Let's once more look at the previous, safe way of calling receive-phone-call, in which we simplify the previously passed defuse-grave-mistake to its very minimum.

```
(handler-bind ((grave-mistake (lambda (condition)
                                (declare (ignore condition))
                                (throw :do-not-answer nil))))
  (dolist (person *phonebook*)
    (catch :do-not-answer
      (receive-phone-call person))))
```

The routing of control is as follows. The function receive-phone-call is called on every member of the *phonebook*. However, it is possible that receive-phone-call may signal an error; if this happens, we want immediately to stop whatever was going on in receive-phone-call and return to the catch form. That form is inside the dolist call, which means that walking the phonebook will continue; if the catch form had encompassed all of dolist, then signaling an error would instead stop iterating through the phonebook.

This is a frequently encountered idiom in programming: attempt to do something, and if doing that something would result in an error, recover and do something else instead. That pattern is called *exception handling* or *try-catch* from the most famous keywords that implement this behavior in many programming languages.

In Lisp, the macro that implements this idiom is named handler-case. In our example, it will have the following syntax:

```
(dolist (person *phonebook*)
  (handler-case (receive-phone-call person)
    (grave-mistake (condition)
      (format t ";; Nope, not this time: ~A~%" (reason condition)))))
```

If, in the preceding example, (receive-phone-call person) returns normally, then—like in handler-bind—no handlers whatsoever are invoked. If, however, an error is signaled and a matching handler-case handler is found, then the condition object becomes bound to the variable condition in the matching handler, and control continues inside that handler. The body of said handler is executed, and it computes the return value for handler-case.

(Detail: in Lisp, handler-case returns a value, as opposed to the try/catch of C-like languages. If the main form returns normally, then its return value is returned from the handler-case; otherwise, the value returned by the handler that handled the signaled condition is returned from the `handler-case`. There is one exception to this rule, which requires the special `:no-error` handler to be defined; if this is present, then its return value is returned in case of no error, and the return value of the main form ends up being ignored.)

We can execute this code snippet and see that it performs as intended:

```
CL-USER> (dolist (person *phonebook*)
           (handler-case (receive-phone-call person)
             (grave-mistake () (format t ";; Nope, not this time.~%"))))
;; Answering a call from MOM.
;; Answering a call from DAD.
;; Answering a call from ALICE.
;; Answering a call from BOB.
;; Answering a call from CATHERINE.
;; About to commit a grave mistake...
;; Nope, not this time.
;; Answering a call from DOROTHY.
;; Answering a call from ERIC.
;; Answering a call from DENTIST.
NIL
```

In other words, `handler-case` is a shorter way of performing a non-local transfer of control, as compared to `handler-bind`—but it is also somewhat less powerful. While `handler-bind` allows one to execute hook functions at the site where a condition is signaled before continuing standard function execution, `handler-case` *always* performs a non-local transfer of control *outside* the expression that was executing, which unconditionally short-circuits the original control flow.

In other words, `handler-case` *always unwinds the stack*, whereas `handler-bind` *does not necessarily unwind the stack*, as it leaves the choice of whether and how to do that to each individual handler.

In yet other words, if `handler-bind` is a way to execute hooks in Lisp, then `handler-case` is a way to execute exception handling. It is possible to implement `handler-case` via `handler-bind` (we have done a simple version of that in the earlier chapter!), but not the other way around.

Finally, if we would like to make our code *very* dirty (e.g., when we are writing quick, temporary hacks that will only last to the end of the current cosmic manifestation), we can use one more operator that is equivalent to creating a `handler-case` handler on all errors: `ignore-errors`. It does what its name says: in case an error is signaled, control is unconditionally transferred outside of the form that is being executed, and no other actions are performed.

```
CL-USER> (dolist (person *phonebook*)
           (ignore-errors (receive-phone-call person)))
;; Answering a call from MOM.
;; Answering a call from DAD.
;; Answering a call from ALICE.
;; Answering a call from BOB.
;; Answering a call from CATHERINE.
;; About to commit a grave mistake...
;; Answering a call from DOROTHY.
;; Answering a call from ERIC.
;; Answering a call from DENTIST.
NIL
```

(Technically speaking, ignore-errors is equivalent to a handler-case with a single handler for error which returns two values: nil and the error object that was being signaled.)

## 2.2.2  Protection against transfers of control

We could complicate the preceding scenario in one more way. Let us assume that Tom has a very broken phone that locks up every time the call finishes. It doesn't matter whether the call was answered and lasted for an hour (for instance, if Tom's girlfriend was calling), whether it was immediately rejected (for instance, if Tom's mother was calling), or even if Tom pretended he did not hear his phone whatsoever (for instance, if Tom's ex was calling): after each of these situations, he needs to pry the battery out of his phone, put it back inside, and start it anew.

Technically speaking, this programming idiom is an extension of the try/catch pattern—usually, it is named finally, giving the pattern the final name of try/catch/finally. The code marked as finally executes unconditionally after the try/catch part, no matter whether the code block in try has returned normally or whether control was transferred out by means of handling an exception.

As mentioned earlier in the book, there are several ways of transferring control in CL: tagbody/go, block/return-from/return, and catch/throw. The form unwind-protect "protects" against all of these means of transferring control outside of the *protected form* (including the situation when control leaves the form normally) and forces the *cleanup forms* to be executed right after control leaves the protected form, before any other code is run.

We could therefore say that `unwind-protect` is Lisp's way of implementing the `finally` part of that idiom. And so, we may utilize that form to implement Tom needing to restart the phone each single time.

Let us work on this example:

```
CL-USER> (dolist (person *phonebook*)
           (catch :do-not-answer
             (handler-case (receive-phone-call person)
               (grave-mistake (e) (defuse-grave-mistake e)))))
;; Answering a call from MOM.
;; Answering a call from DAD.
;; Answering a call from ALICE.
;; Answering a call from BOB.
;; Answering a call from CATHERINE.
;; About to commit a grave mistake...
;; Nope nope nope, not answering - reason was, ABOUT-TO-CALL-YOUR-EX!
;; Answering a call from DOROTHY.
;; Answering a call from ERIC.
;; Answering a call from DENTIST.
NIL
```

(In the preceding example, we use `handler-case`, but `handler-bind` would work as well. The function `defuse-grave-mistake` performs a non-local exit by `throwing` at the `:do-not-answer` catch tag; therefore, it does not matter whether it is called directly, as via `handler-bind`, or with one more indirection, as via `handler-case`.)

It is possible to perform a non-local exit by means of `throwing` anything to the `:do-not-answer` catch tag. This means that the following code (with a reduced phonebook for clarity) will not work correctly in case of an error:

```
CL-USER> (dolist (person '((:bob :classmate :homework)
                           (:catherine :classmate :ex)
                           (:dorothy :classmate :girlfriend :csgo)))
           (catch :do-not-answer
             (handler-case (receive-phone-call person)
               (grave-mistake (e) (defuse-grave-mistake e)))
             (format t ";; Restarting phone.~%")))
;; Answering a call from BOB.
;; Restarting phone.
;; Answering a call from CATHERINE.
;; About to commit a grave mistake...
```

```
;; Nope nope nope, not answering - reason was, ABOUT-TO-CALL-YOUR-EX!
;; Answering a call from DOROTHY.
;; Restarting phone.
NIL
```

We can see that Tom restarted his phone after Bob and Dorothy called him, but we do not see the same happening for Catherine. This is fixable by adding `unwind-protect`:

```
CL-USER> (dolist (person '((:bob :classmate :homework)
                           (:catherine :classmate :ex)
                           (:dorothy :classmate :girlfriend :csgo)))
          (catch :do-not-answer
            (unwind-protect
                (handler-case (receive-phone-call person)
                  (grave-mistake (e) (defuse-grave-mistake e)))
              (format t ";; Restarting phone.~%"))))
;; Answering a call from BOB.
;; Restarting phone.
;; Answering a call from CATHERINE.
;; About to commit a grave mistake...
;; Nope nope nope, not answering - reason was, ABOUT-TO-CALL-YOUR-EX!
;; Restarting phone.
;; Answering a call from DOROTHY.
;; Restarting phone.
NIL
```

To summarize, using `handler-bind` with an unconditional transfer of control, we have constructed `handler-case`: a means of handling errors by transferring control outside of the erroring forms. In addition, we have introduced `unwind-protect`, a means of running cleanup code that is executed even if control leaves a form in an unnatural way.

## 2.2.3  Clustering

One property of handlers which we have not yet touched is *clustering*. In short, clustering handlers together means that a handler does not "see" any handlers bound in the same `handler-bind` form—meaning that it cannot cause itself or its "neighbors" to become invoked.

Let us use a short synthetic example to illustrate. We establish one "outer" handler in one handler-bind form, and then we establish three "inner" handlers inside it, with the second "inner" handler re-signaling the condition that it gets. Finally, as the final form, we signal a single condition. (The same rule applies for handler-case.)

```
CL-USER> (handler-bind ((condition (lambda (condition)
                                     (declare (ignore condition))
                                     (format t ";; Outer handler~%"))))
           (handler-bind ((condition (lambda (condition)
                                        (declare (ignore condition))
                                        (format t ";; Inner handler A~%")))
                          (condition (lambda (condition)
                                       (format t ";; Inner handler B~%")
                                       (signal condition)))
                          (condition (lambda (condition)
                                       (declare (ignore condition))
                                       (format t ";; Inner handler C~%"))))
             (signal 'condition)))
;; Inner handler A
;; Inner handler B
;; Outer handler
;; Inner handler C
;; Outer handler
```

The result is as follows: first, inner handler A is invoked. Second, inner handler B is invoked, and it re-signals that condition. However, due to clustering rules, all of the inner handlers become "invisible" to the signal call within the inner handler B; this is why only the outer handler is invoked. Next, the inner handler C is invoked, and then, finally, the outer handler is invoked *for the second time*. (The second invocation of the outer handler came from the innermost signal call, whereas the first invocation came from the signal call embedded in the inner handler B.)

An important corollary of this fact is that a handler may never call its own self when using standard handler-based mechanisms.

Such a rule, even though it is not fully intuitive, allows for better structuring of distinct layers of handlers. We can rely on all handlers within a single cluster not getting in each other's (and their own) way if they decide to (re-)signal a condition.

## 2.2.4  Summary: The handler subsystem

This concludes the part of this book about the handler subsystem of the Common Lisp condition system. In the earlier sections, we have constructed the basic system of hooks, which turned out to be very similar to the system of condition handlers which we have in the latter sections of this chapter.

In the next section of the book, we will focus on constructing another subsystem of CL, which has a different operating principle.

# 2.3  A simple system of choices

Let us leave Tom for a moment and focus on another person in the story: Catherine.

Catherine, or Kate, had a boyfriend named Tom. That is no longer the case, though, and she has moved on with her life. She has met a marvelous young programmer named Mark, whom she meets in her house when her parents are away, in order to indulge in intense Lisp study sessions.

There is a problem, however. Kate's parents are a pair of hardcore COBOL mainframe programmers of the old generation, who strongly despise dynamic programming and would promptly garbage-collect Mark, sweeping him into the trash bin, the moment they saw him in their household. Then, they would proceed to scold Kate ruthlessly about her life and professional choices as a growing mainframe programmer.

Kate therefore needs to be particularly cautious about her first steps with Mark in the world of interactive programming. If her parents unexpectedly return home while she is in the middle of analyzing a Lisp program with Mark, she needs that fact to go undiscovered, no matter the costs. Since there are many ways in which her mother and father may notice her relationship with Mark, she needs a versatile and adaptive strategy of covering it up. The most important requirement for that new strategy is that Kate needs to be able to **choose** a single option from the various ones she has at any given moment **arbitrarily**, rather than utilizing them all in order.

Because of this last constraint, the previous mechanisms of hooks or handlers are not suited for this kind of use case. Let us construct a mechanism that allows us to inspect the list of available *choices* we have at any given moment and arbitrarily select the ones that we deem to be the most proper.

# 2.3.1 Kate and Mark

First, we need to set the scene. There is a house in which Kate lives. This house has two doors: front door and back door, each of which may be locked or unlocked. Kate's room is on the first floor (meaning that escaping through windows is not a healthy option) and in every scene it initially contains Mark.

We can represent this state as a set of dynamic variables which we will then rebind around calls to our main function.

```
(defvar *mark-safe-p* nil)
(defvar *front-door-locked-p* t)
(defvar *back-door-locked-p* t)
```

We shall also define the main function that will illustrate a situation in which Kate's parents come home. The value of *mark-safe-p* should be true by the time we have finished covering Mark up, which is visible in the following body of code:

```
(defun parents-come-back ()
  (format t ";; Uh oh - Kate's parents are back!~%")
  (try-to-hide-mark)
  (if *mark-safe-p*
      (format t ";; Whew... We're safe! For now.~%")
      (we do not want to be here)))
```

Once again, we do not define the (we do not want to be here form); in the event control reaches this form, we kindly declare that the behavior is undefined, both for Mark and for Kate. To keep our code modular, the functionality for recovering from that situation should stay within the try-to-hide-mark function and within the dynamic scope in which parents-come-back is called.

Therefore, we need to split our implementation between the dynamic scope of parents-come-back and the body of try-to-hide-mark. The former will contain the cover-up choices available for Kate and Mark at any given moment and the latter the actual logic for selecting the proper choice and utilizing it.

# 2.3.2 Choice #1: Escape

In order to implement our system of choices, we will first need to model an individual choice as well as means of interacting with it. First, we will need some means of referring to any given choice, perhaps by a name that could be a Lisp symbol. Second, we will need to be able to execute arbitrary code associated with such a choice, in order actually to affect the state of our code and be able to cover up for Kate and Mark. Third, we will need means of checking whether a given option is applicable to a given moment; there is no worse situation than, for example, Mark trying to escape through a window only to find that Kate's father is standing next to it, giving Mark a surprised stare.

## 2.3.2.1 The CHOICE structure

Each individual choice will have three components: a name, by which we will refer to that choice; an effect function, which will be executed whenever that choice is chosen; and a test function, which will be called to check if a given choice is applicable to the current situation.

While we could model our choice as a list that contains these three elements, we should instead define a proper choice structure that we will later use for code clarity. For that, we will use a Common Lisp facility named defstruct. This tutorial will not go into depth about how to use defstruct; all that matters for us is that evaluating the following form will define the function make-choice for creating new choice objects, as well as functions choice-name, choice-effect-function, and choice-test-function for accessing the values from a choice object.

```
(defstruct choice
  (name (error "Must provide :NAME."))
  (effect-function (error "Must provide :EFFECT-FUNCTION."))
  (test-function (constantly t)))
```

In the preceding defstruct form, the (error "...") subforms mean that assigning a name and effect-function to a newly created choice is mandatory; it is a *default initial form* that, upon evaluation, will signal an error. The (constantly t) subform returns a function which, in turn, always returns true. Therefore, passing this as the default initial form for test-function means that the test function will always return true, and the choice will always be visible. We choose this as a default since we decide that choices, by default, should always be visible—that is, until and unless a programmer decides otherwise.

## 2.3.2.2 Escaping through the front door

The above means that we can now create choice objects that represent means of covering up Kate and Mark's Lisp studies. Let us define one means of escaping for the time being: escaping through the front door. Its effect should be setting *mark-safe-p* to a true value, and it should only be available when *front-door-locked-p* is false, as Mark cannot escape through a locked door.

Let us define a pair of helper functions that will perform these actions along with printing debug information for us.

```
(defun perform-escape-through-front-door ()
  (format t ";; Escaping through the front door.~%")
  (setf *mark-safe-p* t))

(defun escape-through-front-door-p ()
  (format t ";; The front door is~:[ not~;~] locked.~%" *front-door-locked-p*)
  (not *front-door-locked-p*))
```

This allows us to create a choice object and interact with it in the following manner:

```
CL-USER> (defvar *our-first-choice*
           (make-choice
            :name 'escape-through-front-door
            :effect-function #'perform-escape-through-front-door
            :test-function #'escape-through-front-door-p))
*OUR-FIRST-CHOICE*

CL-USER> *our-first-choice*
#S(CHOICE
   :NAME ESCAPE-THROUGH-FRONT-DOOR
   :EFFECT-FUNCTION #<FUNCTION PERFORM-ESCAPE-THROUGH-FRONT-DOOR>
   :TEST-FUNCTION #<FUNCTION ESCAPE-THROUGH-FRONT-DOOR-P>)

CL-USER> (choice-name *our-first-choice*)
ESCAPE-THROUGH-FRONT-DOOR

CL-USER> (choice-effect-function *our-first-choice*)
#<FUNCTION PERFORM-ESCAPE-THROUGH-FRONT-DOOR>

CL-USER> (choice-test-function *our-first-choice*)
#<FUNCTION ESCAPE-THROUGH-FRONT-DOOR-P>
```

## 2.3.2.3  Escaping through the back door

Since Kate's house is symmetrical and we operate the front and back door in the same manner, we can define a pair of helper functions for handling the back door as well.

```
(defun perform-escape-through-back-door ()
  (format t ";; Escaping through the back door.~%")
  (setf *mark-safe-p* t))

(defun escape-through-back-door-p ()
  (format t ";; The back door is~:[ not~;~] locked.~%" *back-door-locked-p*)
  (not *back-door-locked-p*))
```

This means that we can now also create a choice for escaping through the back door via the following form:

```
(make-choice
 :name 'escape-through-back-door
 :effect-function #'perform-escape-through-back-door
 :test-function #'escape-through-back-door-p)
```

## 2.3.2.4  Computing and invoking choices

Now that we have created the logical structures defining our choices, we may use them in future code. Let us first define a variable listing all available choices and give it an empty initial value.

```
(defvar *choices* '())
```

The global value of this dynamic variable should *always* stay empty; we will instead provide new choices by dynamically rebinding that value, meaning that our choices will only be available in some dynamically scoped parts of our program.

This means that only one thing prevents us from executing parents-come-back: we have not yet implemented the function try-to-hide-mark that is called therein. We can do it now.

```
(defun try-to-hide-mark ()
  (let ((choices (loop for choice in *choices*
                       when (funcall (choice-test-function choice))
                         collect choice)))
```

```
(if choices
    (let ((choice (first choices)))
      (format t ";; Performing ~A.~%" (choice-name choice))
      (funcall (choice-effect-function choice)))
    (format t ";; Kate cannot hide Mark!~%"))))
```

The algorithm has the following path. First of all, all the choices from *choices* are scanned to determine whether they apply to a given situation. If yes, such a choice is collected for later processing. Once we have the list of applicable choices, we ensure that it is not empty; once that is done, we perform our logic for choosing and invoking the choices.

For the time being, we simply choose the first choice object that we find. This logic will, however, become more elaborate later in the chapter.

The loop form in the preceding function is somewhat large. We can factor it into a separate function for clarity.

```
(defun compute-choices ()
  (loop for choice in *choices*
        when (funcall (choice-test-function choice))
          collect choice))

(defun try-to-hide-mark ()
  (let ((choices (compute-choices)))
    (if choices
        (let ((choice (first choices)))
          (format t ";; Performing ~A.~%" (choice-name choice))
          (funcall (choice-effect-function choice)))
        (format t ";; Kate cannot hide Mark!~%"))))
```

Now that we have implemented the function try-to-hide-mark, we can construct an example form that represents a situation in which Kate's parents come back and we would like to have the option of escaping through the front or back door.

```
(let ((*choices*
       (list (make-choice
               :name 'escape-through-front-door
               :effect-function #'perform-escape-through-front-door
               :test-function #'escape-through-front-door-p)
             (make-choice
               :name 'escape-through-back-door
               :effect-function #'perform-escape-through-back-door
               :test-function #'escape-through-back-door-p))))
```

```
(let ((*mark-safe-p* nil)
      (*front-door-locked-p* nil)
      (*back-door-locked-p* nil))
  (parents-come-back)))
```

That form is rather unwieldy to type. We can notice that, for the most part, the code consists of a part that is somewhat static: a list of all choices that we offer for successfully covering up Mark's presence in Kate's home.

We can factor this out into a separate function which establishes the proper dynamic environment and then calls a thunk function in that environment.

```
(defun call-with-home-choices (thunk)
  (let ((*choices*
         (list (make-choice
                 :name 'escape-through-front-door
                 :effect-function #'perform-escape-through-front-door
                 :test-function #'escape-through-front-door-p)
               (make-choice
                 :name 'escape-through-back-door
                 :effect-function #'perform-escape-through-back-door
                 :test-function #'escape-through-back-door-p))))
    (funcall thunk)))
```

(In Lisp, this behavior is usually achieved by writing a *macro*, rather than a function; it could be called with-home-choices and accept code that we would want to run in the dynamic scope of that form. For simplicity, we use a function instead to achieve the same result, especially since this situation permits it; it is not easily possible to substitute all macro invocations with function calls.)

The preceding code allows us to shorten our form to the following:

```
(call-with-home-choices
 (lambda ()
   (let ((*mark-safe-p* nil)
         (*front-door-locked-p* nil)
         (*back-door-locked-p* nil))
     (parents-come-back))))
```

## 2.3.2.5  The results

We can now attempt to execute this last form and see how it behaves.

```
CL-USER> (call-with-home-choices
          (lambda ()
            (let ((*mark-safe-p* nil)
                  (*front-door-locked-p* nil)
                  (*back-door-locked-p* nil))
              (parents-come-back))))
;; Uh oh - Kate's parents are back!
;; The front door is not locked.
;; The back door is not locked.
;; Performing ESCAPE-THROUGH-FRONT-DOOR.
;; Escaping through the front door.
;; Whew... We're safe! For now.
NIL
```

If only the front door is unlocked, not much changes:

```
CL-USER> (call-with-home-choices
          (lambda ()
            (let ((*mark-safe-p* nil)
                  (*front-door-locked-p* nil))
              (parents-come-back))))
;; Uh oh - Kate's parents are back!
;; The front door is not locked.
;; The back door is locked.
;; Performing ESCAPE-THROUGH-FRONT-DOOR.
;; Escaping through the front door.
;; Whew... We're safe! For now.
NIL
```

If only the back door is unlocked, then Mark still has a way of escaping:

```
CL-USER> (call-with-home-choices
          (lambda ()
            (let ((*mark-safe-p* nil)
                  (*back-door-locked-p* nil))
              (parents-come-back))))
```

```
;; Uh oh - Kate's parents are back!
;; The front door is locked.
;; The back door is not locked.
;; Performing ESCAPE-THROUGH-BACK-DOOR.
;; Escaping through the back door.
;; Whew... We're safe! For now.
NIL
```

If both doors are locked, well, that is a situation which we do not want to evaluate in practice. We can, however, evaluate `try-to-hide-mark` instead of `parents-come-back` in such an environment—we can assume that Kate tries to hide Mark as a practice exercise for later.

```
CL-USER> (call-with-home-choices
          (lambda ()
            (let ((*mark-safe-p* nil))
              (try-to-hide-mark))))
;; The front door is locked.
;; The back door is locked.
;; Kate cannot hide Mark!
NIL
```

## 2.3.2.6 Same-named choices

The preceding mechanism is based on the assumption that all means of escape are equally desirable and moreover that they do not require any data passed to them from the call site. We are doing it this way since both the choices we have established have functions that accept zero arguments; we can call their effect functions without passing any data to them.

Additionally, both of the choices we have created perform essentially the same thing: they allow Mark to escape without confronting Kate's parents, even if through different means. We shall establish a convention of naming choices that perform the same action with the same symbol. This way, client code could check for presence of *any* choice named escape—without needing to know the exact details of the escape route.

Let us rewrite our code to take this naming convention into account:

```
(defun call-with-home-choices (thunk)
  (let ((*choices*
         (list (make-choice
                 :name 'escape
                 :effect-function #'perform-escape-through-front-door
                 :test-function #'escape-through-front-door-p)
               (make-choice
                 :name 'escape
                 :effect-function #'perform-escape-through-back-door
                 :test-function #'escape-through-back-door-p))))
    (funcall thunk)))
```

Inside call-with-home-choices, we only need to change the names of both choices to escape. Now that we know all desired choices are named identically as escape, we can also change the implementation of try-to-hide-mark to be more precise—instead of calling the first available choice, we can try to *find* a choice named escape. For this search mechanism, we introduce a new function, find-choice, and a convenience function invoke-choice that will call the effect function of the choice with a given name while passing arguments to it.

```
(defun find-choice (name)
  (loop for choice in *choices*
        when (and (funcall (choice-test-function choice))
                  (eq name (choice-name choice)))
          return choice))

(defun invoke-choice (name &rest arguments)
  (let ((choice (find-choice name)))
    (apply (choice-effect-function choice) arguments)))

(defun try-to-hide-mark ()
  (if (find-choice 'escape)
      (invoke-choice 'escape)
      (format t ";; Kate cannot hide Mark!~%")))
```

We can check that our code still works, albeit slightly differently:

```
CL-USER> (call-with-home-choices
          (lambda ()
            (let ((*mark-safe-p* nil)
                  (*front-door-locked-p* nil))
              (parents-come-back))))
;; Uh oh - Kate's parents are back!
;; The front door is not locked.
;; Escaping through the front door.
;; Whew... We're safe! For now.
NIL

CL-USER> (call-with-home-choices
          (lambda ()
            (let ((*mark-safe-p* nil)
                  (*back-door-locked-p* nil))
              (parents-come-back))))
;; Uh oh - Kate's parents are back!
;; The front door is locked.
;; The back door is not locked.
;; Escaping through the back door.
;; Whew... We're safe! For now.
NIL

CL-USER> (call-with-home-choices
          (lambda ()
            (let ((*mark-safe-p* nil))
              (try-to-hide-mark))))
;; The front door is locked.
;; The back door is locked.
;; Kate cannot hide Mark!
NIL
```

## 2.3.3  Choice #2: Excuses

We have unified escape-related choices under a single name, escape. We will now extend our means of Mark's survival with another tactic: allowing him to talk his way out of the difficult situation in which he found himself.

```
(defvar *excuses*
  '("Kate did not divide her program into sections properly!"
    "I was borrowing Kate's books on mainframe programming!"
    "I had COBOL-related homework and hoped Kate could help me!"))

(defun perform-excuse (excuse)
  (format t ";; Mark makes an excuse before leaving:~%;; \"~A\"~%" excuse)
  (setf *mark-safe-p* t))
```

We assume that Mark, when he says one of the preceding excuses, should be able to calm down Kate's parents' suspicion and successfully sneak out of their household. Confronting Kate's parents is nonetheless an option of last resort: if possible, they should not even be aware that Mark visited their daughter. Our logic must take this into account and first try to attempt an escape.

```
(defun try-to-hide-mark ()
  (cond ((find-choice 'escape)
         (invoke-choice 'escape))
        (t (format t ";; Kate cannot hide Mark!~%")
           (when (find-choice 'excuse)
             (let ((excuse-text (elt *excuses* (random (length *excuses*)))))
               (invoke-choice 'excuse excuse-text))))))
```

The preceding code will work, but we have not actually established an excuse choice yet. To do so, we need to modify call-with-home-choices:

```
(defun call-with-home-choices (thunk)
  (let ((*choices*
          (list (make-choice
                  :name 'excuse
                  :effect-function #'perform-excuse)
                (make-choice
                  :name 'escape
                  :effect-function #'perform-escape-through-front-door
                  :test-function #'escape-through-front-door-p)
                (make-choice
                  :name 'escape
                  :effect-function #'perform-escape-through-back-door
                  :test-function #'escape-through-back-door-p))))
    (funcall thunk)))
```

(As mentioned before, we want the excuse choice always to be available; therefore, we do not provide it with a :test-function.)

With this modification in place, we can check whether Kate's and Mark's love for Lisp and each other can survive in the inevitable scenario where the doors are locked and Mark needs to confront Kate's mother and father:

```
CL-USER> (call-with-home-choices
          (lambda ()
            (let ((*mark-safe-p* nil))
              (parents-come-back))))
;; Uh oh - Kate's parents are back!
;; The front door is locked.
;; The back door is locked.
;; Kate cannot hide Mark!
;; Mark makes an excuse before leaving:
;; "Kate did not divide her program into sections properly!"
;; Whew... We're safe! For now.
NIL
```

Looks like Mark is safe... for now.

We are allowed to complicate this example further, both by defining more choices inside the body of call-with-home-choices and by extending the choice-invoking logic inside try-to-hide-mark. Perhaps there should be an option of jumping out the window of Kate's room, if there is a conveniently placed haystack just beneath it and if Mark feels like performing a leap of faith; maybe there could be a laundry pile in Kate's room that Mark could hide in... unless that particular day is laundry day, and Kate's mother comes in to pick the clothes up for washing. Just as in the example with hooks, this means that only these two functions need to be adjusted: one to offer actual choice objects to code executed inside its dynamic scope and the other to compute the available choices and decide which of them should be used and under what conditions. Such enhancement is left as an exercise for the reader.

## 2.3.4  Summary: the choice subsystem

To summarize, we have created a system that internally functions in a similar way to the hook system that we implemented earlier, given that it works based on a single dynamic variable and a list of choice objects bound to it. Invoking a given choice has exactly the same main effect as calling a hook—executing arbitrary code that was provided to us earlier in the dynamic scope.

However, the functioning of this new system is distinct from that of the hook system. In the system of hooks, client code merely calls all hooks that were provided to it; in the system of choices, client code is given much more latitude as to which choices it wants to interact with, both because of the choice objects having names and because of them not always being applicable to a given dynamic situation of the program (as per the test function).

In addition to the preceding data, there is one aspect of the choice system which we have not used in the preceding example. A choice is allowed merely to perform some computation and—contrary to hooks—*return a value*, which is then returned from the place where the choice was invoked. This difference, in addition to the ones described earlier, makes choices a more sophisticated and therefore more versatile toolset than hooks—better suited for situations where client code needs to compute recovery strategies more complex than "let's hope that one of the hooks gets us out of there, and if not, invoke the debugger."

As we have seen so far, choices, just like hooks, are not required to transfer control outside of the normal program control flow. If a choice does not perform a non-local exit and instead returns, the `invoke-choice` call site returns immediately without performing any other actions.

Therefore, choices express a different mechanism of control than hooks do. With hooks, a given situation which has occurred in code may cause one or more externally specified bodies of code to be executed in an order defined by the dynamic scope. With choices, the bodies of code are still provided dynamically, but it is *the invoking code* that chooses which of these code bodies, under what circumstances, and in which order are utilized in order to work with a given situation.

## 2.4  A simple system of restarts

Truth be told, in the previous chapter, we have done a lot of work that was not strictly necessary for production code. This is because, through constructing the choice system from its smallest parts, we have constructed a simple version of a system that already exists in standard CL—a system of *restarts*.

A restart in CL is defined by things similar to the choice objects defined by us: a name (usually), a function utilized for invoking its effects (called a *restart function* in CL), and a test function that checks whether a given restart should be visible, given the current state of the program. (There are other qualities to restarts that I omit here for clarity; we will talk about them later when we discuss the CL debugger.)

To show this system of restarts, we may rewrite the earlier examples while using said restarts. The initial "setting the stage" code will be the same:

```
(defvar *mark-safe-p* nil)
(defvar *front-door-locked-p* t)
(defvar *back-door-locked-p* t)
```

We do not need to create the restart structure manually, since Common Lisp already has created it for us in the form of the restart system class. We are not meant to create instances of that class explicitly, though—Common Lisp provides us with a macro named restart-bind which creates them for us. (The reason for this is that restart objects in Common Lisp have *dynamic extent*; this means that accessing them is only legal within the dynamic scope in which they were created.)

We want to establish a restart named escape-through-front-door, which prints a debug message and unconditionally sets *mark-safe-p* to true. In addition, it must only be visible if the front door is unlocked. Here's an example syntax for such a restart:

```
(restart-bind ((escape-through-front-door
                (lambda ()
                  (format t ";; Escaping through the front door.~%")
                  (setf *mark-safe-p* t))
                :test-function
                (lambda (condition)
                  (declare (ignore condition))
                  (not *front-door-locked-p*))))
  ...)
```

(The test function for a restart must accept one argument, since, in some circumstances, the CL restart system passes a condition object to that function. The purpose of this object will be covered in a later part of this book; for now, the function ignores the argument passed to it.)

For code clarity, let us once again define the helper functions for our restart for escaping through the front door—this time, skipping some verbosity in the test function:

```
(defun perform-escape-through-front-door ()
  (format t ";; Escaping through the front door.~%")
  (setf *mark-safe-p* t))

(defun escape-through-front-door-p (condition)
  (declare (ignore condition))
  (not *front-door-locked-p*))
```

This allows us to shorten our code to the following:

```
(restart-bind ((escape-through-front-door
                 #'perform-escape-through-front-door
                 :test-function #'escape-through-front-door-p))
  ...)
```

We may now compute the restarts available within the dynamic scope of that form. We will print their names to ensure that the restart we have created is on top of that list. For this computation, we will utilize the predefined compute-restarts function, offered to us by CL. It behaves in the same way as compute-choices did for choices from the previous example, offering us a list of restart objects that we can query for their names using the restart-name function.

```
CL-USER> (restart-bind ((escape-through-front-door
                          #'perform-escape-through-front-door
                          :test-function #'escape-through-front-door-p))
           (let ((*mark-safe-p* nil)
                 (*front-door-locked-p* nil))
             (let* ((restarts (compute-restarts))
                    (names (mapcar #'restart-name restarts)))
               (format t "~{;; ~A~%~}" names))))
;; ESCAPE-THROUGH-FRONT-DOOR
;; RETRY
;; ABORT
;; ABORT
NIL
```

The escape-through-front-door restart is available on that list as the first restart, but we also have several restarts that had been established earlier by the particular Lisp implementation in which we happen to be programming. (Since they are established by the system, the list may look different in another Lisp image.) These restarts are not of any relevance to us and are used by the Lisp system as the ultimate means of recovering from errors. We will therefore perform a bit of additional work to filter the system-provided restarts out from the restarts that we establish ourselves.

```
(defvar *toplevel-restarts* '())

(defun compute-relevant-restarts (&optional condition)
  (set-difference (compute-restarts condition) *toplevel-restarts*))
```

(The reason for the existence of that &optional condition argument will be explained later in the book.)

We can bind the variable *toplevel-restarts* to compute the restarts available before entering our dynamic scope and then use our new function compute-relevant-restarts to filter these out from the list.

```
CL-USER> (let ((*toplevel-restarts* (compute-restarts)))
           (restart-bind ((escape-through-front-door
                             #'perform-escape-through-front-door
                             :test-function #'escape-through-front-door-p))
             (let ((*mark-safe-p* nil)
                   (*front-door-locked-p* nil))
               (let* ((restarts (compute-relevant-restarts))
                      (names (mapcar #'restart-name restarts)))
                 (format t "~{;; ~A~%~}" names)))))
;; ESCAPE-THROUGH-FRONT-DOOR
NIL
```

By sticking with the compute-relevant-restarts function instead of the system-given compute-restarts, we'll be safely limiting the restarts to the ones we have created ourselves. We can similarly expand our code with a restart available for escaping through the back door:

```
(defun perform-escape-through-back-door ()
  (format t ";; Escaping through the back door.~%")
  (setf *mark-safe-p* t))

(defun escape-through-back-door-p (condition)
  (declare (ignore condition))
  (not *back-door-locked-p*))

CL-USER> (let ((*toplevel-restarts* (compute-restarts)))
           (restart-bind ((escape-through-front-door
                             #'perform-escape-through-front-door
                             :test-function #'escape-through-front-door-p)
```

```
                        (escape-through-back-door
                          #'perform-escape-through-back-door
                          :test-function #'escape-through-back-door-p))
              (let ((*mark-safe-p* nil)
                    (*front-door-locked-p* nil)
                    (*back-door-locked-p* nil))
                (let* ((restarts (compute-relevant-restarts))
                       (names (mapcar #'restart-name restarts)))
                  (format t "~{;; ~A~%~}" names)))))
;; ESCAPE-THROUGH-BACK-DOOR
;; ESCAPE-THROUGH-FRONT-DOOR
NIL
```

Our code is now starting to become unwieldy. To nip this in the bud, we can separate it into three logical where we declare the state of the world and the third where we utilize the available restarts in some way (so far, to print their names). This separation will achieve greater code clarity and isolate the different concerns of our program.

Let us separate the first part from the rest. We will factor it out into a function call-with-home-restarts that, just like call-with-home-choices from the earlier section, will establish the new restarts for us; in addition, however, it will also set the *toplevel-restarts* variable for filtering out the restarts not relevant for us.

```
(defun call-with-home-restarts (thunk)
  (let ((*toplevel-restarts* (compute-restarts)))
    (restart-bind ((escape-through-front-door
                     #'perform-escape-through-front-door
                     :test-function #'escape-through-front-door-p)
                   (escape-through-back-door
                     #'perform-escape-through-back-door
                     :test-function #'escape-through-back-door-p))
      (funcall thunk))))
```

We can verify that our code, when called by call-with-home-restarts, behaves in the expected manner. If we call it with both doors unlocked, we have both restarts available:

```
CL-USER> (call-with-home-restarts
           (lambda ()
             (let ((*mark-safe-p* nil)
                   (*front-door-locked-p* nil)
                   (*back-door-locked-p* nil))
```

```
            (let* ((restarts (compute-relevant-restarts))
                   (names (mapcar #'restart-name restarts)))
              (format t "~{;; ~A~%~}" names)))))
;; ESCAPE-THROUGH-BACK-DOOR
;; ESCAPE-THROUGH-FRONT-DOOR
NIL
```

On the other hand, if both doors are locked, we have no way to let Mark escape:

```
CL-USER> (call-with-home-restarts
          (lambda ()
            (let ((*mark-safe-p* nil))
              (let* ((restarts (compute-relevant-restarts))
                     (names (mapcar #'restart-name restarts)))
                (format t "~{;; ~A~%~}" names)))))
NIL
```

This brings our restart-based implementation on par with the choice-based one that we created ourselves. We will use the same main function as we did in the earlier chapter:

```
(defun parents-come-back ()
  (format t ";; Uh oh - Kate's parents are back!~%")
  (try-to-hide-mark)
  (if *mark-safe-p*
      (format t ";; Whew... We're safe! For now.~%")
      (we do not want to be here)))
```

The try-to-hide-mark function will also be very similar to the one we created for choices. Other than performing a s/choice/restart/g inside it and substituting compute-restarts with compute-relevant-restarts, we are allowed to use the system-defined function invoke-restart on it from the very start:

```
(defun try-to-hide-mark ()
  (let ((restarts (compute-relevant-restarts)))
    (if restarts
        (let ((restart (first restarts)))
          (format t ";; Performing ~A.~%" (restart-name restart))
          (invoke-restart restart))
        (format t ";; Kate cannot hide Mark!~%"))))
```

This means that we can execute `parents-come-back` in the dynamic environment created by `call-with-home-restarts` in various states of the doors' openness:

```
CL-USER> (call-with-home-restarts
           (lambda ()
             (let ((*mark-safe-p* nil)
                   (*front-door-locked-p* nil))
               (parents-come-back))))
;; Uh oh - Kate's parents are back!
;; Performing ESCAPE-THROUGH-FRONT-DOOR.
;; Escaping through the front door.
;; Whew... We're safe! For now.
NIL

CL-USER> (call-with-home-restarts
           (lambda ()
             (let ((*mark-safe-p* nil)
                   (*back-door-locked-p* nil))
               (parents-come-back))))
;; Uh oh - Kate's parents are back!
;; Performing ESCAPE-THROUGH-BACK-DOOR.
;; Escaping through the back door.
;; Whew... We're safe! For now.
NIL
```

How about the situation in which no doors are open? (Note that, again, for Kate's and Mark's well-being, we demonstrate this in a safe environment—we do not call `parents-come-back`, but only `try-to-hide-mark`.)

```
CL-USER> (call-with-home-restarts
           (lambda ()
             (let ((*mark-safe-p* nil))
               (try-to-hide-mark))))
;; Kate cannot hide Mark!
NIL
```

Similarly, we can refactor the preceding code to allow the use of a single escape restart name for the different escape methods that we have. We will also modify try-to-hide-mark to use the system-provided find-restart function, analogous to find-choice which we defined earlier ourselves.

```
(defun call-with-home-restarts (thunk)
  (let ((*toplevel-restarts* (compute-restarts)))
    (restart-bind ((escape #'perform-escape-through-back-door
                           :test-function #'escape-through-back-door-p)
                   (escape #'perform-escape-through-front-door
                           :test-function #'escape-through-front-door-p))
      (funcall thunk))))

(defun try-to-hide-mark ()
  (cond ((find-restart 'escape)
         (invoke-restart 'escape))
        (t (format t ";; Kate cannot hide Mark!~%"))))
```

And these are the examples of the preceding code in use:

```
CL-USER> (call-with-home-restarts
          (lambda ()
            (let ((*mark-safe-p* nil)
                  (*front-door-locked-p* nil))
              (parents-come-back))))
;; Uh oh - Kate's parents are back!
;; Escaping through the front door.
;; Whew... We're safe! For now.
NIL

CL-USER> (call-with-home-restarts
          (lambda ()
            (let ((*mark-safe-p* nil)
                  (*back-door-locked-p* nil))
              (parents-come-back))))
;; Uh oh - Kate's parents are back!
;; Escaping through the back door.
;; Whew... We're safe! For now.
NIL
```

```
CL-USER> (call-with-home-restarts
           (lambda ()
             (let ((*mark-safe-p* nil))
               (try-to-hide-mark))))
;; Kate cannot hide Mark!
NIL
```

This also allows us easily to bind a restart with a different name and a different implementation: our excuse restart from earlier.

```
(defvar *excuses*
  '("Kate did not divide her program into sections properly!"
    "I was borrowing Kate's books on mainframe programming!"
    "I had COBOL-related homework and hoped Kate could help me!"))

(defun perform-excuse (excuse)
  (format t ";; Mark makes an excuse before leaving:~%;; \"~A\"~%" excuse)
  (setf *mark-safe-p* t))
```

We will modify try-to-hide-mark and call-with-home-restarts in the same way we have modified the choice-based implementation. (The latter function, obviously, will need a slightly different syntax provided by the restart-bind macro.)

```
(defun try-to-hide-mark ()
  (cond ((find-restart 'escape)
         (invoke-restart 'escape))
        (t
         (format t ";; Kate cannot hide Mark!~%")
         (when (find-restart 'excuse)
           (let ((excuse-text (elt *excuses* (random (length *excuses*)))))
             (invoke-restart 'excuse excuse-text))))))

(defun call-with-home-restarts (thunk)
  (let ((*toplevel-restarts* (compute-restarts)))
    (restart-bind ((escape #'perform-escape-through-back-door
                           :test-function #'escape-through-back-door-p)
                   (escape #'perform-escape-through-front-door
                           :test-function #'escape-through-front-door-p)
                   (excuse #'perform-excuse))
      (funcall thunk))))
```

(One difference from the choice system: in `restart-bind`, restarts are established in order from the last one to the first one; this means that the `excuse` restart will be the on top of the list returned by `compute-relevant-restarts`, even though here in the code it is on the bottom.)

Is Mark safe in a restart-based situation where no escape is possible? Let us find out!

```
CL-USER> (call-with-home-restarts
          (lambda ()
            (let ((*mark-safe-p* nil))
              (parents-come-back))))
;; Uh oh - Kate's parents are back!
;; Kate cannot hide Mark!
;; Mark makes an excuse before leaving:
;; "I was borrowing Kate's books on mainframe programming!"
;; Whew... We're safe! For now.
NIL
```

Again, we can see that the system of choices that we have created maps perfectly into the restart system. (Almost as if the author did that on purpose!...) Of course, this apparent perfect mapping exists only to the extent to which we have used the restart system so far; while the preceding exercises display the internal structure and workings of the restart system, they do *not* represent the canonical way of using restarts. The next section will elaborate on that.

## 2.4.1  Interactive restarts

There is one more function provided by standard CL that we have not implemented in the choice system from the previous chapter; we will instead discuss it now. It is most commonly used from within the debugger, since it is used *interactively* to prompt the user for arguments which are then used to call a given restart. However, user code is also allowed to call this function on its own.

That function is named `invoke-restart-interactively`, and it does not accept any arguments other than the *restart designator* for the restart that it is meant to invoke. The restart arguments are instead retrieved by calling one aspect of the restart system that we have not touched—the restart's "*interactive function*".

Let us imagine a situation in which we may supply Mark with new excuses interactively. Only if the excuse we supply is empty, will Mark resort to one of the classical ones which we have stored in the value of *excuses*. This requires us to change the function try-to-hide-mark so it calls invoke-restart-interactively instead of a non-interactive invoke-restart.

```
(defun try-to-hide-mark ()
  (cond ((find-restart 'escape)
         (invoke-restart 'escape))
        (t
         (format t ";; Kate cannot hide Mark!~%")
         (when (find-restart 'excuse)
           (invoke-restart-interactively 'excuse)))))
```

This function will compile without complaints; however, attempting to execute it will not work. The default interactive function for all restarts returns an empty list of arguments, whereas our excuse restart needs exactly one argument to be passed to it. This means that we need to define an interactive function for our excuse restart, which we then pass to the created excuse restart. We can do this by modifying call-with-home-restarts.

```
(defun provide-excuse ()
  (format t ";; Mark is thinking of an excuse...~%")
  (let ((excuse-text (read-line)))
    (list (if (string/= "" excuse-text)
              excuse-text
              (elt *excuses* (random (length *excuses*)))))))
```

Calling this function and passing it some text causes this text to be returned, wrapped in a list. (The outer list is required, since invoke-restart-interactively is expected to return a list of arguments.)

```
CL-USER> (provide-excuse)
;; Mark is thinking of an excuse...
I was discussing the distinct aspects of mainframe repair!     ; text input by the user
("I was discussing the distinct aspects of mainframe repair!")
```

If we instead provide no input (an empty line), this function instead picks a random predefined excuse.

```
CL-USER> (provide-excuse)
;; Mark is thinking of an excuse...
                                                   ; empty line provided
("I was borrowing Kate's books on mainframe programming!")
```

Now that the provide-excuse function works as intended, we can add it to the excuse restart

```
(defun call-with-home-restarts (thunk)
  (let ((*toplevel-restarts* (compute-restarts)))
    (restart-bind ((escape #'perform-escape-through-back-door
                           :test-function #'escape-through-back-door-p)
                   (escape #'perform-escape-through-front-door
                           :test-function #'escape-through-front-door-p)
                   (excuse #'perform-excuse
                           :interactive-function #'provide-excuse))
      (funcall thunk))))
```

and try running our code!

```
CL-USER> (call-with-home-restarts
           (lambda ()
             (let ((*mark-safe-p* nil))
               (parents-come-back))))
;; Uh oh - Kate's parents are back!
;; Kate cannot hide Mark!
;; Mark is thinking of an excuse...
I was working on getting a mainframe installed in Kate's room! ; text input by the user
;; Mark makes an excuse before leaving:
;; "I was working on getting a mainframe installed in Kate's room!"
;; Whew... We're safe! For now.
NIL

CL-USER> (call-with-home-restarts
           (lambda ()
             (let ((*mark-safe-p* nil))
               (parents-come-back))))
;; Uh oh - Kate's parents are back!
;; Kate cannot hide Mark!
;; Mark is thinking of an excuse...
                                         ; empty line provided
;; Mark makes an excuse before leaving:
;; "Kate did not divide her program into sections properly!"
;; Whew... We're safe! For now.
NIL
```

Of course, the interactive function for a given restart may call `read-line` multiple times in order to get more than one textual argument. It may also call other query functions, such as `read` for reading Lisp data, or `parse-integer` to try and parse a user-input string into an integer usable by Lisp. In more creative cases, the `invoke-restart-interactively` function may also, for example, invoke GUI toolkits to prompt the user for data input or for selecting some of the options available to them by using mouse.

# 2.5  A simple system of actually restarting restarts

While a restart is not strictly required to "restart" any abstract process in the code, the usual way to use restarts is exactly this: "rolling back" the code to some previously established good point, with an optional step of performing some recovery action earlier.

Just as `handler-case` is much, much more commonly used in practice than `handler-bind`, the macro `restart-case` is more frequently used than `restart-bind`. This is not to say that `restart-bind` is never used—there are sometimes practical uses for it—just that the macro `restart-case` (which, like `handler-case`, always performs a non-local transfer of control) is the more commonly used part of the restart facility, compared to `restart-bind`.

This turns out to be because restarts which do *not* perform non-local transfers of control do not integrate well with one other CL facility: the debugger. As mentioned earlier, there is no programmatic way of leaving the debugger; and even with a programmer interacting with the debugger, the only way of escaping it is to perform a non-local transfer of control outside the debugger. If a restart function returns normally, then such a normal return is not enough to leave a debugger, even if that function performs some side effects which otherwise modify the state of the program.

We will describe the debugger itself in a later part of this book; for now, we will focus on the two macros which establish restarts that always perform a non-local exit: `restart-case` and `with-simple-restart`.

## 2.5.1  Restarts that perform a non-local exit

First, we need to describe the means by which a restart established by `handler-bind` is capable of transferring control outside of a form executed within it.

Instead of using `catch` and `throw`, as we did with handlers, we will utilize a different pair of operators: `block` and `return-from`. This pair of operators is lexical in scope and therefore less footgun-shaped than `catch` and `throw`.

We will begin by creating a *named block*. A block, in CL, is a form that gives special meaning to return-from forms that execute within its lexical scope; it becomes possible to short-circuit the execution of code inside the block in order to return from it (and, optionally, return a value). (If a block is not named (or rather, named nil), then return can be used in place of return-from. return is a shorthand for return-from nil.)

Therefore, the following code will work correctly and will return without printing anything:

```
CL-USER> (block restart
           (restart-bind ((abort (lambda () (return-from restart))))
             (invoke-restart 'abort)
             (format t ";; We do not want to be here.~%")))
NIL
```

However, let us suppose that we want to perform some action in addition to a simple non-local exit; let us say that, after transferring control outside of the affected form, we want to print a different debug message. For this extra action, we may use one more lexical mechanism of control flow: tagbody and go. Just like the dreaded goto of other programming languages, the lexically scoped tagbody and go allow control to be transferred out from arbitrary places in the code and into one of the *tagbody tags* stored in the body of tagbody.

The following example illustrates this:

```
CL-USER> (block restart
           (tagbody
              (restart-bind ((abort (lambda () (go :abort))))
                (invoke-restart 'abort)
                (format t ";; We do not want to be here.~%"))
            :abort
              (format t ";; Whew. That was close.~%")
              (return-from restart)))
;; Whew. That was close.
NIL
```

It is possible to extend this example into multiple restarts. This requires the list of restarts bound in restart-bind to be appropriately extended with new restart forms and the body of tagbody to be similarly expanded with new tags and the bodies that execute associated restart cases.

However, a keen eye may notice that this example assumes that the lambda list of a given restart is always empty, that is, that the abort restart defined earlier does not accept any arguments. For example, if our abort restart accepted a single argument, reason for the abort, the preceding mechanism would not be able to handle that properly.

We may begin fixing this issue by wrapping the restart case in a function that accepts such a single argument. Once that is done, we may route the arguments that are actually passed to the bound restart by means of a *local variable* whose value will be the arguments with which the restart function was called. Once that is done, we will call the restart case with these arguments:

```
CL-USER> (block restart
          (let (restart-arguments)
            (tagbody
              (restart-bind ((abort (lambda (&rest arguments)
                                       (setf restart-arguments arguments)
                                       (go :abort))))
                (invoke-restart 'abort :about-to-error)
                (format t ";; We do not want to be here.~%"))
             :abort
              (return-from restart
                (apply (lambda (reason) (format t ";; Whew: ~A.~%" reason))
                       restart-arguments)))))
;; Whew: ABOUT-TO-ERROR.
NIL
```

This implementation outlines the difference between a *restart function* and a *restart case*. In restart-bind, all code is allowed to run within the restart function, because there is no requirement to leave the dynamic scope of restart-bind before executing our code. For restart-case, however, the stack must first be unwound in order to, among other things, disestablish the original restart that we bind via handler-bind and to execute any cleanup forms established by unwind-protect in the dynamic scope. Therefore, the only effective responsibility of the *restart function* inside restart-case is to pass the arguments it was called with outside and transfer control to code that calls the *restart case*.

## 2.5.2 From RESTART-BIND to RESTART-CASE

We can see that the code from the last example is complex and therefore unwieldy to write on one's own. This is why the standard macro restart-case implements that idiom. First, a non-local transfer of control is made; second, the restart forms are executed; third, the value returned by the restart forms is returned from the outermost block created by the restart-case.

The restart-case code equivalent to the preceding form looks like this:

```
CL-USER> (restart-case (progn (invoke-restart 'abort :about-to-error)
                              (format t ";; We do not want to be here.~%"))
           (abort (reason) (format t ";; Whew: was ~A.~%" reason)))
;; Whew: was ABOUT-TO-ERROR.
NIL
```

We can see that it is much shorter than the earlier one. It also fulfills our requirement of first disestablishing the dynamic scope and only then calling the code contained in the restart case:

```
CL-USER> (restart-case
            (unwind-protect
                (progn (invoke-restart 'abort :about-to-error)
                       (format t ";; We do not want to be here.~%"))
              (format t ";; Leaving the dynamic scope.~%"))
           (abort (reason)
             (format t ";; Whew: was ~A.~%" reason)))
;; Leaving the dynamic scope.
;; Whew: was ABOUT-TO-ERROR.
NIL
```

Let us apply this knowledge to rework the earlier example of Kate and Mark trying to cover up for themselves. Because the restarts established by restart-case always transfer control outside of the restarting forms, we need to modify parents-come-back in order to move the established restarts inside its body. That, in turn, will require us to modify call-with-home-restarts, where the restarts will actually be established.

```
(defun parents-come-back ()
  (format t ";; Uh oh - Kate's parents are back!~%")
  (call-with-home-restarts
   (lambda ()
```

```
    (try-to-hide-mark)
    (we do not want to be here)))
  (format t ";; Whew... We're safe! For now.~%"))
```

The preceding function now forces `call-with-home-restarts` to accept a single lambda that will be called. The function `try-to-hide-mark` is now forced to transfer control outside of the lambda, in order to prevent the `(we do not want to be here)` form from being evaluated and wreaking havoc upon the professional lives of Mark and Kate.

This also means that the variable which we have used previously, `*mark-safe-p*`, is now unnecessary. If we want our code to be clean, we can remove the global variable definition from our code and remove now dangling references to it from the bodies of all the functions that used it: `perform-escape-through-front-door`, `perform-escape-through-back-door`, and `perform-excuse`.

```
(makunbound '*mark-safe-p*)
```

```
(defun perform-escape-through-front-door ()
  (format t ";; Escaping through the front door.~%"))
```

```
(defun perform-escape-through-back-door ()
  (format t ";; Escaping through the back door.~%"))
```

```
(defun perform-excuse (excuse)
  (format t ";; Mark makes an excuse before leaving:~%;; \"~A\"~%" excuse))
```

Let us now appropriately modify `call-with-home-restarts` to utilize `restart-case` instead of `restart-bind`.

```
(defun call-with-home-restarts (thunk)
  (let ((*toplevel-restarts* (compute-restarts)))
    (restart-case (funcall thunk)
      (escape () :test escape-through-back-door-p
        (perform-escape-through-back-door))
      (escape () :test escape-through-front-door-p
        (perform-escape-through-front-door))
      (excuse (reason) :interactive provide-excuse
        (perform-excuse reason)))))
```

(A keen eye can notice that the test/interactive functions are now provided using a different protocol. Where `handler-bind` had keywords `:test-function` and `:interactive-function`, `handler-case` has `:test` and `:interactive`; in addition, we now pass function

91

names—without the #' reader macro—instead of passing function objects. This inconsistency is an unfortunate result of CL syntax being the product of certain compromises to achieve backward compatibility with earlier Lisp dialects.)

This modification is enough to trigger the new behavior: what is noteworthy is that we do not have to perform any modifications to the body of try-to-hide-mark. If either door is unlocked, Mark is able to escape that way:

```
CL-USER> (let ((*front-door-locked-p* nil))
           (parents-come-back))
;; Uh oh - Kate's parents are back!
;; Escaping through the front door.
;; Whew... We're safe! For now.
NIL

CL-USER> (let ((*back-door-locked-p* nil))
           (parents-come-back))
;; Uh oh - Kate's parents are back!
;; Escaping through the back door.
;; Whew... We're safe! For now.
NIL
```

In case Mark needs to make an excuse:

```
CL-USER> (parents-come-back)
;; Uh oh - Kate's parents are back!
;; Kate cannot hide Mark!
;; Mark is thinking of an excuse...
I was checking if floor is even in all the rooms!     ; text input by the user
;; Mark makes an excuse before leaving:
;; "I was checking if floor is even in all the rooms!"
;; Whew... We're safe! For now.
NIL
```

We can see that our restart-binding code is now fully contained within the body of parents-come-back, and the only modifications to the dynamic environment around it are forms that state which doors are unlocked. This has effectively simplified the control flow of our functions: when a suitable restart is visible, invoking it inside try-to-hide-mark now causes an unconditional transfer control back to call-with-home-restarts where a proper restart case is executed.

Whether such simplification is beneficial for us depends on our exact use case: in some cases, we may want a more intricate flow of possible actions where restart-bind may be of more use, but in other situations—especially when we get to deal with the Lisp debugger—we might prefer the more "get me out of here" style of restart-case.

## 2.5.3 Simple restarts

There is one more operator that simplifies the syntax of restart-case even further. It allows the binding of a single restart only, and if that restart is invoked, it returns two values: nil as the primary value and t as the secondary one.

The name of that macro is with-simple-restart, and its syntax is even simpler than that of restart-case.

```
CL-USER> (with-simple-restart (escape "Wake up from the bad dream.")
           (parents-come-back))
;; Uh oh - Kate's parents are back!
NIL
T
```

Inside the macro, we define the name of that restart, but also *a format control, and optional format arguments.* (Why—we will explain in the next sections.) The forms executed within the scope of with-simple-restart will have this new restart bound. In the preceding case, the escape restart that we bind immediately transfers control outside of parents-come-back without printing anything else to the screen, returning values nil and t.

(These return values are meaningful if the forms within with-simple-restart are supposed to return a non-nil primary value and either return nil as the secondary value or not to return a secondary value at all. This means that it is possible to check the secondary value to determine whether the particular call has been restarted with the restart bound by with-simple-restart; if that is the case, the code that invoked a with-simple-restart-wrapped form may use that information for recovery.)

We can therefore see the parallel between ignore-errors and with-simple-restart. Both of them establish a dynamic binding: ignore-errors binds a condition handler, with-simple-restart—a restart. Both of these, when the object from that binding is invoked, immediately transfer control outside of their form, returning nil as the first value and a meaningful non-nil secondary value: a condition object for ignore-errors and t for with-simple-restart. (It is impossible to return a restart object as a secondary value, since restart objects always have *dynamic extent*; to repeat the definition, it is not valid to return them outside the dynamic scope in which they were bound.)

## 2.5.4  Standard restarts and restart-invoking functions

Before we explain the unusual syntax of with-simple-restart, let us take a small detour to talk about the standard restarts which portable Common Lisp programs may expect to use. There are five such restarts: abort, continue, use-value, store-value, and muffle-warning, and these are always meant to perform non-local transfers of control.

The first restart, abort, should always be bound by the Lisp system. Its role is to terminate the current computation and transfer control to a known location in the program where it may be possible to specify another command for the Lisp system. In case of interactive usage, such as communicating with Lisp via the read-eval-print loop, the abort restart should make it possible to input another command into the REPL; in case of programmatic or batch usage, such a restart is allowed to terminate the Lisp system altogether and return control to the operating system.

The restart continue is meant to allow the computation to proceed. It is up to the restart function of an individual continue restart to define what "proceeding" means in its particular context; it might mean simply continuing the standard control flow from some defined point in the program, but it might also mean interactively querying the programmer for some data before execution is continued.

The restarts use-value and store-value are usually bound when some block of code decides that a piece of Lisp data that was passed to it may be, for whatever reason, unfit for processing; for instance, they may be bound by a Lisp function that accepts only strings, in order to protect against a case when someone passes it, for example, an integer. Invoking such a restart then means that the original datum (meaning a single piece of data) that the function was invoked with is discarded, and another datum is supplied in its stead to continue program execution. The difference between the two is that use-value only utilizes the value once and then discards it, whereas store-value also stores the value in some proper place of the Lisp system, so it will also be used again in the future. (The precise *place* where the datum is stored in the second case is, again, defined by the piece of code that binds the store-value restart.)

The restart muffle-warning is established by the warn function; they will both be discussed in detail in the next section.

The programmer is free to bind these standard restarts on their own. This allows the programmer to implement these restarts in their own way that makes sense for a given program; as long as they are bound to the standard symbols listed earlier, the standard restart-invoking functions will be able to find these restarts and invoke them.

## 2.5.5  Defining custom restart-invoking functions

Each of the aforementioned restarts has an associated standard function which invokes that restart. The functions abort, continue, and muffle-warning each invoke the same-named restart without requiring any arguments, whereas use-value and store-value must be given one mandatory argument. (For completeness, all of these functions accept an optional argument, which must be a condition object. The reason for that will be explained in later chapters, since it is the same reason that compute-restarts and find-restart also accept condition objects as optional arguments.)

In addition, the functions abort and muffle-warning are unique, as they explicitly expect their respective restarts to be bound. Otherwise, they signal a control-error. Invoking continue, use-value, and store-value is safe, however; these functions do nothing if they cannot find a restart named after them.

It is actually a Lisp idiom to define functions named after individual restarts. These functions invoke their same-named restarts with any arguments they might need.

Let us utilize that knowledge to refactor further the one function that was untouched by our earlier transition from handler-bind to handler-case: try-to-hide-mark. Its implementation looked like this:

```
(defun try-to-hide-mark ()
  (cond ((find-restart 'escape)
         (invoke-restart 'escape))
        (t
         (format t ";; Kate cannot hide Mark!~%")
         (when (find-restart 'excuse)
           (invoke-restart-interactively 'excuse)))))
```

We can see that there is a pair of restarts which are invokable within its body. We shall define a pair of restart-invoking functions for restarts escape and excuse. The former is a non-interactive restart; for the latter, we will specify an option of invoking that restart interactively. If an excuse is provided, it will be used to invoke the restart function; otherwise, the user will be queried for the excuse.

```
(defun escape (&optional condition)
  (let ((restart (find-restart 'escape condition)))
    (when restart (invoke-restart restart))))

(defun excuse (&optional excuse-text condition)
  (if excuse-text
      (invoke-restart 'excuse excuse-text)
      (invoke-restart-interactively 'excuse)))
```

(These functions accept the optional `condition` argument and pass it over to `find-restart`; again, explanation of this phenomenon will become available later in the book.)

We can see that these two functions follow the logic of our program. The restart `escape` is not always available, for example, when both doors are locked; therefore, it makes sense for its restart-invoking function first to check whether such a restart is available. The restart-invoking function for `excuse`, though, assumes that it is always possible for Mark to make an excuse; it therefore assumes that an `excuse` restart is always bound.

Now that these functions are available, we can rewrite `try-to-hide-mark` to use them.

```
(defun try-to-hide-mark ()
  (escape)
  (format t ";; Kate cannot hide Mark!~%")
  (excuse))
```

We see that the control flow logic of `try-to-hide-mark` has disappeared altogether, having been offloaded onto the restart system. A keen eye may notice that our restarts have been established via `restart-case`; therefore, we can depend on the fact that they will always perform a non-local transfer of control. That is why simply calling `(escape)` will either unwind the stack to the matching `escape` handler or simply return if no such restart is available. Once that happens, debug information is printed, and `(excuse)` is called to ultimately save Mark and Kate from the doom of becoming mainframe programmers for the rest of their lives.

We have not utilized the optional `excuse-text` argument to the function `excuse` in the given scenario; however, it is worthwhile to keep that option inside the function body, since it may be utilized in other situations. For instance, Kate may notice that a particular set of excuses—for example, talking about C++—works particularly well on her father. To model that behavior, the only required modification will be changing `try-to-hide-mark` to call the `excuse` function explicitly with a suitable, C++-mentioning excuse text.

This mechanism is a part of a whole other part of the condition system which we have not yet touched: reporting condition objects and restarts. We will do that now.

# 2.6  Reporting conditions and restarts

One thing that we have not explained in the previous chapter is the fact that `with-simple-restart` requires us to pass *a format control string* and allows us to pass in optional *format arguments*. This ties in with the fact that, so far, we have been discussing conditions and restarts in a non-interactive context. The conditions we have signaled and the restarts we have invoked were all handled programmatically. Even in such a fully automated environment, though, it might be worthwhile to have observability into what is happening inside the program.

One common use of condition handlers is to insert logging into programs which is triggered by signaled conditions. In addition, such logging might be a part of the functioning of restarts; the program logs may want to include information about which restart is being invoked and in which context.

CL provides functionality that dovetails well with these goals. Both condition objects and restarts have the ability to be *reported*—which means the process of extracting human-readable information about the details of a given condition or restart. This chapter shall elaborate on the details of programming this process.

## 2.6.1  Printing vs. reporting

If we were to attempt to print a condition object or a restart object, it is most likely that we would get an *unreadable* object, which is printed by `print-unreadable-object`. It would likely look similar to `# <CONDITION 012345ABCDEF>` or `#<RESTART FOO 012345FEDCBA>`. (This behavior is not mandated by the Common Lisp standard, but is nonetheless exhibited by all Common Lisp implementations the author is aware of.) This syntax is called "unreadable" since it is impossible to read these objects back into Lisp by using the standard `read` function; the Lisp reader signals an error every time it encounters the character `#<` at the beginning of the read object.

The way to force a condition or a restart to be *reported* is by setting the global variable *print-escape*. This is a system variable which is initially set to true, and that is what causes the condition and restart objects to be printed in the unreadable way. Binding it to nil and then printing causes the object's report function to be invoked instead, and the data output by that function to the reporting stream then becomes the report of that condition.

(The variable *print-escape* is implicitly bound by some of the printing functions and some of the format directives. It is implicitly bound to true by, for example, the function prin1 and the format directive ~S; it is implicitly bound to false by, for example, the function princ and the format directive ~A. Functions write, write-string, and write-to-string and the format directive ~W do not bind that variable themselves; they simply use its value from the dynamic environment in which they are executed.)

For conditions and restarts with no specified report function, the reported data is implementation-dependent. Therefore, not only to provide proper content to be reported but also to ensure overall consistency across all conditions and restarts which may be reported in our program, it is important to specify the report functions in all define-condition, restart-bind, and restart-case macros which we write.

This fact also means that the code examples from the earlier chapters are not suited for situations where the condition or restart objects might have been reported. No such situation occurred in the preceding examples; however, from now on, our code will contain proper report functions for all defined conditions and bound restarts.

## 2.6.2  Custom condition reports

Condition objects are printed in their unreadable form if the dynamic variable *print-escape* is bound to t. However, when that same variable is bound to nil, printing a restart objects causes its *report function* to be invoked. That report function accepts a pair of arguments: the condition object itself and the reporting stream that the report should be written to. This means that the report function is capable of querying the condition object for all the information that is needed for generating a proper report; it is good style for condition reporting functions to be self-contained, which means not to depend on any Lisp data other than the condition object itself.

Let us come back to the earlier example of Tom and his phonebook. We will not focus on the calling algorithm this time; we will instead spend our time on the condition objects themselves, in particular: on ensuring that they are reported properly.

The three conditions we have defined in that example are:

```
(define-condition before-call ()
  ((%person :reader person :initarg :person)))

(define-condition after-call ()
  ((%person :reader person :initarg :person)))

(define-condition grave-mistake (error)
  ((%reason :reader reason :initarg :reason)))
```

We see that the earlier two are similar, since both of them refer to a person who is about to be called or whom was just called. We will return to the third one in a moment; for now, we will utilize the condition inheritance that is possible in CL to refactor the first two conditions slightly.

```
(define-condition person-condition ()
  ((%person :reader person :initarg :person)))

(define-condition before-call (person-condition) ())

(define-condition after-call (person-condition) ())
```

We have extracted the common slot into a single condition type named person-condition and caused before-call and after-call to inherit from it. This allows us to reduce code duplication slightly, since the report functions for both before-call and after-call can now call the function person on the condition object in order to be able to fetch the person who was, respectively, about to be called or actually called.

Let us write report functions for these two conditions.

```
(define-condition before-call (person-condition) ()
  (:report (lambda (condition stream)
             (format stream "We are about to call ~A." (person condition)))))

(define-condition after-call (person-condition) ()
  (:report (lambda (condition stream)
             (format stream "We have just called ~A." (person condition)))))
```

This ensures that the conditions we have created are reported correctly.

```
CL-USER> (let ((*print-escape* nil))
           (write-to-string (make-condition 'before-call :person :mom)))
"We are about to call MOM."
```

```
CL-USER> (let ((*print-escape* nil))
           (write-to-string (make-condition 'after-call :person :mom)))
"We have just called MOM."
```

As we come back to the condition grave-mistake, let us focus for a moment on the :report option. These three means of defining are all valid (even though the first one does not utilize the reason slot in our condition):

```
(define-condition grave-mistake (error)
  ((%reason :reader reason :initarg :reason))
  (:report "We are committing a grave mistake."))

(define-condition grave-mistake (error)
  ((%reason :reader reason :initarg :reason))
  (:report (lambda (condition stream)
             (format stream "We are committing a grave mistake: ~A."
                     (reason condition)))))

(defun report-grave-mistake (condition stream)
  (format stream "We are committing a grave mistake: ~A."
          (reason condition)))

(define-condition grave-mistake (error)
  ((%reason :reader reason :initarg :reason))
  (:report report-grave-mistake))
```

In the first case, the report for the given condition is a static string. (Even though the report does not utilize the reason slot in any way, this slot is still accessible to handlers; this is why removing it altogether is not a valid move.) The second case passes a lambda form as the option value, and the third one passes the name of a function.

From these examples, we are able to induce that the :report option has multiple ways of specifying the actual report contents. The first example shows that it accepts a string, which then becomes the condition report as is. This string is written to the reporting stream as if by write-string. The second example shows that it can accept an anonymous function which can then explicitly output a string to the reporting stream. And in the third example, the condition supplies :report with the symbol report-grave-mistake— which is the name of a function bound elsewhere. (The actual function may be bound globally, as via defun, or locally, as via flet or labels.)

## 2.6.3 Custom restart reports

For restarts, the situation is similar to that which we have encountered for conditions. Restart objects are printed in their unreadable form if the dynamic variable *print-escape* is bound to t. However, when *print-escape* is bound to nil, printing a restart object causes its *report function* to be invoked. However, since restarts are objects of dynamic extent that are not usually utilized directly, report functions suitable for use in restarts only accept one argument: the stream to which they are expected to output their information.

Let us consider a simplified version of the earlier example with Kate and Mark. For brevity, we will completely ignore the restart functions (which will be empty) and test functions (which will be defaulted). We will only focus on the parts of code that are relevant to *reporting* the restarts in question and completely neuter all logic related to actually handling the situations Kate and Mark are finding themselves in. ~~(Poor Mark.)~~

The simplified code from the earlier example is:

```
(defvar *toplevel-restarts* '())

(defun compute-relevant-restarts (&optional condition)
  (set-difference (compute-restarts condition) *toplevel-restarts*))

(defvar *excuses*
  '("Kate did not divide her program into sections properly!"
    "I was borrowing Kate's books on mainframe programming!"
    "I had COBOL-related homework and hoped Kate could help me!"))

(defun call-with-home-restarts (thunk)
  (let ((*toplevel-restarts* (compute-restarts))
        (excuse (elt *excuses* (random (length *excuses*)))))
    (flet ((report-excuse (stream) (format stream "Make an excuse, ~S." excuse)))
      (restart-case (funcall thunk)
        (escape ()
          :report "Escape through the back door.")
        (escape ()
          :report (lambda (stream)
                    (write-string "Escape through the front door." stream)))
        (excuse ()
          :report report-excuse)))))
```

The first two forms are still relevant to us, since we only want to concern ourselves with restarts that we bind ourselves.

The third form is a collection of excuses that Mark is allowed to make; in the interest of simplicity, once again we will allow Mark to choose only from these three excuses. In addition, one can see that the excuse is now randomly chosen inside the body of `call-with-home-restarts`. One reason for that is to simplify our code, but the other is the fact that the excuse is now used inside the local function `report-excuse`.

Instead of starting with a full explanation of the preceding code, we will instead begin with a more hands-on example.

```
CL-USER> (call-with-home-restarts
           (lambda ()
             (let ((*print-escape* nil))
               (format t ";; Available restarts:~%;;~%~{;; ~W~%~}"
                       (compute-relevant-restarts)))))
;; Available restarts:
;;
;; Make an excuse, "I had COBOL-related homework and hoped Kate could help me!".
;; Escape through the front door.
;; Escape through the back door.
NIL
```

The anonymous function we call here first binds the dynamic variable *print-escape* to nil, causing the report function of the restart objects to be invoked. This is how we are able to print human-readable reports for each individual restart that is returned from compute-relevant-restarts.

Let us take a closer look at the restart-case form from earlier.

```
(...
 (restart-case (funcall thunk)
   (escape ()
     :report "Escape through the back door.")
   (escape ()
     :report (lambda (stream)
               (write-string "Escape through the front door." stream)))
   (excuse ()
     :report report-excuse)))
```

We can see that the `:report` option for each restart case accepts three different kinds of arguments, just like in `define-condition`. This "do-what-I-mean"-style richness is not shared by `restart-bind`, however. The two differences in how `restart-bind` treats restart reports are, first, the difference in keyword used for report functions (`restart-case` uses `:report`, whereas `restart-bind` uses `:report-function`) and, second, that `restart-bind` explicitly requires *function objects* to be passed as their arguments. (This means that, contrary to `restart-case`, it is not possible to pass function names there; this inconsistency is yet another compromise made by the CL standard committee.)

If we wanted to replicate the preceding functionality via `restart-bind` instead of `restart-case` (while still ignoring all actual restarting behavior), then we could implement `call-with-home-restarts` in the following way:

```
(defun call-with-home-restarts (thunk)
  (let ((*toplevel-restarts* (compute-restarts))
        (excuse (elt *excuses* (random (length *excuses*)))))
    (flet ((report-excuse (stream) (format stream "Make an excuse, ~S." excuse)))
      (restart-bind
          ((escape (lambda ())
                   :report-function
                   (lambda (stream)
                     (write-string "Escape through the back door." stream)))
           (escape (lambda ())
                   :report-function
                   (lambda (stream)
                     (write-string "Escape through the front door." stream)))
           (excuse (lambda ())
                   :report-function #'report-excuse))
        (funcall thunk)))))
```

We can evaluate the same form as before to confirm that this behavior is consistent with the previous example.

```
CL-USER> (call-with-home-restarts
           (lambda ()
             (let ((*print-escape* nil))
               (format t ";; Available restarts:~%;;~%~{;; ~W~%~}"
                       (compute-relevant-restarts)))))
```

```
;; Available restarts:
;;
;; Make an excuse, "I was borrowing Kate's books on mainframe programming!".
;; Escape through the front door.
;; Escape through the back door.
NIL
```

One more notable detail is that the local function `report-excuse` accesses the `excuse` variable from earlier in its scope in order to print its value in the report. Also note that, every time the `excuse` restart is established inside `call-with-home-restarts`, the excuse for the restart will be chosen randomly from the three available ones; this excuse will be used both for reporting the restart and for letting Mark use it on Kate's parents. (Note also that, if we somehow invoke the same `excuse` restart multiple times, the excuse given will remain the same between the distinct invocations.)

Creating *closures* is the way to work around the fact that report functions for restarts, unlike those for conditions, accept no user-programmable objects which could be queried for more information about the report. (Restarts, unlike conditions, cannot be subclassed or otherwise extended by the user.)

# 2.7  Warnings

Now that we know how to report conditions properly, we can describe one more standard CL operator that makes use of that information. The function `warn` is one more means of signaling a condition, in addition to the functions `signal` and `error`. If the signaled condition is not handled, `signal` simply returns `nil` and `error` invokes the debugger; `warn` instead reports the condition to the stream that is the value of `*error-output*` before returning `nil`. Additionally, it must be used to signal conditions of type `warning`, which is a subtype of `condition`.

One more fact that we have yet to talk about is that the data accepted by all these functions—`signal`, `warn`, and `error`—are versatile. Each function may accept either a condition object itself, a set of arguments suitable for `make-condition`, or a format string and arguments that are then used to construct a condition of type `simple-warning`.

# 2.7.1 Different ways of warning

We will draw on the preceding knowledge to demonstrate warn. However, for such a demonstration, we will need to define a warning condition. Let us derive from our previous grave-mistake condition, defining a condition that is not an error, but a warning.

```
(defun report-grave-warning (condition stream)
  (format stream "We are committing a grave warning: ~A."
          (reason condition)))

(define-condition grave-warning (warning)
  ((%reason :reader reason :initarg :reason))
  (:report report-grave-warning))
```

Now, let's attempt to warn this condition in two cases: without handling it and while handling it to return its report instead.

```
CL-USER> (warn 'grave-warning :reason :about-to-call-your-ex)
;; WARNING: We are committing a grave warning: ABOUT-TO-CALL-YOUR-EX.
NIL

CL-USER> (handler-case (warn 'grave-warning :reason :about-to-call-your-ex)
           (warning (condition)
             (let ((*print-escape* nil))
               (write-to-string condition))))
"We are committing a grave warning: ABOUT-TO-CALL-YOUR-EX."
```

The same can be achieved if we instead use make-condition explicitly:

```
CL-USER> (warn (make-condition 'grave-warning :reason :about-to-call-your-ex))
;; WARNING: We are committing a grave warning: ABOUT-TO-CALL-YOUR-EX.
NIL
CL-USER> (handler-case (warn (make-condition 'grave-warning :reason :about-to-call-your-ex))
           (warning (condition)
             (let ((*print-escape* nil))
               (write-to-string condition))))
"We are committing a grave warning: ABOUT-TO-CALL-YOUR-EX."
```

Finally, if we do not care about signaling a particular warning type (and are therefore fine with simple-warning that warn will implicitly create for us), we may pass a format control (with optional format arguments) to warn.

```
CL-USER> (warn "Example warning with no arguments.")
;; WARNING: Example warning with no arguments.
NIL

CL-USER> (handler-case (warn "Example warning with no arguments.")
           (warning (condition)
             (let ((*print-escape* nil))
               (write-to-string condition))))
"Example warning with no arguments."
NIL

CL-USER> (warn "Example warning with argument ~S." 42)
;; WARNING: Example warning with argument 42.
NIL

CL-USER> (handler-case (warn "Example warning with argument ~S." 42)
           (warning (condition)
             (let ((*print-escape* nil))
               (list (write-to-string condition) (type-of condition)))))
("Example warning with argument 42." SIMPLE-WARNING)
```

## 2.7.2  Muffling warnings

Additionally, there is a particular restart, and its matching restart-invoking function, which is of particular interest when considering the function warn. The name of that restart is muffle-warning, and it is established inside warn in a way that makes it visible in the dynamic scope of the signaled condition. Invoking the muffle-warning restart informs the Lisp system that the warning has been accounted for in some way and that execution of the program may continue without any other actions, for example, reporting the warning to *error-output*. We can observe this behavior on the following example:

```
CL-USER> (warn "Example warning with argument ~S." 42)
;; WARNING: Example warning with argument 42.
NIL

CL-USER> (handler-bind ((warning #'muffle-warning))
           (warn "Example warning with argument ~S." 42))
NIL
```

# 2.8 Assertions

Now that we have covered the topic of restarts, we can touch one more topic that utilizes both condition handling and restarts. CL includes certain operators which act as *assertions*: unless some condition is met, they signal errors, which—unless they are handled—force entry into the debugger. Some of these assertions bind restarts around the error sites, which allows execution to proceed if those restarts are invoked and—in case of assert and check-type—if some additional conditions are met.

## 2.8.1 Simple assertions via ASSERT

The macro assert, in its simplest form, checks whether its test form evaluates to true (i.e., non-NIL) or not. If it does, it returns nil; if it doesn't, it signals an error.

```
CL-USER> (handler-case (assert (= (+ 2 2) 4)))
NIL

CL-USER> (handler-case (assert (= (+ 2 2) 5))
          (error () :HANDLED))
:HANDLED
```

However, assert also establishes a continue restart that allows the programmer to retry the assertion. This ability is most useful in interactive programming environments where the programmer may, for example, *redefine* a failing function while still in the debugger and then invoke the restart. However, it can also be used, for example, to retry some process in a brute-force manner.

```
CL-USER> (handler-bind ((error (lambda (condition)
                                 (declare (ignore condition))
                                 (format t ";; Retrying...~%")
                                 (continue))))
          (assert (= (random 10) 0)))
;; Retrying...
;; Retrying...
;; Retrying...
;; Retrying...
;; Retrying...                              ; the number of retries
;; Retrying...                              ; will vary randomly
;; Retrying...
```

```
;; Retrying...
;; Retrying...
;; Retrying...
NIL
```

The optional arguments to assert allow the programmer to alter the functionalities of the restart further: if they pass a non-empty collection of Lisp *places* to the macro, then the continue restart will prompt the programmer with the option to populate these places with new, interactively provided values.

```
CL-USER> (handler-bind ((error #'continue))
           (let ((x nil))
             (assert x (x))))
;; The old value of X is NIL.
;; Do you want to supply a new value? (y or n) y     ; user input here
;; Type a form to be evaluated: t                    ; user input here
NIL
```

The further optional arguments consist of a datum and arguments that should be passed to the error call that reports the error. This means that we can pass a symbol naming the condition type and initialization arguments for the constructed condition; we can also provide a format control and format arguments that should be passed along to the condition reporter.

```
CL-USER> (handler-case (assert (= (+ 2 2) 5) ()
                               'type-error :datum 5 :expected-type '(eql 4))
           (error (condition)
             (let ((*print-escape* nil))
               (format t ";; ~W~%" condition))))
;; The value 5 is not of type (EQL 4).
NIL

CL-USER> (handler-case (assert (= (+ 2 2) 5) ()
                               "The numbers ~D and ~D do not sum up to ~D." 2 2 5)
           (error (condition)
             (let ((*print-escape* nil))
               (format t ";; ~W~%" condition))))
;; The numbers 2 and 2 do not sum up to 5.
NIL
```

## 2.8.2  Type checking via CHECK-TYPE

The macro check-type functions similarly to assert; however, it requires specifying exactly one place and a type form. A check is then made to see whether the value in that place is of the provided type; if not, a type-error is signaled.

```
CL-USER> (let ((x 42))
           (check-type x integer))
NIL

CL-USER> (let ((x "42"))
           (handler-case (check-type x integer)
             (type-error () :oops)))
:OOPS
```

This macro binds a store-value restart around the error site; invoking that restart causes the user to be prompted for a new value of that place, after which the type check is repeated.

It is noteworthy that, while assert binds a continue restart, check-type binds a store-value restart; this distinction is important. check-type always works on a single place, whereas assert can work on an arbitrary number of places.

```
CL-USER> (let ((x "42"))
           (handler-bind ((type-error (lambda (condition)
                                        (declare (ignore condition))
                                        (store-value 42))))
             (check-type x integer)
             x))
42
```

The only optional argument to check-type is a string that describes, in human-readable form, the type that is to be checked; this argument is used during the construction of the condition report for the signaled error.

```
CL-USER> (let ((x 24))
           (handler-case (check-type x (eql 42) "the ultimate answer to everything")
             (type-error (condition)
               (let ((*print-escape* nil))
                 (format t ";; ~W~%" condition)))))
;; The value of X is 24, which is not the ultimate answer to everything.
NIL
```

## 2.8.3  Case assertions

The macros ecase and etypecase are variants of case and typecase. The latter two return nil when no case matches the provided test key; the former two instead signal a type-error.

```
CL-USER> (let ((x 24))
           (handler-case (ecase x
                           (42 :integer)
                           (:forty-two :keyword)
                           ("42" :string))
             (type-error (condition)
               (let ((*print-escape* nil))
                 (format t ";; ~W" condition)))))
;; 24 fell through ECASE expression. Wanted one of (42 :FORTY-TWO "42").
NIL
```

ecase ensures that the test key is *of type* (member key-1 key-2 key-3 ...), where key-n are all the keys provided to ecase in case forms.

```
CL-USER> (let ((x nil))
           (handler-case (etypecase x
                           (integer :integer)
                           (keyword :keyword)
                           (string :string))
             (type-error (condition)
               (let ((*print-escape* nil))
                 (format t ";; ~W" condition)))))
;; NIL fell through ETYPECASE expression. Wanted one of (INTEGER KEYWORD STRING).
NIL
```

etypecase ensures that the test key is of type (or type-1 type-2 type-3 ...), where type-n are all the types provided to etypecase in typecase forms.

## 2.8.4  Correctable case assertions

The macros ccase and ctypecase are variants of ecase and etypecase. They function in the same way as their e* counterparts, except that they also establish a store-value restart around the type-error that they signal. This means that it is possible to continue program execution even after the error is signaled by invoking the store-value restart with the proper argument. The ccase or ctypecase is then retried with the newly stored value.

```
CL-USER> (let ((x nil))
           (handler-bind ((type-error (lambda (condition)
                                        (declare (ignore condition))
                                        (store-value 42))))
             (ctypecase x
               (integer :integer)
               (keyword :keyword)
               (string :string))))
:INTEGER

CL-USER> (let ((x nil))
           (handler-bind ((type-error (lambda (condition)
                                        (declare (ignore condition))
                                        (store-value :forty-two))))
             (ccase x
               (42 :integer)
               (:forty-two :keyword)
               ("42" :string))))
:KEYWORD
```

In Lisp jargon, the behavior of ccase and ctypecase is called signaling a *correctable error*. It is implemented by the function cerror, which is, likewise, a variant of error. The function cerror takes one more required argument: a format control, which is used by the report function of the established restart.

## 2.8.5  Arguments for continuable errors

An interesting feature of cerror is that the optional arguments passed to the function are used *both* for constructing the condition object *and* as format arguments for the passed format string. Let us analyze the following form:

```
(cerror "Continue after signaling a SIMPLE-ERROR ~
         with arguments: ~S ~S ~S ~S."
        'simple-error
        :format-control "A simple error signaled with ~A."
        :format-arguments '(42))
```

Executing this form will cause the system to signal a simple-error; we expect the report of that condition object to be A simple error signaled with 42.. In addition, we expect a new restart to be bound around the error site; the restart will have a longer report form, reading Continue after signaling a SIMPLE-ERROR with arguments: and then listing all the optional arguments that cerror was called with.

We can verify our assumptions by handling the signaled simple-error and printing out information about the condition object and the most recently established restart. This is one of the situations where handler-bind is required over handler-case; if we had used the latter, we would have managed successfully to inspect the condition object, but the continue restart bound by cerror would have been disestablished already by the time control reached the handler case.

```
CL-USER> (block nil
           (flet ((print-reports (condition)
                    (let ((*print-escape* nil))
                      (format t ";; Condition report: ~W~%;; Restart report: ~W~%"
                              condition (first (compute-restarts)))
                      (return))))
             (handler-bind ((simple-error #'print-reports))
               (cerror "Continue after signaling a SIMPLE-ERROR ~
                        with arguments:~%;;    ~S ~S ~S ~S"
                       'simple-error
                       :format-control "A simple error signaled with ~A."
                       :format-arguments '(42)))))
;; Condition report: A simple error signaled with 42.
;; Restart report: Continue after signaling a SIMPLE-ERROR with arguments:
;;    :FORMAT-CONTROL "A simple error signaled with ~A." :FORMAT-ARGUMENTS (42)
NIL
```

# 2.9  A simple debugger

So far in the book, we have avoided talking in detail about the debugger. Moreover, we have completely avoided invoking it. However, in the end, there is no escaping the fact that automated error handling is never going to be good enough to take care of all erroneous situations. Sometimes, the only recourse that a program may have is to put itself into the hands of the programmer. The debugger is the utility via which Lisp achieves that goal.

# 2.9.1 Reporting the condition in the debugger

To follow the general spirit of our book, we begin not by describing the Lisp debugger, but by introducing the system-defined variable *debugger-hook*. This variable's full description will come later. For now, let us define a very simple *debugger function* that produces some output and then handles all conditions by invoking the abort restart.

```
(defun debugger (condition hook)
  (declare (ignore hook))
  (let ((*print-escape* nil))
    (format t ";; Aborting: ~W~%" condition))
  (abort condition))
```

We will, for the time being, ignore the second argument passed to that function. Let us rebind *debugger-hook* and explicitly call invoke-debugger for the first time in this book:

```
CL-USER> (let ((*debugger-hook* #'debugger)
               (condition (make-condition 'simple-error
                                          :format-control "We are in trouble.")))
           (invoke-debugger condition))
;; Aborting: We are in trouble.
;;
;; ABORT restart invoked; returning to top level.
```

We can see that the code inside our debugger function was evaluated and that the abort restart established by the Lisp system was invoked. (The message printed to the screen by that second part, if any, is implementation-dependent.) This has effectively brought us back to the read-eval-print loop, allowing us to specify the next command to be evaluated.

We can simplify the preceding example by using the fact that the function error calls invoke-debugger internally if the condition signaled by it is not handled.

```
CL-USER> (let ((*debugger-hook* #'debugger))
           (error "We are in trouble."))
;; Aborting: We are in trouble.
;;
;; ABORT restart invoked; returning to top level.
```

By performing this exercise, we have demonstrated the functioning of the *debugger-hook* variable. The function invoke-debugger first checks whether that variable is bound; if yes, then the debugger hook function is called with the condition passed to invoke-debugger. If the debugger hook function returns, for any reason, then the system-provided debugger is ultimately invoked to handle the condition.

One more step done by invoke-debugger is to bind the variable *debugger-hook* to nil. This is to ensure that, if an unexpected error is signaled *inside* the debugger hook, the debugger that is invoked recursively is the debugger provided by the Lisp system; this allows system-provided recovery from errors in the user-provided debugger. The value of *debugger-hook* is passed as the second argument to the debugger hook function, which, in our case, is the hook variable which we have ignored.

In other words, by defining one function and by binding one variable, we have defined our own custom Lisp debugger. This debugger is a very primitive one, however; it provides absolutely no interaction with the programmer and tells them little to nothing about what exactly happened. It also utilizes only one restart strategy, which is invoking the abort restart; the programmer has no chance to attempt to utilize a different one.

## 2.9.2  Reporting the condition type in the debugger

Let's breathe a bit more life into our debugger function. First of all, let us print both the condition report and the condition type before invoking the abort restart:

```
(defun debugger (condition hook)
  (declare (ignore hook))
  (let ((*print-escape* nil))
    (format t ";;~%;; Debugger entered on ~S:~%" (type-of condition))
    (format t ";; ~W~%" condition))
  (abort condition))
```

The preceding example adds another piece of information to our program: now we know the condition type of the signaled condition.

```
CL-USER> (let ((*debugger-hook* #'debugger))
           (invoke-debugger (make-condition 'simple-error
                                             :format-control "We are in trouble.")))
;;
;; Debugger entered on SIMPLE-ERROR:
```

```
;; We are in trouble.
;;
;; ABORT restart invoked; returning to top level.
```

## 2.9.3  Reporting the restarts in the debugger

Let us now list the restarts available to the user.

```
(defun debugger (condition hook)
  (declare (ignore hook))
  (let ((*print-escape* nil))
    (format t ";;~%;; Debugger entered on ~S:~%" (type-of condition))
    (format t ";; ~W~%" condition)
    (let ((restarts (compute-restarts condition)))
      (format t ";;~%;; Available restarts:~%")
      (dolist (restart restarts)
        (format t ";; [~W] ~W~%" (restart-name restart) restart))))
  (abort condition))
```

This version gives the programmer even more information about the available restarting options.

```
CL-USER> (let ((*debugger-hook* #'debugger))
           (invoke-debugger (make-condition 'simple-error
                                     :format-control "We are in trouble.")))
;;
;; Debugger entered on SIMPLE-ERROR:
;; We are in trouble.
;;
;; Available restarts:
;; [RETRY] Retry evaluating the form.
;; [ABORT] Return to the top level.
;;
;; ABORT restart invoked; returning to top level.
```

(The preceding restarts are established by the Lisp system and therefore implementation-dependent; they are allowed to look different on different implementations.)

## 2.9.4  Choosing the restarts in the debugger

Now that the restart options are listed, we should allow the programmer some simple way to choose from among them. We will assign numbers to the restarts and define a function that reads input from the user until it manages to read a valid restart number; at that point, our debugger will invoke the corresponding restart.

```
(defun read-valid-restart-number (number-of-restarts)
  (loop (format t ";;~%;; Invoke restart number: ")
        (let* ((line (read-line *query-io*))
               (integer (parse-integer line :junk-allowed t)))
          (when (and integer (< -1 integer number-of-restarts))
            (return integer)))))

(defun debugger (condition hook)
  (let ((*print-escape* nil))
    (format t ";;~%;; Debugger entered on ~S:~%" (type-of condition))
    (format t ";; ~W~%" condition)
    (let ((restarts (compute-restarts condition)))
      (format t ";;~%;; Available restarts:~%")
      (loop for i from 0
            for restart in restarts do
              (format t ";; ~D [~W] ~W~%" i (restart-name restart) restart))
      (let ((chosen-restart (read-valid-restart-number (length restarts)))
            (*debugger-hook* hook))
        (invoke-restart-interactively (nth chosen-restart restarts)))
      (debugger condition hook))))
```

This setup allows the programmer the most basic amount of interactivity, allowing them to choose which restart should be invoked. (We also rebind the *debugger-hook* variable; in case the restart function signals an error, this binding will cause our debugger function to be invoked recursively instead of escalating to the system-provided debugger.)

One more change we add in the preceding example is to call the debugger recursively at the very end of the code. This is required in case a restart returns normally instead of performing a non-local transfer of control; if a restart returns normally, we must assume that the condition was not handled and that the programmer should still remain in the debugger.

```
CL-USER> (let ((*debugger-hook* #'debugger))
           (invoke-debugger (make-condition 'simple-error
                                       :format-control "We are in trouble.")))
;;
;; Debugger entered on SIMPLE-ERROR:
;; We are in trouble.
;;
;; Available restarts:
;; 0 [RETRY] Retry evaluating the form.
;; 1 [ABORT] Return to the top level.
;;
;; Invoke restart number: 0                      ; user input here
;;
;; Debugger entered on SIMPLE-ERROR:
;; We are in trouble.
;;
;; Available restarts:
;; 0 [RETRY] Retry evaluating the form.
;; 1 [ABORT] Return to the top level.
;;
;; Invoke restart number: 3                      ; user input here
;;
;; Invoke restart number: forty-two              ; user input here
;;
;; Invoke restart number:                        ; empty line provided
;;
;; Invoke restart number: 1                      ; user input here
;;
;; ABORT restart invoked; returning to top level.
```

We can see that this simple input loop is robust enough to survive the programmer attempting to break it; the only available options which allow the programmer to leave this debugger are 0 (which immediately casts the programmer back inside, because evaluating that form again immediately invokes the debugger once more) and 1 (which aborts evaluation and brings the programmer back to the read-eval-print loop).

# 2.9.5  Installing a custom debugger

We have already come far in our debugger journey—and yet, there is a technique possible in standard CL that will defeat our current approach. Our preceding debugger depends on the Lisp system calling it when the debugger is invoked by means of the variable *debugger-hook*. This dependence means that if some code binds this variable differently—for example, to another debugger function or to nil in order to invoke the system debugger directly—then we will not be able to handle that error via our custom debugger function at all.

There is even worse news: there is a standard CL function which does exactly that kind of binding. The function is named break, and it is utilized to insert temporary *breakpoints* into a program for debugging purposes. This function internally binds *debugger-hook* to nil just before calling invoke-debugger. This means not only that no handlers are allowed to fire (because no condition is being signaled), but also that our custom debugger function has no chance of being executed!

This conundrum means that we need to seek a stronger solution than the *debugger-hook*. Such a solution, however, is not defined by the ANSI CL standard; it is up to each CL implementation to define some means of replacing the standard Lisp debugger in a way that makes it possible to capture break.

To address this issue, the author of this book has created a *portability library* named trivial-custom-debugger, available on GitHub at the time of this writing. If the reader is a Quicklisp user, it should be possible to load this library via (ql:quickload :trivial-custom-debugger); otherwise, it should be enough to (load "trivial-custom-debugger.lisp") contained within that repository.

We can then attempt to use the with-debugger macro from that package to tame the uncivilized beast that is break, by using our custom debugger function which we previously passed to *debugger-hook*:

```
CL-USER> (trivial-custom-debugger:with-debugger (#'debugger)
           (break "Breaking with ~D." 42))
;;
;; Debugger entered on SIMPLE-CONDITION:
;; Breaking with 42.
;;
;; Available restarts:
;; 0 [CONTINUE] Return from BREAK.
;; 1 [RETRY] Retry evaluating the form.
```

```
;; 2 [ABORT] Return to the top level.
;;
;; Invoke restart number: 0                              ; user input here
NIL
```

We can observe that the function break establishes a single continue restart, which is the conventional way to quit the debugger from inside a breakpoint. (It is not possible to customize the report of that restart, unless we were to perform the exercise of re-implementing break from scratch; an example implementation of break, along with the whole condition system, is available in the last chapters of this book.)

The function break is also useful in one case which we have yet to mention: in some cases, it can be invoked directly by the function signal (and its derivatives, such as warn, error, or cerror). Namely, signal is equipped with the capability to enter the debugger directly for some condition types before they are actually signaled; this allows the programmer quickly and at once to generate break calls for a whole group of conditions.

This behavior is driven by a standard variable named *break-on-signals*. Its initial value is nil, which matches no condition types; however, when we set it to an actual condition type, all signal calls which signal a condition matching that condition type will first break with that condition instead.

```
CL-USER> (trivial-custom-debugger:with-debugger (#'debugger)
           (let ((*break-on-signals* 'error))
             (handler-case (signal 'simple-error :format-control "Error: ~D."
                                                 :format-arguments '(42))
               (error (condition)
                 (format t ";; Handling a ~W.~%" (type-of condition))))))
;;
;; Debugger entered on SIMPLE-CONDITION:
;; Error: 42.
;; (BREAK was entered because of *BREAK-ON-SIGNALS*.)
;;
;; Available restarts:
;; 0 [CONTINUE] Return from BREAK.
;; 1 [RESET] Set *BREAK-ON-SIGNALS* to NIL and continue.
;; 2 [REASSIGN] Return from BREAK and assign a new value to *BREAK-ON-SIGNALS*.
;; 3 [RETRY] Retry evaluating the form.
;; 4 [ABORT] Return to the top level.
;;
```

```
;; Invoke restart number: 0                              ; user input here
;; Handling a SIMPLE-ERROR.
NIL
```

From the preceding example we see that with *break-on-signals* bound, merely signaling a condition is enough to enter the debugger directly by means of a break. Only after the continue restart is invoked are the condition handlers for that condition allowed to execute.

We can also see that our Lisp implementation has gone ahead and established additional, non-standard restarts around the *break-on-signals*-invoked break call: in this case, they are named reset and reassign. We will not go in detail into them and instead leave their presence as an example of permitted implementation-defined behavior. Implementing them is left as an exercise for the reader.

## 2.9.6  Recursive debugger

It might be desirable to equip the debugger function with even more functionalities. For instance, the current version of our debugger is not particularly well-equipped to deal with recursive errors, which may happen, for example, when one of the restarts chosen by the programmer enters the debugger again as a part of the restart function, without first routing control out of the previous instance of the debugger.

One of the ways our current debugger falls short is that it does not provide the programmer with any information regarding how many recursive invocations of the debugger have happened so far. We will implement a solution to this issue by creating a new dynamic variable that stores the current debugger level. We will then rebind this variable on every successive debugger invocation.

In addition, our debugger function has grown large, especially with I/O-specific code. Let us try to decompose that function, abstracting specific parts of it into new functions.

```
(defvar *debugger-level* 0)

(defun print-banner (condition)
  (format t ";;~%;; Debugger level ~D entered on ~S:~%"
          *debugger-level* (type-of condition))
  (format t ";; ~W~%" condition))
```

```
(defun print-restarts (restarts)
  (format t ";;~%;; Available restarts:~%")
  (loop for i from 0
        for restart in restarts do
          (format t ";; ~D [~W] ~W~%" i (restart-name restart) restart)))

(defun read-valid-restart-number (number-of-restarts)
  (loop (format t ";;~%;; Invoke restart number: ")
        (let* ((line (read-line *query-io*))
               (integer (parse-integer line :junk-allowed t)))
          (when (and integer (< -1 integer number-of-restarts))
            (return integer)))))

(defun debugger (condition hook)
  (let ((*print-escape* nil)
        (*debugger-level* (1+ *debugger-level*)))
    (print-banner condition)
    (let ((restarts (compute-restarts condition)))
      (print-restarts restarts)
      (let ((chosen-restart (read-valid-restart-number (length restarts)))
            (*debugger-hook* hook))
        (invoke-restart-interactively (nth chosen-restart restarts)))
      (debugger condition hook))))
```

Now we have indeed factored the code and introduced a new dynamic variable, *debugger-level*; we rebind this variable inside debugger and print it inside print-banner. Let's try it out with check-type:

```
CL-USER> (trivial-custom-debugger:with-debugger (#'debugger)
           (let ((x 42))
             (check-type x string)
             x))
;;
;; Debugger level 1 entered on SIMPLE-TYPE-ERROR:
;; The value of X is 42, which is not of type STRING.
;;
;; Available restarts:
;; 0 [STORE-VALUE] Supply a new value for X.
;; 1 [RETRY] Retry evaluating the form.
;; 2 [ABORT] Return to the top level.
;;
```

```
;; Invoke restart number: 0                              ; user input here
;;
;; Enter a form to be evaluated:                         ; user input here

(let ((maybe-result "some string"))
  (cerror "Continue." "About to supply ~S." maybe-result)
  maybe-result)

;;
;; Debugger level 2 entered on SIMPLE-ERROR:
;; About to supply "some string".
;;
;; Available restarts:
;; 0 [CONTINUE] Continue.
;; 1 [RETRY] Retry evaluating the form.
;; 2 [ABORT] Return to the top level.
;;
;; Invoke restart number: 0                              ; user input here

"some string"
```

This is already better—the programmer can now see the debugger level inside the banner printed by the debugger, just above the condition. However, the programmer still does not have an easy way of routing control from the nested debugger back up to a shallower level of nesting.

We can fix this issue by wrapping the invoke-restart-interactively form in the debugger function inside a with-simple-restart form. This form will provide a non-local-exit-performing abort restart, which will allow the programmer to return to a less deeply nested level of the debugger.

```
(defun debugger (condition hook)
  (let ((*print-escape* nil)
        (*debugger-level* (1+ *debugger-level*)))
    (print-banner condition)
    (let ((restarts (compute-restarts condition)))
      (print-restarts restarts)
      (let ((chosen-restart (read-valid-restart-number (length restarts)))
            (*debugger-hook* hook)
            (current-debugger-level *debugger-level*))
```

```
      (with-simple-restart
          (abort "Return to level ~D of the debugger." current-debugger-level)
        (invoke-restart-interactively (nth chosen-restart restarts))))
    (debugger condition hook))))
```

(The new lexical variable, current-debugger-level, is required in order to remember the debugger level at the moment of establishing the restart. If we instead were to supply *debugger-level* directly as a format argument, it would have been rebound with a new value by the time this restart were reported.)

We can now verify that the new restart is available and works as intended:

```
CL-USER> (trivial-custom-debugger:with-debugger (#'debugger)
           (let ((x 42))
             (check-type x string)
             x))
;;
;; Debugger level 1 entered on SIMPLE-TYPE-ERROR:
;; The value of X is 42, which is not of type STRING.
;;
;; Available restarts:
;; 0 [STORE-VALUE] Supply a new value for X.
;; 1 [RETRY] Retry evaluating the form.
;; 2 [ABORT] Return to the top level.
;;
;; Invoke restart number: 0                        ; user input here
;;
;; Enter a form to be evaluated:                   ; user input here
(let ((maybe-result "some string"))
  (cerror "Continue." "About to supply ~S." maybe-result)
  maybe-result)

;;
;; Debugger level 2 entered on SIMPLE-ERROR:
;; About to supply "some string".
;;
;; Available restarts:
;; 0 [CONTINUE] Continue.
;; 1 [ABORT] Return to level 1 of the debugger.
;; 2 [RETRY] Retry evaluating the form.
;; 3 [ABORT] Return to the top level.
;;
```

```
;; Invoke restart number: 1                                    ; user input here
;;
;; Debugger level 1 entered on SIMPLE-TYPE-ERROR:
;; The value of X is 42, which is not of type STRING.
;;
;; Available restarts:
;; 0 [STORE-VALUE] Supply a new value for X.
;; 1 [RETRY] Retry evaluating the form.
;; 2 [ABORT] Return to the top level.
;;
;; Invoke restart number: 2                                    ; user input here
;;
;; ABORT restart invoked; returning to top level.
```

We see that the programmer has left the level 2 debugger via the newly established abort restart, which has once again invoked the level 1 debugger with its condition. This approach will continue to work in cases with more debugger nesting. For instance, a programmer from a level 5 debugger will have restarts that make it possible to drop to any debugger from levels 1 to 4.

## 2.9.7  Adding a REPL to the debugger

Another noteworthy idea is to allow the programmer to evaluate arbitrary Lisp code instead of merely picking a restart. The moment that the programmer has a read-eval-print loop available inside the debugger is the moment that they not only can compute, find, and invoke restarts but also can inspect and modify their Lisp environment in order better to deal with the erroneous situation. For these reasons, debuggers used in real-life situations typically include such evaluation functionality.

At the same time as adding this extra flexibility, we would still like to retain the convenience of selecting a restart by simply typing its number. One way to achieve this convenience is to modify the standard behavior of a Lisp read-eval-print loop slightly, by introducing one more stage between its read and eval steps. If the programmer enters an integer, we will attempt to match it against our list of restarts; otherwise, we will evaluate the read form normally.

This will require us to modify read-valid-restart-number to handle a wider variety of user input. At this juncture, we note that this function will not be expected just to read a number anymore: it will be used to query the programmer for general Lisp expressions.

We can still keep the restart-number-checking logic in that function, though, while we keep evaluating arbitrary Lisp forms until the user inputs a number that matches an available restart.

```lisp
(makunbound 'read-valid-restart-number)

(defun read-debug-expression (number-of-restarts)
  (format t ";; Enter a restart number to be invoked~%")
  (format t ";; or an expression to be evaluated.~%")
  (loop (format t "Debug> ")
        (let* ((form (read)))
          (if (and (integerp form) (< -1 form number-of-restarts))
              (return form)
              (print (eval form))))))

(defmacro with-abort-restart (&body body)
  (let ((level (gensym)))
    `(let ((,level *debugger-level*))
       (with-simple-restart (abort "Return to level ~D of the debugger." ,level)
         ,@body))))

(defun debugger (condition hook)
  (let ((*print-escape* nil)
        (*debugger-level* (1+ *debugger-level*)))
    (print-banner condition)
    (let ((restarts (compute-restarts condition)))
      (print-restarts restarts)
      (let* ((*debugger-hook* hook)
             (chosen-restart
              (with-abort-restart (read-debug-expression (length restarts)))))
        (when chosen-restart
          (with-abort-restart
            (invoke-restart-interactively (nth chosen-restart restarts)))))
      (let ((*debugger-level* (1- *debugger-level*)))
        (debugger condition hook)))))
```

We have additionally introduced a *macro* named with-abort-restart, which establishes an abort restart around the function read-debug-expression (which contains our debug REPL) and around the restart invocation. Both of these places are now allowed to signal arbitrary errors and therefore invoke the debugger recursively; therefore, we will want a way to reduce the debugger level from both of these places. Additionally, now that with-abort-restart is allowed to return nil, we have wrapped the restart invocation within an additional when to check for cases where we immediately want to drop into the debugger again instead. We also bind *debugger-level* to its previous value before calling the debugger again. (In case the syntax of the preceding with-abort-restart macro and other upcoming macros in this book are not clear to the reader, a short macro writing (and reading) tutorial is provided as an appendix to this book.)

Now we can utilize this REPL to change the state of the program without leaving the debugger. This ability, in turn, will allow us, for example, to continue from a simple assert form, from which we would not previously have been able to continue normally.

```
CL-USER> (defvar *x* 24)
*X*

CL-USER> (trivial-custom-debugger:with-debugger (#'debugger)
           (assert (= *x* 42)))
;;
;; Debugger level 1 entered on SIMPLE-ERROR:
;; The assertion (= *X* 42) failed.
;;
;; Available restarts:
;; 0 [CONTINUE] Retry assertion.
;; 1 [RETRY] Retry evaluating the form.
;; 2 [ABORT] Return to the top level.
;;
;; Enter a restart number to be invoked
;; or an expression to be evaluated.

Debug> (setf *x* 42)                          ; user input here
42

Debug> 0                                      ; user input here
NIL

CL-USER>
```

# 2.9.8 Backtraces

One more utility frequently provided by a debugger is a *backtrace*. A backtrace is a list of all functions that were *on the stack* at the moment of entering the debugger; programmers frequently utilize these as debugging aids. A backtrace often contains the names of functions that were previously called, their arguments, and sometimes the values of local variables within these functions.

The CL standard does not contain any standardized functions related to accessing backtraces at any point in program execution; it is therefore up to every implementation to implement such functionality and optionally to provide it for programmers. The library Dissect is a portability library, which means that it is similar to `trivial-custom-debugger` that we have mentioned earlier; but while `trivial-custom-debugger` provides the ability to modify the system debugger portably, Dissect provides a portable means of retrieving and analyzing detailed stack information such as function names, arguments, or source locations for individual forms on the backtrace.

If we use Quicklisp, then, after issuing (`ql:quickload :dissect`), we can begin utilizing the Dissect functionality. For instance, we can ask Dissect to "present" everything that it knows about our environment, in the form of a backtrace. A fragment of example output of (`dissect:present t`) may look like this:

```
CL-USER> (dissect:present t)
#<ENVIRONMENT {10059B6B83}>
   [Environment of thread #<THREAD "new-repl-thread" RUNNING {100237A133}>]

Available restarts:
 0: [RETRY] Retry evaluating the form.
 1: [ABORT] Return to the top level.

Backtrace:
 13: (DISSECT:PRESENT T T)
 14: (SI:SIMPLE-EVAL (DISSECT:PRESENT T) #<NULL-LEXENV>)
 15: (EVAL (DISSECT:PRESENT T))
 16: (REPL-EVAL-FROM-STRING "(dissect:present t)")
     ...
```

Extending our hand-written debugger with a Dissect-provided backtrace (returned via calling (`dissect:with-capped-stack () (dissect:stack))`) is left as an exercise for the reader.

## 2.9.9  Associating conditions with restarts

The interactive REPL within our debugger allows the programmer to execute arbitrary code: among other consequences, this capability means that the programmer is now allowed to commit arbitrary programming mistakes—mistakes such as common typos.

```
CL-USER> (setf *x* 42)
42

CL-USER> (trivial-custom-debugger:with-debugger (#'debugger)
           (check-type *x* string))
;;
;; Debugger level 1 entered on SIMPLE-TYPE-ERROR:
;; The value of *X* is 42, which is not of type STRING.
;;
;; Available restarts:
;; 0 [STORE-VALUE] Supply a new value for *X*.
;; 1 [RETRY] Retry evaluating the form.
;; 2 [ABORT] Return to the top level.
;;
;; Enter a restart number to be invoked
;; or an expression to be evaluated.

Debug> (setg *x* "forty-two")                        ; user input here

;;
;; Debugger level 2 entered on UNDEFINED-FUNCTION:
;; The function COMMON-LISP-USER::SETG is undefined.
;;
;; Available restarts:
;; 0 [CONTINUE] Retry using SETG.
;; 1 [USE-VALUE] Use specified function
;; 2 [ABORT] Return to level 1 of the debugger.
;; 3 [RETRY] Retry evaluating the form.
;; 4 [ABORT] Return to the top level.
;;
;; Enter a restart number to be invoked
;; or an expression to be evaluated.

Debug>
```

Even though everything seems normal in the level 2 debugger which was invoked, a particularly keen eye might notice a unique restart-related behavior. Before continuing with the next paragraph, the reader may want to pause for a moment and focus on the list of restarts available in the level 2 debugger and ask themselves: *hasn't something gone missing in between these two debug levels?*

*(\*jazz music plays\*)*

That "something" is the `store-value` restart which was available inside the level 1 debugger and is now not visible anymore since we have entered the level 2 debugger— even though we are clearly still in the dynamic scope in which that restart was established, due to the level 1 debugger (in which the `store-value` restart was visible) still being active when the level 2 debugger was invoked. At the same time, we can be sure that the `store-value` restart has no `:test-function` specified and therefore should always be visible regardless of the state of the dynamic environment.

Therefore, we may observe a particular behavior that is related to the *condition* with which the debugger is invoked. When we invoked the level 1 debugger with the original `type-error` coming from `check-type`, the `store-value` restart was indeed accessible. However, when we entered the debugger one more time, with the `undefined-function` error coming from the user attempting to call the undefined function `setg`, the `store-value` restart had disappeared!

This behavior is actually defined in CL. It is the reason why we have been passing around that optional `condition` argument in all of our restart-based functions, most notably, `compute-restarts` and `find-restart`. For user convenience, we will add one more modification to our debugger, making the condition object accessible to us via a newly created *debugger-condition* dynamic variable:

```
(defvar *debugger-condition* nil)

(defun debugger (condition hook)
  (let ((*print-escape* nil)
        (*debugger-condition* condition)
        (*debugger-level* (1+ *debugger-level*)))
    (print-banner condition)
    (let ((restarts (compute-restarts condition)))
      (print-restarts restarts)
      (let* ((*debugger-hook* hook)
             (chosen-restart
               (with-abort-restart (read-debug-expression (length restarts)))))
```

```
      (when chosen-restart
        (with-abort-restart
          (invoke-restart-interactively (nth chosen-restart restarts)))))
    (let ((*debugger-level* (1- *debugger-level*)))
      (debugger condition hook)))))
```

This modification will allow us to see the difference that we get when calling compute-restarts with and without the condition argument passed to it.

```
CL-USER> (trivial-custom-debugger:with-debugger (#'debugger)
           (check-type *x* string))
;;
;; Debugger level 1 entered on SIMPLE-TYPE-ERROR:
;; The value of *X* is 42, which is not of type STRING.
;;
;; Available restarts:
;; 0 [STORE-VALUE] Supply a new value for *X*.
;; 1 [RETRY] Retry evaluating the form.
;; 2 [ABORT] Return to the top level.
;;
;; Enter a restart number to be invoked
;; or an expression to be evaluated.

Debug> (setg *x* "forty-two")                          ; user input here

;;
;; Debugger level 2 entered on UNDEFINED-FUNCTION:
;; The function COMMON-LISP-USER::SETG is undefined.
;;
;; Available restarts:
;; 0 [CONTINUE] Retry using SETG.
;; 1 [USE-VALUE] Use specified function
;; 2 [ABORT] Return to level 1 of the debugger.
;; 3 [RETRY] Retry evaluating the form.
;; 4 [ABORT] Return to the top level.
;;
;; Enter a restart number to be invoked
;; or an expression to be evaluated.

Debug> *debugger-condition*
#<UNDEFINED-FUNCTION SETG {100D2AF073}>
```

```
Debug> (let ((*print-escape* nil))
         (format t "~&~{;; ~W~%~}" (compute-restarts)))
;; Return to level 2 of the debugger.
;; Retry using SETG.
;; Use specified function
;; Return to level 1 of the debugger.
;; Supply a new value for *X*.
;; Retry evaluating the form.
;; Return to the top level.
NIL

Debug> (let ((*print-escape* nil))
         (format t "~&~{;; ~W~%~}" (compute-restarts *debugger-condition*)))
;; Return to level 2 of the debugger.
;; Retry using SETG.
;; Use specified function
;; Return to level 1 of the debugger.
;; Retry evaluating the form.
;; Return to the top level.
NIL
```

Let us differentiate these two lists of restarts via set-difference to find restarts which appear in the first list but don't in the other:

```
Debug> (let ((*print-escape* nil))
         (format t "~&~{;; ~W~%~}"
                  (set-difference
                   (compute-restarts *debugger-condition*)
                   (compute-restarts))))
;; Supply a new value for *X*.
NIL
```

We can see that calling compute-restarts *without* passing it the undefined-function condition object has caused one more restart to appear—the missing store-value restart, with a report "Supply a new value for *X*.", which was bound by the store-value form which we originally evaluated. From this observation, we may induce that there must be some sort of relationship between condition objects and restart objects that is checked by compute-restarts and find-restart, among other functions. This relationship in CL is named *condition-restart association*.

In the preceding example, first we were dealing with a type-error coming from check-type, but then the object of our focus changed: we started to deal with an undefined-function coming from our typo while trying to type setf. This is the reason for the existence of condition-restart association, which works by *hiding* the restarts which are *not associated* with the *currently handled* condition.

In this particular situation, the store-value restart was associated with the type-error; when the debugger is invoked on undefined-function, this restart stops being relevant to the currently handled condition and is therefore hidden from the programmer's view to let them see only restarts which are either explicitly associated with the new undefined-function error or not associated with any condition in particular.

This association is always established by with-simple-restart and, sometimes, by handler-case. (Detailed explanation: restart-case is required to detect when the form that it directly invokes is a signal, warn, error, or cerror call or a form which macroexpands into such a call. In such a case, the condition signaled by that form becomes associated with all restarts bound by that particular handler-case.)

The programmer is also allowed to associate conditions with restarts manually when they decide that the association automatically performed by with-simple-restart and handler-case is not suited to their needs. The operator in question is named with-condition-restarts. To demonstrate it, we will revive one variable and one function which we defined in the restart-related chapters.

```
(defvar *toplevel-restarts* '())

(defun compute-relevant-restarts (&optional condition)
  (set-difference (compute-restarts condition) *toplevel-restarts*))
```

A synthetic example for the association behavior can be seen here:

```
CL-USER> (let ((*toplevel-restarts* (compute-restarts))
               (condition-1 (make-instance 'condition))
               (condition-2 (make-instance 'condition)))
           (restart-bind ((restart-1 (lambda ()))
                          (restart-2 (lambda ())))
             (with-condition-restarts condition-1 (list (find-restart 'restart-1))
               (with-condition-restarts condition-2 (list (find-restart 'restart-2))
                 (format t ";; All restarts:~%")
                 (format t ";; ~S~%" (mapcar #'restart-name
                                             (compute-relevant-restarts)))
```

```
        (format t ";; Restarts applicable for condition-1:~%")
        (format t ";; ~S~%" (mapcar #'restart-name
                                    (compute-relevant-restarts condition-1)))
        (format t ";; Restarts applicable for condition-2:~%")
        (format t ";; ~S~%" (mapcar #'restart-name
                                    (compute-relevant-restarts condition-2)))))))
;; All restarts:
;; RESTART-2 RESTART-1
;; Restarts applicable for condition-1:
;; (RESTART-1)
;; Restarts applicable for condition-2:
;; (RESTART-2)
NIL
```

We first create two distinct condition objects, then bind two distinct restarts, and then associate the restart objects with the conditions. This association is then reflected when we list all restarts, or list restarts associated with the first condition, or list those with the second condition.

(It is noteworthy that, while many other Lisp forms operate on condition types and restart names as monikers for the actual objects, with-condition-restarts operates on the actual *condition/restart instances themselves*. The association does not happen between condition types or restart names—it happens between individual condition and restart object instances. This distinction exists because association based on condition types or restart names would be too general—for example, if we were to make several typos in a row and end up recursively invoking the debugger with several undefined-function errors in a row, then with type-based associations they would all end up with the same list of restarts, which likely is not our intention.)

# CHAPTER 3

# Implementing the Common Lisp condition system

(I kind of wish I could title this chapter "A simple Common Lisp condition system"—unfortunately, the matters that we touch in this chapters are not as simple anymore as I had first envisioned.)

So far in this book, we have built the handler and restart subsystems of standard CL, constructing the basics of these from scratch. Equipped with this knowledge, we can now proceed into the ultimate chapters of this book, in which we describe an example implementation of a full, standard-compliant condition system for CL.

The condition system defined in this book is adapted from Portable Condition System (henceforth referred to as PCS), which, in turn, was adapted from the original condition system written for the first versions of CL by Kent M. Pitman. The "portable" in its name refers to the fact that it is defined without using the CL-provided versions of any operators that it defines itself, and therefore its code is suitable for implementing, for example, condition systems in CL implementations which themselves do not have a condition system. It also means that it enjoys complete independence from any native condition system that the host may have—allowing for easier introspection and debugging.

PCS purports to comply with the ANSI CL standard and, at the time of writing, passes the applicable tests from the ANSI-TEST test suite related to the condition system and assertion operators. (If any issues are found and fixed in PCS code, then this book shall be amended and/or errata shall be published to take that into account.)

For brevity, we will omit the less interesting and more repetitive parts of the full code, such as package definition and the list of definitions for the standard condition types.

© Michał "phoe" Herda 2020
M. "phoe" Herda, *The Common Lisp Condition System*, https://doi.org/10.1007/978-1-4842-6134-7_3

Readers interested in these parts of the code may see them in the full repository linked earlier or fetch and install it themselves, for local inspection and interaction, by issuing (`ql:quickload :portable-condition-system`) on a Quicklisp-enabled Lisp REPL.

If the reader would like instead to follow this book, evaluating forms incrementally as they are listed herein, it will be enough for them to load the file `package.lisp` from the aforementioned PCS repository, in order to establish the requisite package structure. Then, they can do (`in-package :portable-condition-system`) to make current a suitable package in which to evaluate our code.

One more issue that will become visible in this part of the book is that we will take greater care to use proper *input/output streams* when reading input and communicating to the user. Previously, all of our `format` calls were using the `t` value for the stream, meaning that they printed to the standard output; likewise for our `read` calls and standard input.

That pattern was a big simplification of the CL stream structure which we are now going to fix: from now on, depending on the particular situation, we will be deliberate in choosing the stream with which we want to interact. In some cases, we will interact with `*debug-io*`, which is a stream meant for interactive debugging; in other cases, we will print to `*error-output*`, an output stream meant for logging error and warning information; in yet other cases, we will interact with `*query-io*`, which is a stream responsible for interactively querying the user for data.

Such care is required in order to comply with the ANSI CL standard and to ensure that our condition system will work with CL implementations which rebind these variables, for example, routing error streams to a different file/window than standard output or presenting query windows to the user when input is requested from `*query-io*`.

# 3.1 Package definition

The package for our condition system is allowed to use all CL exported symbols, except for symbols related to the condition system. To achieve this setup, we need to define a list of all these condition system–related symbols, *shadow* them in our package, and export them to allow other people to use them. The shadowing is needed to ensure that our package uses its own versions of these symbols rather than importing them from the host's `common-lisp` package; exporting them is needed in order to ensure that the people using our condition system will be able to use our package's functionality without needing to prepend our package name to symbols in the code.

Our package will be named `portable-condition-system`. Here is the complete list of all symbols shadowed and exported by it, grouped by their role within the condition system:

- Creating conditions: `define-condition`, `make-condition`

- Standard condition types and their readers: `condition`, `warning`, `serious-condition`, `error`, `style-warning`, `simple-condition`, `simple-warning`, `simple-error`, `simple-condition-format-control`, `simple-condition-format-arguments`, `storage-condition`, `type-error`, `type-error-datum`, `type-error-expected-type`, `simple-type-error`, `control-error`, `program-error`, `cell-error`, `cell-error-name`, `unbound-variable`, `undefined-function`, `unbound-slot`, `unbound-slot-instance`, `stream-error`, `stream-error-stream`, `end-of-file`, `parse-error`, `reader-error`, `package-error`, `package-error-package`, `arithmetic-error`, `arithmetic-error-operands`, `arithmetic-error-operation`, `division-by-zero`, `floating-point-invalid-operation`, `floating-point-inexact`, `floating-point-overflow`, `floating-point-underflow`, `file-error`, `file-error-pathname`, `print-not-readable`, `print-not-readable-object`

- Handling conditions: `*break-on-signals*`, `signal`, `warn`, `cerror`, `error`, `cerror`, `handler-case`, `handler-bind`, `ignore-errors`

- Assertions: `assert`, `check-type`, `etypecase`, `ctypecase`, `ecase`, `ccase`

- Binding and accessing restarts: `restart`, `restart-name`, `find-restart`, `compute-restarts`, `invoke-restart`, `invoke-restart-interactively`, `with-condition-restarts`, `restart-case`, `restart-bind`, `with-simple-restart`, `abort`, `continue`, `muffle-warning`, `store-value`, `use-value`

- Interfacing with the debugger: `*debugger-hook*`, `break`, `invoke-debugger`

In addition, we will prepare a package named `common-lisp+portable-condition-system`, which imports and reexports all the symbols from `common-lisp` *except* for symbols from the preceding list, which will be imported and reexported from `portable-condition-system`. This package will be useful for people who want to start using PCS in their programs right away.

(For brevity, this book will also nickname this package pcs; this nickname is not present in the package definitions present in the repository.)

# 3.2  Conditions

In the previous chapters, we used a CL macro named defstruct to define a structure for our choice objects. This tool was good enough for the job at the time, given that choices (just like restart objects) are very static in CL: they have a limited, strictly defined set of functionalities that cannot be extended in any way. Contrary to restarts, however, condition types can be defined with a wide variety of options: they may exhibit *multiple inheritance* by being subtypes of multiple distinct condition types; their slots may have multiple *reader, writer,* and/or *accessor* functions; their slots can be *class-allocated* or *instance-allocated*; they may have a *default initialization argument* list; and so on and so forth.

All that richness exists because CL condition types defined via define-condition are very closely related to classes defined by Common Lisp Object System's defclass. The only practical difference between define-condition and defclass is the presence of an additional :report option in define-condition, used to define a report function for condition objects. This allows define-condition to be implemented elegantly via defclass, which is exactly the way many CL implementations do it. (As for impractical differences, the ANSI specification for define-condition contradicts itself on the details of how this macro should work on matters like *slot inheritance*; CL implementers generally agree that define-condition should work like defclass.)

(Teaching the details of classes, defclass, or the Common Lisp Object System in general is not in scope of this book; the readers who would like to learn more about these topics can consult *Practical Common Lisp* by Peter Seibel or *Object-Oriented Programming in Common Lisp: A Programmer's Guide to CLOS* by Sonya Keene.)

## 3.2.1  Base class for conditions

First of all, let us define the root of our condition tree: the condition class, along with a pair of methods that describe the printing and reporting mechanism.

```
(defclass condition () ())

(defmethod print-object ((object condition) stream)
  (format stream "Condition ~S was signaled." (type-of object)))
```

```
(defmethod print-object :around ((object condition) stream)
  (if *print-escape*
      (print-unreadable-object (object stream :type t :identity t))
      (call-next-method)))
```

We define a pair of methods on `print-object`, which is the generalized object printer that is invoked every time `print`, `print`, `princ`, or `format` is used to print Lisp objects.

The first method *specializes* on all objects of class `condition` which we define in the `defclass` form; it means that, whenever `print-object` is called with an object of class `condition`, it is possible that this method will be invoked. Note that it is *possible*, but not guaranteed—that uncertainty is because the second method we define, while it also specializes on the `condition` class, is in addition an `:around` method. The consequence of using an `:around` method in this context is that it will be called *before* any method that is not an `:around` method and therefore will take precedence over the first method we define.

This second method defines a "wrapper" over condition reporting. In particular, we want to ensure that the condition is reported (by means of `call-next-method`) only when the special variable `*print-escape*` is false. If that variable is true, then we want to print the condition object in an unreadable way—which is implemented by the `print-unreadable-object` macro.

We can immediately test this behavior in our REPL:

```
PCS> (defvar *condition* (make-instance 'condition))
*CONDITION*

PCS> (let ((*print-escape* t))
       (format nil "~W" *condition*))
"#<CONDITION {100F8112B3}>"

PCS> (let ((*print-escape* nil))
       (format nil "~W" *condition*))
"Condition CONDITION was signaled."
```

One issue here is the fact that `make-instance` is not the standard-defined way to create condition objects—`make-condition` is. However, since the syntax used in both operators is identical, we can define our `make-condition` in terms of `make-instance`.

```
(defun make-condition (type &rest args)
  (apply #'make-instance type args))
```

We may immediately test it:

```
PCS> (make-condition 'condition)
#<CONDITION {1010744EB3}>
```

## 3.2.2 Defining new condition types

We can now create individual condition objects. The next step is to be able to define new condition types, which requires us to *define a new macro*, define-condition. In particular, if we have the following define-condition form:

```
(define-condition foo-condition (condition)
  ((foo-slot :reader foo-condition-slot :initarg :slot)))
```

then we would like it to expand into the equivalent of the following form:

```
(defclass foo-condition (condition)
  ((foo-slot :reader foo-condition-slot :initarg :slot)))
```

Based on this case, the expansion seems simple—apparently we need merely to translate define-condition into defclass. However, there are two special cases that we need to support inside our macro:

- The first is that all condition types must be supertypes of the condition class. Therefore, if the programmer provides an empty list of superclasses, then we must ensure that the omission is corrected before the list is passed along to defclass.

- The other special case is that we need to handle the :report option, which may not be passed directly to defclass. So we need to extract that option and honor it by generating a print-object method specializing on the newly created condition class.

Therefore, if we have the following code:

```
(defun report-foo-condition (condition stream)
  (format stream "A foo happened: ~A"
          (foo-condition-slot condition)))

(define-condition foo-condition ()
  ((foo-slot :reader foo-condition-slot :initarg :slot))
  (:report report-foo-condition))
```

we may expect the preceding `define-condition` form to expand into an equivalent of the following code:

```
(progn
  (defclass foo-condition (condition)
    ((foo-slot :reader foo-condition-slot :initarg :slot)))
  (defmethod print-object ((condition foo-condition) stream)
    (funcall #'report-foo-condition condition stream))
  'foo-condition)
```

Note that our macro needed to expand into a `progn` in order to accommodate more than one generated form. We can see that the superclass list in `defclass` now contains the name of the `condition` class and that the `:report` option has been rendered into its separate `print-object` method. In addition, we return the name of the condition from the final form, as dictated by the Common Lisp standard.

For clarity, we will separate our macro into two logical parts. The first will be a function named `define-condition-make-report-method` that will be used for generating the `defmethod print-object` form.

```
(defun define-condition-make-report-method (name report-option)
  (let* ((condition (gensym "CONDITION"))
         (stream (gensym "STREAM"))
         (report (second report-option))
         (report-form (if (stringp report)
                          `(write-string ,report ,stream)
                          `(funcall #',report ,condition ,stream))))
    `(defmethod print-object ((,condition ,name) ,stream)
       ,report-form)))
```

It is not within this book's scope to explain the art of writing Lisp macros, backquote notation, or the use of symbols returned by `gensym` calls. (Readers interested in pursuing this fascinating topic can consult *On Lisp* by Paul Graham and/or *Let over Lambda* by Doug Hoyte.) Here, we will essentially treat macros and code-generating functions as black boxes, only outlining important details of their internal structure and testing them in the REPL. An appendix to this book describes the most important parts of the new syntax; the reader may want to skim that appendix before proceeding with this chapter, if the use of Lisp macros here proves discomforting or distracting.

The function `define-condition-make-report-method` accepts two arguments: the name of the condition being defined and the whole `:report` option passed to `define-condition`. Its output is a *backquoted* `defmethod print-object` form that defines a corresponding reporting method on the new condition.

Inside the backquoted structure, we can see that the condition variable (represented by the unquoted `condition` variable) is going to be specialized to the unquoted `name`, which is the name of the condition class which we define. The body of the defined method is going to be the value of `report-form`, which—as we can see in the variable bindings—will be calculated based on the type of the `report` variable which was extracted from the report option. This is consistent with the behavior of `define-condition`: if the value passed to `:report` is a string, then it should be written to the stream (and so a `write-string` form is generated). Otherwise, that value denotes a function, which must be called with the condition and stream passed as its arguments (embodied by the `funcall` form).

We can test the preceding function by giving it the same arguments that we passed into the example (`define-condition foo-condition ...`) form earlier: the symbol `foo` and the report option containing a function name.

```
PCS> (define-condition-make-report-method
       'foo '(:report report-foo-condition))
(DEFMETHOD PRINT-OBJECT ((#:CONDITION576 FOO) #:STREAM577)
  (FUNCALL #'REPORT-FOO-CONDITION #:CONDITION576 #:STREAM577))
```

The *gensyms* in the preceding form denote the variables with which the method will be called; they are passed as is to the `funcall` form, which calls the function named `report-foo-condition`. If we were to pass a lambda form instead, it would work as well, since the `#'` syntax also accepts lambda forms. However, the situation will change if we decide that `foo-condition` should have a static report instead:

```
PCS> (define-condition-make-report-method
       'foo '(:report "A foo happened."))
(DEFMETHOD PRINT-OBJECT ((#:CONDITION578 FOO) #:STREAM579)
  (WRITE-STRING "A foo happened." #:STREAM579))
```

Here we can see that the `funcall` form has been replaced with a `write-string` form, suitable for reporting static strings passed to the `:report` option. This works for creating new methods or *redefining* old ones; however, `define-condition` can also be used to *redefine* a condition, meaning that the `:report` option can disappear from the `define-condition` form. To account for this eventuality, we must also have an option for removing the method that we define: that is implemented by our define-condition-remove-report-method function.

```
(defun define-condition-remove-report-method (name)
  (let ((method (gensym "CONDITION")))
    `(let ((,method (find-method #'print-object '() '(,name t) nil)))
       (when ,method (remove-method #'print-object ,method)))))
```

We may test this with the name of our foo-condition to see the generated code:

```
PCS> (define-condition-remove-report-method 'foo-condition)
(LET ((#:CONDITION617 (FIND-METHOD #'PRINT-OBJECT 'NIL '(FOO-CONDITION T) NIL)))
  (WHEN #:CONDITION617 (REMOVE-METHOD #'PRINT-OBJECT #:CONDITION617)))
```

We see that we test for presence of a method defined on print-object with no qualifiers and specialized on foo-condition. If such a method is found, we call remove-method on it to remove it from the system.

The choice of whether we should generate a defmethod form or a remove-method form depends on whether the :report option was passed to define-condition. We will check for presence of that option inside the body of our next function, expand-define-condition; we will use that function to generate the full expansion of the define-condition macro.

```
(defun expand-define-condition (name supertypes direct-slots options)
  (let* ((report-option (find :report options :key #'car))
         (other-options (remove report-option options))
         (supertypes (or supertypes '(condition))))
    `(progn (defclass ,name ,supertypes ,direct-slots ,@other-options)
            ,@(if report-option
                  `(,(define-condition-make-report-method name report-option))
                  `(,(define-condition-remove-report-method name)))
            ',name)))

(defmacro define-condition (name (&rest supertypes) direct-slots &rest options)
  "Defines or redefines a condition type."
  (expand-define-condition name supertypes direct-slots options))
```

This function accepts four arguments: the condition name, a list of supertypes of that condition, a list of direct slots, and a list of options. All four are passed from the macro, which additionally performs proper structuring of them inside its *macro lambda list.*

In the first two lines of the body of expand-define-condition, we separate the :report option, if any, from the list of all other options provided to the macro. The third line checks whether the supertypes argument is empty and, if so, replaces it with a static list containing only the condition symbol.

This takes care of the two edge cases we identified for our define-condition implementation, so now we can proceed to generate the expansion itself. The expansion contains a defclass form and a conditional for handling the print-object method. If the report-option was found, we will want it to expand into a defmethod print-object form and, otherwise, into a remove-method print-object form.

(We have separated the function expand-define-condition from define-condition for slightly easier testing in the REPL. It is more common to include macro bodies directly within defmacro forms.)

We can test expand-define-condition in the REPL now, checking for both presence and absence of the :report option.

```
PCS> (expand-define-condition
       'foo-condition '()
       '((foo-slot :reader foo-condition-slot :initarg :slot))
       '((:report report-foo-condition)))
(PROGN
  (DEFCLASS FOO-CONDITION (CONDITION)
    ((FOO-SLOT :READER FOO-CONDITION-SLOT :INITARG :SLOT)))
  (DEFMETHOD PRINT-OBJECT ((#:CONDITION624 FOO-CONDITION) #:STREAM625)
    (FUNCALL #'REPORT-FOO-CONDITION #:CONDITION624 #:STREAM625))
 'FOO-CONDITION)

PCS> (expand-define-condition
       'foo-condition '()
       '((foo-slot :reader foo-condition-slot :initarg :slot))
       '())
(PROGN
  (DEFCLASS FOO-CONDITION (CONDITION)
    ((FOO-SLOT :READER FOO-CONDITION-SLOT :INITARG :SLOT)))
  (LET ((#:CONDITION626 (FIND-METHOD #'PRINT-OBJECT 'NIL '(FOO-CONDITION T) NIL)))
    (WHEN #:CONDITION626 (REMOVE-METHOD #'PRINT-OBJECT #:CONDITION626)))
 'FOO-CONDITION)
```

Now that we have confirmed the correct workings of our code-generation functions, we can use macroexpand-1 on sample uses of the macro, to ensure that they will expand as expected:

```
PCS> (macroexpand-1
       '(define-condition foo-condition ()
          ((foo-slot :reader foo-condition-slot :initarg :slot))
          (:report report-foo-condition)))
(PROGN
  (DEFCLASS FOO-CONDITION (CONDITION)
    ((FOO-SLOT :READER FOO-CONDITION-SLOT :INITARG :SLOT)))
  (DEFMETHOD PRINT-OBJECT ((#:CONDITION627 FOO-CONDITION) #:STREAM628)
    (FUNCALL #'REPORT-FOO-CONDITION #:CONDITION627 #:STREAM628))
 'FOO-CONDITION)
T

PCS> (macroexpand-1
       '(define-condition foo-condition ()
          ((foo-slot :reader foo-condition-slot :initarg :slot))))
(PROGN
  (DEFCLASS FOO-CONDITION (CONDITION)
    ((FOO-SLOT :READER FOO-CONDITION-SLOT :INITARG :SLOT)))
  (LET ((#:CONDITION629 (FIND-METHOD #'PRINT-OBJECT 'NIL '(FOO-CONDITION T) NIL)))
    (WHEN #:CONDITION629 (REMOVE-METHOD #'PRINT-OBJECT #:CONDITION629)))
 'FOO-CONDITION)
T
```

This concludes the implementation of our first macro, define-condition, which defines new condition types. (When defclass defines a class, it also defines a matching CL type with the same name as the class.) This operator is enough for us to define the entirety of the Common Lisp condition type hierarchy, replete with matching condition readers and report functions.

(For brevity, we omit the actual definition from the book; interested readers can inspect the file condition-hierarchy.lisp inside the PCS repository. The only parts of this file that we will include here are two non-standard condition types, which we define for the convenience of implementing case assertions and restart functions; they shall be defined in their respective chapters.)

# 3.3 Coercing data to conditions

Before we continue implementing the outward visible parts of the condition system, we will focus on one internal utility that will be used by signal, warn, error, cerror, and—implicitly—restart-case. The interface to the condition system allows the user to create condition objects in a multitude of ways: for instance, it is possible to (signal "foo"), (signal 'condition), (signal (formatter "foo")), or (signal (make-condition 'condition)); all of these are valid ways of signaling a condition within signal, warn, error, and cerror. To sum up, the datum argument that is passed to one of these four functions may legally be a string, a symbol, a function, or a condition object.

That variability in the type of the datum argument makes it useful to have a single function that can handle parsing the arguments for all four of these cases and return condition objects that will do their signaling properly. We will create such a function, named coerce-to-condition, and equip it to deal with all four of these situations, as well as with a fifth situation—one in which the user has passed a datum that is not of the aforementioned four types.

To separate these four cases from one another and incidentally to demonstrate a bit of Lisp syntax, we will create a new *generic function*—a function that, just like the print-object function we have seen before, may specialize on its arguments.

```
(defgeneric coerce-to-condition (datum arguments default-type name))
```

This function will accept four arguments. Obviously, it needs the datum and arguments passed to the signaling function that will be used for constructing the condition object. In case a string is passed as datum, though, the function will need a default simple condition type to be constructed, which will be passed as the third argument. The fourth argument is the name of the signaling function that is calling coerce-to-condition: its purpose is only to be displayed in error messages, if any occur.

Let us start with the seemingly simplest case: passing a condition object to the signaling function, exemplified by (signal (make-condition 'condition)).

```
(defmethod coerce-to-condition ((datum condition) arguments default-type name)
  (when arguments
    (cerror "Ignore the additional arguments." 'simple-type-error
            :datum arguments
            :expected-type 'null
            :format-control "You may not supply additional arguments when giving ~S to ~S."
            :format-arguments (list datum name)))
  datum)
```

146

We can see that the datum is returned, but not immediately; first, a check is made that the argument list is empty (since it is illegal to, e.g., (signal (make-condition 'condition) 42)); if not, a continuable error is signaled.

```
(defmethod coerce-to-condition ((datum symbol) arguments default-type name)
  (apply #'make-condition datum arguments))
```

The second case is the *actually* simplest one: if we receive a condition type and a list of arguments, we can directly call make-condition with them.

```
(defmethod coerce-to-condition ((datum string) arguments default-type name)
  (make-condition default-type :format-control datum :format-arguments arguments))

(defmethod coerce-to-condition ((datum function) arguments default-type name)
  (make-condition default-type :format-control datum :format-arguments arguments))
```

The third and fourth cases are identical: if a string or a function is passed as the datum, then we instantiate a simple condition of default-type, passing the datum and arguments as the format control and format arguments. (This is possible because format accepts *formatter functions* as format controls; the reader may verify this by playing with forms such as (format t (lambda (stream &rest args) (declare (ignore args)) (write-string "Test!" stream))).)

```
(defmethod coerce-to-condition (datum arguments default-type name)
  (error 'simple-type-error :datum datum
                            :expected-type '(or condition symbol function string)
                            :format-control "~S is not coercible to a condition."
                            :format-arguments (list datum)))
```

The fifth and final case is the saddest one; if the datum is not of any recognized type, coerce-to-condition signals a type error of its own.

A possible issue that we will encounter here is the fact that this method refers to an undefined function, error. This is a function that we will properly define later, since we need coerce-to-condition for it to function properly. However, CL allows functions to be *redefined*, which means that we can create a stub implementation of error now and use it for our testing, only to replace it with a proper definition of error later in the code.

```
(defun error (datum &rest arguments)
  (declare (ignore arguments))
  (format *error-output* ";; Error: ~A~%" datum)
  (throw :error nil))
```

Our stub implementation requires a `catch` tag to be present in order to transfer control, which means that testing our error situations will require wrapping the tested form with (`catch :error ...`) until we define `error` in the proper, standard-compliant way. This stub will work well for us until that time.

We can now test all five cases of this function in the REPL.

```
PCS> (coerce-to-condition (make-condition 'condition) '() 'simple-condition 'signal)
#<CONDITION {1003271693}>

PCS> (coerce-to-condition 'condition '() 'simple-condition 'signal)
#<CONDITION {1003272D63}>

PCS> (coerce-to-condition "A condition was signaled." '() 'simple-condition 'signal)
#<SIMPLE-CONDITION {1003273B23}>

PCS> (coerce-to-condition (lambda (stream) (write-string "A condition was signaled." stream))
                          '() 'simple-condition 'signal)
#<SIMPLE-CONDITION {100336B663}>

PCS> (catch :error (coerce-to-condition 42 '() 'simple-condition 'signal))
;; Error: SIMPLE-TYPE-ERROR
NIL
```

# 3.4  Restart basics

The next part of the condition system that we are going to touch is the restart subsystem. This does not strictly follow the order in which we have discussed the condition system in the book; however, it is necessary to touch it now for bootstrapping reasons. In order to implement assertions like `cerror` or `check-type`, which bind restarts as a part of their functioning, we need to implement the macros that are used to bind restarts; and to do that, we need to implement restarts themselves.

## 3.4.1  Restart class

Let us start with the `restart` structure, which is similar to the choice structure we defined in the earlier chapters. (To repeat, using `defstruct` in place of `defclass` is okay, since we will not allow the user to extend the restart structure.) We will follow it with a pair of `print-object` methods, similar in functioning to the methods we defined on the condition class.

```
(defstruct restart
  (name (error "NAME required."))
  (function (constantly nil))
  (report-function nil)
  (interactive-function nil)
  (test-function (constantly t))
  (associated-conditions '()))

(defmethod print-object :around ((restart restart) stream)
  (if *print-escape*
      (print-unreadable-object (restart stream :type t :identity t)
        (prin1 (restart-name restart) stream))
      (call-next-method)))

(defmethod print-object ((restart restart) stream)
  (cond ((restart-report-function restart)
         (funcall (restart-report-function restart) stream))
        ((restart-name restart)
         (format stream "Invoke restart ~A." (restart-name restart)))
        (t
         (format stream "Invoke the anonymous restart ~S." restart))))
```

We can see that the main reporting method for the restart is somewhat larger than the one for condition. This is because restarts, while not extensible by the user, by default contain more logic than conditions. A part of this logic is to accommodate the fact that each restart has a report function that, if present, is used to report the restart. Otherwise, if the restart has no report function but does have a name, we use that name to report the restart; and finally, if we have a truly "incognito" restart without a report function or a name, we also need to account for that in the report.

(A keen eye or a working compiler may also notice that we are using the error function, which we have not yet properly defined. Do note, however, that even if error were completely undefined, using such an undefined function is permitted by the CL standard. This function will work later, after it is compiled, even if it will not work at this juncture. We are nonetheless still able to create restart objects right now, as long as we are careful always to provide a :name argument for them.)

(Additionally, the standard specifies that restart objects have *dynamic extent*, meaning that accessing them outside the dynamic scope in which they are bound has undefined consequences. For ease of testing and clarity of code, we will not apply that trait to our implementation of restarts.)

# 3.4.2  Restart visibility and computing restarts

We may now implement a test for restart visibility. First and foremost, a restart should not be visible if its test function returns nil. If its test function returns true, then we may begin checking the condition-restart association. For a restart to be visible, either we must have no condition to test against, or the restart must have no conditions associated with it, or the condition must be present among the associated conditions. The function restart-visible-p implements exactly this logic:

```
(defun restart-visible-p (restart condition)
  (and (funcall (restart-test-function restart) condition)
       (or (null condition)
           (let ((associated-conditions (restart-associated-conditions restart)))
             (or (null associated-conditions)
                 (member condition associated-conditions))))))
```

One implementation detail for the preceding function is that associated-conditions is a slot within each restart that is modified each time the association is required to change. The change occurs within macro with-condition-restarts, which we may now implement.

The macro will work as follows: given a condition object and a list of restart objects, it will push the condition object to each restart's list of associated conditions, and only then it will execute the body. We delegate the task of disassociating them to another form that pops the conditions off the lists; we also ensure that this popping always happens upon leaving the body's dynamic scope, by the use of unwind-protect.

```
(defun expand-with-condition-restarts (condition restarts body)
  (let ((condition-var (gensym "CONDITION"))
        (restarts-var (gensym "RESTARTS"))
        (restart (gensym "RESTART")))
    `(let ((,condition-var ,condition)
           (,restarts-var ,restarts))
       (unwind-protect
           (progn
             (dolist (,restart ,restarts-var)
               (push ,condition-var (restart-associated-conditions ,restart)))
             ,@body)
         (dolist (,restart ,restarts-var)
           (pop (restart-associated-conditions ,restart)))))))
```

```
(defmacro with-condition-restarts (condition (&rest restarts) &body body)
  (expand-with-condition-restarts condition restarts body))
```

This macro will, in effect, transform a form like this:

```
(with-condition-restarts condition (list restart-1 restart-2 ...)
  ...)
```

into the equivalent of a form like this:

```
(let ((restarts (list restart-1 restart-2 ...)))
  (unwind-protect
      (progn (dolist (restart restarts)
                (push condition (restart-associated-conditions restart)))
             ...)
    (dolist (restart restarts)
      (pop (restart-associated-conditions restart)))))
```

In order to test this macro, we need some means of finding restarts based on their association with condition objects. This means that we need to implement compute-restarts and find-restart—and, in order to implement these, we will need a dynamic variable that shall host our restarts.

```
(defvar *restart-clusters* '())

(defun compute-restarts (&optional condition)
  (loop for restart in (apply #'append *restart-clusters*)
        when (restart-visible-p restart condition)
          collect restart))

(defun find-restart (name &optional condition)
  (dolist (cluster *restart-clusters*)
    (dolist (restart cluster)
      (when (and (or (eq restart name)
                     (eq (restart-name restart) name))
                 (restart-visible-p restart condition))
        (return-from find-restart restart)))))
```

(While *restart-clusters* holds restarts in clusters, restarts do not follow the same clustering behavior as handlers. The specification is not very clear on this issue, but within contemporary CL implementations, a restart function is allowed to call any restart available within the dynamic environment—including its "neighbors" and the restarts which were defined later in dynamic scope.)

We can see that compute-restarts first appends the list of all restart clusters into a flat list of restarts and then walks this flat list, collecting into a new list all restarts which should be visible. find-restarts works slightly differently, as it does not need to collect its results; it walks each cluster and then checks if each restart inside that cluster is eligible for being returned from the function.

We may now test these functions by rebinding *restart-clusters* to some meaningful value manually. What is important for us are their names, test functions, and associations with conditions.

Our sandbox will have the following contents:

```
(defvar *abort-restart-2-visible-p* t)
(defvar *test-condition-1* (make-instance 'condition))
(defvar *test-condition-2* (make-instance 'condition))

(defvar *example-clusters*
  (let ((abort-1 (make-restart :name 'abort
                                :function (lambda () 'abort-1)))
        (retry (make-restart :name 'retry))
        (fail (make-restart :name 'fail
                            :associated-conditions
                            (list *test-condition-1*)))
        (abort-2 (make-restart :name 'abort
                                :function (lambda () 'abort-2)
                                :test-function
                                (lambda (condition)
                                  (declare (ignore condition))
                                  *abort-restart-2-visible-p*))))
    (list (list abort-2 retry)
          (list fail)
          (list abort-1))))
```

Let us first compute all restarts and verify that they are listed in the correct order.

```
PCS> (let ((*restart-clusters* *example-clusters*))
       (format t "~{;; ~S~%~}" (compute-restarts)))
;; #<RESTART ABORT {1014C89C13}>
;; #<RESTART RETRY {1014C89B53}>
;; #<RESTART FAIL {1014C89BB3}>
;; #<RESTART ABORT {1014C89AF3}>
NIL
```

Then, we should ensure that binding the *abort-restart-2-visible-p* variable affects the visibility of one of the abort restarts.

```
PCS> (let ((*restart-clusters* *example-clusters*)
           (*abort-restart-2-visible-p* nil))
      (format t "~{;; ~S~%~}" (compute-restarts)))
;; #<RESTART RETRY {101759EB53}>
;; #<RESTART FAIL {101759EBE3}>
;; #<RESTART ABORT {101759EAD3}>
NIL
```

Finally, let us verify that the fail restart stays visible when we look for restarts associated with *test-condition-1*, but disappears for *test-condition-2*.

```
PCS> (let ((*restart-clusters* *example-clusters*))
      (format t "~{;; ~S~%~}" (compute-restarts *test-condition-1*)))
;; #<RESTART ABORT {1017184ED3}>
;; #<RESTART RETRY {1017184DE3}>
;; #<RESTART FAIL {1017184E73}>
;; #<RESTART ABORT {1017184D63}>
NIL

PCS> (let ((*restart-clusters* *example-clusters*))
      (format t "~{;; ~S~%~}" (compute-restarts *test-condition-2*)))
;; #<RESTART ABORT {1017184ED3}>
;; #<RESTART RETRY {1017184DE3}>
;; #<RESTART ABORT {1017184D63}>
NIL
```

## 3.4.3  Invoking restarts

Now that we can find restarts, we should also be able to invoke them. Let us implement invoke-restart and invoke-restart-interactively, starting with the first one.

```
(defun invoke-restart (restart &rest arguments)
  (typecase restart
    (restart (apply (restart-function restart) arguments))
    (symbol (let ((real-restart (find-restart restart)))
              (unless real-restart (error "Restart ~S is not active." restart))
              (apply #'invoke-restart real-restart arguments)))
    (t (error "Wrong thing passed to INVOKE-RESTART: ~S" restart))))
```

The preceding code dispatches based on the type of the `restart` argument passed to it. If this argument is a restart object, then its restart function is applied to the provided arguments; if it is a symbol, then it is treated as a restart name, and the first restart with that name is found and invoked. In case there is no visible restart with that name or when `restart` is not a *restart designator*, calling `invoke-restart` results in an error.

```
(defun invoke-restart-interactively (restart)
  (typecase restart
    (restart (let* ((function (restart-interactive-function restart))
                    (arguments (if function (funcall function) '())))
               (apply (restart-function restart) arguments)))
    (symbol (let ((real-restart (find-restart restart)))
              (unless real-restart (error "Restart ~S is not active." restart))
              (invoke-restart-interactively real-restart)))
    (t (error "Wrong thing passed to INVOKE-RESTART-INTERACTIVELY: ~S"
              restart))))
```

The implementation of `invoke-restart-interactively` is the same in two `typecase` branches out of three. The third branch is the most interesting: first, the restart is queried for its interactive function. If it is present, it is called to retrieve the list of arguments that will be used to apply the restart function to; otherwise, the argument list is assumed to be the empty list. The restart function is then called.

We may now test invoking our restarts. First, let us attempt to invoke a restart non-interactively:

```
PCS> (let* ((restart (make-restart :name 'add-42
                                   :function (lambda (x) (+ 42 x))))
            (*restart-clusters* (list (list restart))))
       (invoke-restart 'add-42 4200))
4242
```

Then, let us add a trivial interactive function to the restart and call `invoke-restart-interactively`:

```
PCS> (let* ((restart (make-restart :name 'add-42
                                   :function (lambda (x) (+ 42 x))
                                   :interactive-function (lambda () '(4200))))
            (*restart-clusters* (list (list restart))))
       (invoke-restart-interactively 'add-42))
4242
```

Let us also try to invoke non-existing restarts:

```
PCS> (catch :error (invoke-restart 'foo))
;; Error: Restart ~S is not active.
NIL

PCS> (catch :error (invoke-restart-interactively 'foo))
;; Error: Restart ~S is not active.
NIL
```

# 3.5  Binding restarts

By now, we have all the parts required to find and invoke our restart objects, as well as to create them manually. The CL standard does not, however, provide that last part to the programmer. Instead, restarts must be established within dynamic scope by means of restart-binding macros, which we will now implement.

The simplest one of the three is restart-bind, which accepts a list of restart bindings, creates new restart objects based on them, and attaches a list of newly created restarts to the overall list of restart clusters. This is exactly what our macro is going to do.

```
(defun restart-bind-transform-binding (binding)
  (destructuring-bind (name function . arguments) binding
    `(make-restart :name ',name :function ,function ,@arguments)))

(defun expand-restart-bind (bindings body)
  (let ((cluster (mapcar #'restart-bind-transform-binding bindings)))
    `(let ((*restart-clusters* (cons (list ,@cluster) *restart-clusters*)))
       ,@body)))

(defmacro restart-bind (bindings &body body)
  (expand-restart-bind bindings body))
```

We see that there are two logical parts to our macro. The first part is a function that accepts a raw binding the way it is listed inside handler-bind and turns it into a make-restart form that will construct our restart object with the provided data. The second part is the main body of the macro which calls restart-bind-transform-binding on all bindings passed to handler-bind and then rebinds *restart-clusters* by adding a new list element—our new handler cluster—atop them.

Let us perform some basic tests of these functions, starting with the binding transform.

```
PCS> (restart-bind-transform-binding
      '(return-42 (lambda () 42)))
(MAKE-RESTART :NAME 'FOO-RESTART
              :FUNCTION (LAMBDA () 42))

PCS> (restart-bind-transform-binding
      '(return-42 (lambda () 42)
                  :test-function (lambda (condition) (typep condition 'error))
                  :report-function "Return 42 if an error is being signaled."))
(MAKE-RESTART :NAME 'RETURN-42
              :FUNCTION (LAMBDA () 42)
              :TEST-FUNCTION (LAMBDA (CONDITION) (TYPEP CONDITION 'ERROR))
              :REPORT-FUNCTION "Return 42 if an error is being signaled.")
```

Then, the body generator:

```
PCS> (expand-restart-bind
      '((return-42 (lambda () 42)
         :test-function (lambda (condition) (typep condition 'error))
         :report-function "Return 42 if an error is being signaled."))
      '((let ((restart (find-restart 'return-42)))
         (when restart (invoke-restart restart)))))
(LET ((*RESTART-CLUSTERS*
       (CONS
        (LIST
         (MAKE-RESTART :NAME 'RETURN-42
                       :FUNCTION (LAMBDA () 42)
                       :TEST-FUNCTION (LAMBDA (CONDITION) (TYPEP CONDITION 'ERROR))
                       :REPORT-FUNCTION "Return 42 if an error is being signaled."))
         *RESTART-CLUSTERS*)))
  (LET ((RESTART (FIND-RESTART 'RETURN-42)))
    (WHEN RESTART (INVOKE-RESTART RESTART))))
```

And finally, the macro body (which is, in a way, just a formality; we only effectively test the macro lambda list, which ensures that the arguments inside the macro are structured properly):

```
PCS> (macroexpand-1
       '(restart-bind
           ((return-42 (lambda () 42)
             :test-function (lambda (condition) (typep condition 'error))
             :report-function "Return 42, but only if an error is being signaled."))
          (let ((restart (find-restart 'return-42)))
            (when restart (invoke-restart restart)))))
(LET ((*RESTART-CLUSTERS*
       (CONS
        (LIST
         (MAKE-RESTART :NAME 'RETURN-42
                       :FUNCTION (LAMBDA () 42)
                       :TEST-FUNCTION (LAMBDA (CONDITION) (TYPEP CONDITION 'ERROR))
                       :REPORT-FUNCTION "Return 42 if an error is being signaled."))
         *RESTART-CLUSTERS*)))
  (LET ((RESTART (FIND-RESTART 'RETURN-42)))
    (WHEN RESTART (INVOKE-RESTART RESTART))))
T
```

Now that we have verified our expansions, we can test the macro itself:

```
PCS> (restart-bind
         ((return-42 (lambda () 42)
                     :test-function (lambda (condition) (typep condition 'error))
                     :report-function "Return 42 if an error is being signaled."))
       (let ((restart (find-restart 'return-42)))
         (when restart (invoke-restart restart))))
NIL

PCS> (restart-bind
         ((return-42 (lambda () 42)
                     :test-function (lambda (condition) (typep condition 'error))
                     :report-function "Return 42 if an error is being signaled."))
       (let ((restart (find-restart 'return-42 (make-condition 'error))))
         (when restart (invoke-restart restart))))
42
```

# 3.6  Restart cases

A functioning `restart-bind` is the most important building block for the more commonly used restart operator, `restart-case`. It is not the only building block required, however; due to the keyword differences between `restart-bind` and `restart-case`, the need to parse keyword-value pairs from the body of each restart case, and the requirement to detect common signaling operators for automatic condition-restart association, `restart-case` is the most complex macro in the whole condition system.

Therefore, we will construct the fully conforming macro incrementally. We will start with a basic version that only performs a non-local transfer of control and then add the preceding differences one by one.

## 3.6.1  First iteration: basics

The non-expanded `restart-case` accepts its input as an expression to execute (which, for now, we may pass as is without any transformations) and a list of cases. Each case needs to be transformed into a pair of subforms: one that will be a `restart-bind` binding and another that will form the restart case. The binding is responsible for passing the arguments passed to the restart binding and transferring control to the restart case, which, in turn, executes the body forms of the given case.

Therefore, we will need a function to parse a restart case and annotate it with a unique symbol which will be used to perform the transfer of control. Such a parsed and annotated case can then be passed to a pair of functions whose purpose will be to generate proper restart binding and restart case forms ready to be spliced into the macro body. This strategy, along with the need of a function which will generate the proper body of `restart-case`, means that the first iteration of our macro will be achievable by defining four separate functions.

Let us start with the first one, for parsing a restart case. For simplicity, let us assume that the cases passed to `restart-case` have the same form as `restart-bind` bindings.

```
(defun restart-case-parse-case (case)
  (destructuring-bind (name function . options) case
    (let ((tag (gensym (format nil "~A-RESTART-CASE" name))))
      (list tag name function options))))
```

Invoking this function on a restart case gives us a four-element list containing a unique tag symbol, the restart name, restart function, and a list of options.

```
(defun report-return-42 (stream)
  (write-string "Return 42 if an error is being signaled." stream))

PCS> (restart-case-parse-case
       '(return-42 (lambda () 42)
         :test-function (lambda (condition) (typep condition 'error))
         :report-function #'report-return-42))
(#:RETURN-42-RESTART-BINDING616 RETURN-42 (LAMBDA () 42)
 (:TEST-FUNCTION (LAMBDA (CONDITION) (TYPEP CONDITION 'ERROR))
  :REPORT-FUNCTION #'REPORT-RETURN-42))
```

We can use this structure in the pair of functions that will generate the parts of our macro for us. First, let us make the restart binding:

```
(defun restart-case-make-restart-binding (parsed-case temp-var)
  (destructuring-bind (tag name function options) parsed-case
    (declare (ignore function))
    (let ((lambda-var (gensym "RESTART-ARGS")))
      `(,name
        (lambda (&rest ,lambda-var) (setf ,temp-var ,lambda-var) (go ,tag))
        ,@options))))
```

The preceding function requires two arguments: the parsed case from restart-case-parse-case and the name of the temporary variable that it should set in order to pass the restart arguments outside of the restart binding. We will see this mechanism in action when we come to the main body of restart-case; for now, let us assume that the temporary variable is the symbol named temp-var.

```
PCS> (let ((case (restart-case-parse-case
                   '(return-42 (lambda () 42)
                     :test-function (lambda (condition) (typep condition 'error))
                      :report-function #'report-return-42))))
       (restart-case-make-restart-binding case 'temp-var))
(RETURN-42
 (LAMBDA (&REST #:RESTART-ARGS622)
   (SETF TEMP-VAR #:RESTART-ARGS622)
   (GO #:RETURN-42-RESTART-BINDING621))
 :TEST-FUNCTION (LAMBDA (CONDITION) (TYPEP CONDITION 'ERROR))
 :REPORT-FUNCTION #'REPORT-RETURN-42)
```

We can see that this `restart-case-make-restart-binding` returned, indeed, a restart binding. It binds a restart named `return-42` with a test function and report function that we have seen before. The restart function accepts a `&rest` argument, which gathers into a list all arguments with which that restart was invoked. This list is then set to the `temp-var` symbol which we have passed, and a `go` call then transfers control to the unique tag the case has been annotated with.

Let us compare this with the function generating the other half of the mechanism.

```
(defun restart-case-make-restart-case (parsed-case temp-var block-name)
  (destructuring-bind (tag name function options) parsed-case
    (declare (ignore name options))
    `(,tag (return-from ,block-name (apply ,function ,temp-var)))))
```

This function accepts three arguments in total: the parsed case, the temporary variable, and a *block name* from which it should return the results of the restart function. We can see that the original function passed to the restart binding is ignored inside the result of `restart-case-make-restart-binding`; it is instead executed here, after control has been transferred, applied to the arguments from `temp-var`—the temporary variable that has been set by the restart binding.

This function returns a subform that starts with the tag; its purpose is to be spliced into a `tagbody` form, where the unique symbol will be recognized as a `go` tag to which control may be transferred. Because `tagbody` returns `nil`, a valid `block` that wraps the `tagbody` is required in order to transfer return values outside.

We can test this function in order to see the output that will be spliced into `tagbody` from our `return-42` restart.

```
PCS> (let ((case (restart-case-parse-case
                  '(return-42 (lambda () 42)
                    :test-function (lambda (condition) (typep condition 'error))
                    :report-function #'report-return-42))))
       (restart-case-make-restart-case case 'temp-var 'block-name))
(#:RETURN-42-HANDLER-BINDING623
 (RETURN-FROM BLOCK-NAME (APPLY (LAMBDA () 42) TEMP-VAR)))
```

As expected, we can see a unique symbol that will become the `go` tag and a `return-from` form that will return the values from evaluating (apply (lambda () 42) temp-var) outside a block named `block-name`.

The preceding knowledge allows us to understand the general structure of the code into which restart-case will expand. We need to have a temporary variable that will allow us to transfer restart arguments outside the binding; we need to have a block to return values from; and we need to have a tagbody that will allow us to transfer control outside the restart bindings. Using this knowledge, we may now construct the main body of restart-case.

```
(defun expand-restart-case (expression cases)
  (let ((block-name (gensym "RESTART-CASE-BLOCK"))
        (temp-var (gensym "RESTART-CASE-VAR"))
        (parsed-cases (mapcar #'restart-case-parse-case cases)))
    (flet ((make-restart-binding (case)
             (restart-case-make-restart-binding case temp-var))
           (make-restart-case (case)
             (restart-case-make-restart-case case temp-var block-name)))
      `(let ((,temp-var nil))
         (declare (ignorable ,temp-var))
         (block ,block-name
           (tagbody
             (restart-bind ,(mapcar #'make-restart-binding parsed-cases)
               (return-from ,block-name ,expression))
             ,@(apply #'append (mapcar #'make-restart-case parsed-cases))))))))

(defmacro restart-case (expression &body cases)
  (expand-restart-case expression cases))
```

First of all, we define gensyms for the block name and our temporary variable. Next, we parse all the cases using restart-case-parse-case. Then, we define a pair of *local* functions, make-restart-binding and make-restart-case. We do that in order to have one-argument functions suitable for passing to mapcar later in code. (Technical detail: the block name and temporary variable name, which are the additional arguments that restart-case-make-restart-binding and restart-case-make-restart-case accept, are going to be constant throughout the function call; this is why we may use a technique called *partial application* and construct functions that have these constant arguments already "filled in" and therefore no longer require them to be passed.)

After constructing the local functions, we begin to construct our body. We define our temporary variable (and make it *ignorable*, in case restart-case is called without any restarts and therefore the variable goes unused), and we define our block and tagbody.

Inside, we can see a restart-bind that contains a list of restart bindings returned by mapcar make-restart-binding and a return-from form that will return the values of our expression in case none of the freshly bound restarts are invoked. The result of appending all calls to make-restart-case is also spliced into our tagbody form; this will provide the tags that are recognized by tagbody, thereby providing a means of transferring control outside of restart-bind.

Let us test the expander function with the same restart binding with which we worked earlier, introducing a small modification to the expression which we want to evaluate.

```
PCS> (expand-restart-case
       '(let ((restart (find-restart 'return-42)))
          (when restart (invoke-restart restart))
          24)
       '((return-42
          (lambda () 42)
          :test-function (lambda (condition) (typep condition 'error))
          :report-function #'report-return-42)))
(LET ((#:RESTART-CASE-VAR631 NIL))
  (DECLARE (IGNORABLE #:RESTART-CASE-VAR631))
  (BLOCK #:RESTART-CASE-BLOCK630
    (TAGBODY
      (RESTART-BIND ((RETURN-42 (LAMBDA (&REST #:RESTART-ARGS633)
                                  (SETF #:RESTART-CASE-VAR631 #:RESTART-ARGS633)
                                  (GO #:RETURN-42-HANDLER-BINDING632))
                      :TEST-FUNCTION
                      (LAMBDA (CONDITION) (TYPEP CONDITION 'ERROR))
                      :REPORT-FUNCTION #'REPORT-RETURN-42))
        (RETURN-FROM #:RESTART-CASE-BLOCK630
          (LET ((RESTART (FIND-RESTART 'RETURN-42)))
            (WHEN RESTART (INVOKE-RESTART RESTART))
            24)))
      #:RETURN-42-HANDLER-BINDING632
      (RETURN-FROM #:RESTART-CASE-BLOCK630
        (APPLY (LAMBDA () 42) #:RESTART-CASE-VAR631)))))
```

Here we can see our restart-case expansion in its full glory. We bind a variable, create a block and a tagbody, bind a restart by means of restart-bind, and begin evaluating our expression, preparing to return its value from the block which we have declared.

If the restart is invoked, the temporary variable (here named #:restart-case-var631) is set to the list of restart arguments (in this case, empty!), control is transferred outside the dynamic scope of restart-bind, and our 42-returning function is applied to the (empty) list of arguments, yielding 42.

If the restart is not invoked, however, our expression returns 24—and that value is then immediately returned from the block and, therefore, from the whole of the expanded handler-case.

Let us confirm that these expansions work as expected:

```
PCS> (restart-case (let ((restart (find-restart 'return-42)))
                     (when restart (invoke-restart restart))
                     24)
        (return-42
         (lambda () 42)
         :test-function (lambda (condition) (typep condition 'error))
         :report-function #'report-return-42))
24

PCS> (restart-case (let* ((condition (make-condition 'error))
                          (restart (find-restart 'return-42 condition)))
                     (when restart (invoke-restart restart))
                     24)
        (return-42
         (lambda () 42)
         :test-function (lambda (condition) (typep condition 'error))
         :report-function #'report-return-42))
42
```

## 3.6.2  Second iteration: Forms instead of a function

Our first iteration of restart-case works well. Now we can proceed to work on shaping it toward compliance with the Common Lisp standard. First, we need to notice that the forms inside a restart-case are spliced into the case itself; the keyword-value pairs are placed between the restart case lambda list and the actual body forms. This means that the restart-case body from the preceding example should instead look like this:

```
(restart-case (let* ((condition (make-condition 'error))
                     (restart (find-restart 'return-42 condition)))
                (when restart (invoke-restart restart))
                24)
```

```
(return-42 ()
  :test-function (lambda (condition) (typep condition 'error))
  :report-function #'report-return-42
  42))
```

To support this protocol, we must modify our case-parsing function to separate our case into five distinct parts: the unique tag, restart name, lambda list, keyword-value pairs, and the body of the restart case. The new structure must then be accounted for in the parts that generate restart bindings and the proper restart case.

Let us first construct a function that parses the part of the restart case after the lambda list and returns two values—the keyword-value pairs, if any, and the remaining body forms:

```
(defun restart-case-pop-keywords (case)
  (let ((things case)
        (keywords '(:report-function :interactive-function :test-function)))
    (loop for thing = (first things)
          if (member thing keywords)
            collect (pop things) into pairs
            and collect (pop things) into pairs
          else return (list pairs things))))
```

Our function iterates over the Lisp data inside things. If the form matches one of the three recognized keywords, the loop collects the keyword and its matching value from the list. If the next form awaiting processing is not a known keyword, the iteration stops, and the body and keyword-value pairs are returned.

Let us test this newly modified function on the form of our restart case.

```
PCS> (restart-case-pop-keywords
       '(:test-function (lambda (condition) (typep condition 'error))
         :report-function #'report-return-42
         42))
((:TEST-FUNCTION (LAMBDA (CONDITION) (TYPEP CONDITION 'ERROR))
  :REPORT-FUNCTION #'REPORT-RETURN-42)
 (42))
```

We can see that the body, (42), is correctly returned, so are the values for the report function, interactive function (none), and test function.

We can utilize this function inside our `restart-case-parse-case`. We will account for the fact that we now need to pop keyword-value pairs from our case body and return five values instead of four.

```
(defun restart-case-parse-case (case)
  (destructuring-bind (name lambda-list . rest) case
    (destructuring-bind (options body) (restart-case-pop-keywords rest)
      (let ((tag (gensym (format nil "~A-RESTART-BINDING" name))))
        (list tag name lambda-list options body)))))
```

Let us test our function by passing a full restart case to it:

```
PCS> (restart-case-parse-case
       '(return-42 ()
         :test-function (lambda (condition) (typep condition 'error))
         :report-function #'report-return-42
         42))
(#:RETURN-42-RESTART-BINDING743 RETURN-42 NIL
 (:TEST-FUNCTION (LAMBDA (CONDITION) (TYPEP CONDITION 'ERROR))
  :REPORT-FUNCTION #'REPORT-RETURN-42)
 (42))
```

We get a tag, restart name, restart lambda list (empty), a list of keywords, and the body of the case—which is exactly what we wanted. Now, we need to adjust `restart-case-make-restart-binding` and `restart-case-make-restart-case` to use the new five-element structure—starting with the former.

```
(defun restart-case-make-restart-binding (parsed-case temp-var)
  (destructuring-bind (tag name lambda-list options body) parsed-case
    (declare (ignore lambda-list body))
    (let ((lambda-var (gensym "RESTART-ARGS")))
      `(,name
        (lambda (&rest ,lambda-var) (setf ,temp-var ,lambda-var) (go ,tag))
        ,@options))))
```

The only required change here is splitting the old `function` argument into separate `lambda-list` and `body` arguments; both of them are not used in the binding and therefore ignored. These two arguments will indeed be used in the case-making function though:

```
(defun restart-case-make-restart-case (parsed-case temp-var block-name)
  (destructuring-bind (tag name lambda-list options body) parsed-case
    (declare (ignore name options))
    `(,tag
      (return-from ,block-name (apply (lambda ,lambda-list ,@body) ,temp-var)))))
```

Once again, the change here is minor: we have replaced `function` with an explicit `lambda` form which accepts our lambda list and case body.

We may now test both functions with the new form of the restart case:

```
PCS> (let ((parsed-case (restart-case-parse-case
                          '(return-42 ()
                            :test-function (lambda (condition) (typep condition 'error))
                            :report-function #'report-return-42
                            42))))
       (restart-case-make-restart-binding parsed-case 'temp-var))
(RETURN-42
 (LAMBDA (&REST #:RESTART-ARGS756)
   (SETF TEMP-VAR #:RESTART-ARGS756)
   (GO #:RETURN-42-RESTART-BINDING755))
 :TEST-FUNCTION (LAMBDA (CONDITION) (TYPEP CONDITION 'ERROR))
 :REPORT-FUNCTION #'REPORT-RETURN-42)

PCS> (let ((parsed-case (restart-case-parse-case
                          '(return-42 ()
                            :test-function (lambda (condition) (typep condition 'error))
                            :report-function #'report-return-42
                            42))))
       (restart-case-make-restart-case parsed-case 'temp-var 'block-name))
(#:RETURN-42-RESTART-BINDING757
 (RETURN-FROM BLOCK-NAME (APPLY (LAMBDA () 42) TEMP-VAR)))
```

Both of these functions return what they should (and what they did in the preceding example!), which means that no modifications to expand-restart-case are required. We may now test whether the restart-case macro accepts our new syntax:

```
PCS> (restart-case (let* ((restart (find-restart 'return-42)))
                     (when restart (invoke-restart restart))
                     24)
        (return-42 ()
          :test-function (lambda (condition) (typep condition 'error))
          :report-function #'report-return-42
          42))
24

PCS> (restart-case (let* ((condition (make-condition 'error))
                          (restart (find-restart 'return-42 condition)))
                     (when restart (invoke-restart restart))
                     24)
        (return-42 ()
          :test-function (lambda (condition) (typep condition 'error))
          :report-function #'report-return-42
          42))
42
```

# 3.6.3  Third iteration: Managing the keyword differences

The third iteration of our restart-case macro will extend the keyword-parsing mechanism that we created in the second iteration. Not only are the keywords used by restart-case different from the ones used by restart-bind, but their functioning is distinct as well: whereas for restart-bind we may pass any function objects, restart-case accepts only lambda forms or function names (or strings, for its :report option).

We will modify restart-case-pop-keywords to call one more function, restart-case-transform-subform, on the keyword and value that it finds. In addition, we must modify the set of keywords that it recognizes.

```
(defun restart-case-pop-keywords (case)
  (let ((things case)
        (keywords '(:report :interactive :test)))
```

```
(loop for thing = (first things)
      if (member thing keywords)
        append (restart-case-transform-subform (pop things) (pop things))
          into pairs
      else return (list pairs things))))
```

Now, we need to define restart-case-transform-subform.

```
(defun restart-case-transform-subform (keyword value)
  (case keyword
    (:report
     (if (stringp value)
         `(:report-function (lambda (stream) (write-string ,value stream)))
         `(:report-function #',value)))
    (:interactive `(:interactive-function #',value))
    (:test `(:test-function #',value))))
```

The preceding function dispatches on the keyword. If the keyword is :interactive or :test, a matching :interactive-function or :test-function is returned. The situation is slightly more complicated in case of :report, since—just like in define-condition—we need to account for the possibility of a string being passed as the value, around which we must construct a write-string call.

We may now test restart-case-transform-subform to verify that all four of its branches are taken into account—and then test restart-case-pop-keywords on our venerable example return-42 restart.

```
PCS> (restart-case-transform-subform :report "Test report")
(:REPORT-FUNCTION (LAMBDA (STREAM) (WRITE-STRING "Test report" STREAM)))

PCS> (restart-case-transform-subform :report 'report-return-42)
(:REPORT-FUNCTION #'REPORT-RETURN-42)

PCS> (restart-case-transform-subform :test (lambda (condition) (typep condition 'error)))
(:TEST-FUNCTION #'#<FUNCTION (LAMBDA (CONDITION)) {52E349AB}>)

PCS> (restart-case-transform-subform :interactive (lambda () '(42)))
(:INTERACTIVE-FUNCTION #'#<FUNCTION (LAMBDA ()) {52E34F4B}>)

PCS> (restart-case-pop-keywords
      '(:test (lambda (condition) (typep condition 'error))
        :report report-return-42
        42))
```

```
((:TEST-FUNCTION #'(LAMBDA (CONDITION) (TYPEP CONDITION 'ERROR))
  :REPORT-FUNCTION #'REPORT-RETURN-42)
 (42))
```

That is all that's required. The modification is complete, and our `restart-case` is now syntactically compliant with ANSI CL.

```
PCS> (restart-case (let* ((condition (make-condition 'error))
                          (restart (find-restart 'return-42 condition)))
                     (when restart (invoke-restart restart))
                     24)
       (return-42 ()
         :test (lambda (condition) (typep condition 'error))
         :report report-return-42
         42))
42

PCS> (restart-case (let* ((restart (find-restart 'return-42)))
                     (when restart (invoke-restart restart))
                     24)
       (return-42 ()
         :test (lambda (condition) (typep condition 'error))
         :report report-return-42
         42))
24
```

## 3.6.4  Fourth iteration: Associating conditions with restarts

Our `restart-case` already spans six distinct functions. We will need to increase that number in order to add one final standard feature of `restart-case`. However, the required modification will be completely separated from the ones we have done so far: the change will be related to the *expression* that is passed to `handler-case`, which, so far, we have been splicing into the resulting macroexpansion without any alterations.

That final standard feature is implicit condition-restart association, which we have already described earlier; it is triggered only when the form passed to `restart-case`, *or the result of its macroexpansion*, is a direct call to `signal`, `warn`, `error`, or `cerror`. This implies that `restart-case` must have the capability to macroexpand the expressions that are passed to it, detect whether the expression is a call to one of the four aforementioned functions, and *rewrite* such a form into one utilizing `with-condition-restarts`.

This is not a trivial task. Let us start by slightly modifying `restart-case` and `restart-case-expand` to suit our needs:

```
(defun expand-restart-case (expression cases environment)
  (let ((block-name (gensym "RESTART-CASE-BLOCK"))
        (temp-var (gensym "RESTART-CASE-VAR"))
        (parsed-cases (mapcar #'restart-case-parse-case cases)))
    (flet ((make-restart-binding (case)
             (restart-case-make-restart-binding case temp-var))
           (make-restart-case (case)
             (restart-case-make-restart-case case temp-var block-name)))
      `(let ((,temp-var nil))
         (declare (ignorable ,temp-var))
         (block ,block-name
           (tagbody
             (restart-bind ,(mapcar #'make-restart-binding parsed-cases)
               (return-from ,block-name
                 ,(if (restart-case-signaling-form-p expression environment)
                      (restart-case-expand-signaling-form expression environment)
                      expression)))
             ,@(apply #'append (mapcar #'make-restart-case parsed-cases))))))))

(defmacro restart-case (expression &body cases &environment environment)
  (expand-restart-case expression cases environment))
```

We can see that the macro definition has been expanded to include a special *environment* object inside its lambda list; this object is not directly passed to it by the programmer, but is usually provided by the Lisp implementation as part of calling its macroexpander. While we will not describe environment objects in detail, we will note their traits which are most relevant to us for the matter at hand. This environment argument is available only in macros; it holds, among other things, information about local macro definitions—information which is important for passing into the `macroexpand` calls of our new functions. Since these calls must perform macroexpansion of their own, it is important that they receive this environment argument to be able to expand macros correctly. That is why `restart-case` passes the argument to `expand-restart-case`, which—in turn—passes it into our yet-undefined functions `restart-case-signaling-form-p` and `restart-case-expand-signaling-form`.

Let us continue by defining the predicate function. This function needs to macroexpand the form and return true if the form is a list whose first element turns out to be a standard condition-signaling operator:

```
(defun restart-case-signaling-form-p (expression env)
  (let ((expansion (macroexpand expression env)))
    (and (consp expansion)
         (member (car expansion) '(signal warn error cerror)))))
```

Now we can perform quick REPL tests for this predicate, passing nil as the second argument to signify a *null environment.*

```
PCS> (restart-case-signaling-form-p '(+ 2 2) nil)
NIL

PCS> (restart-case-signaling-form-p '(error 2 2) nil)
(ERROR CERROR)
```

(In the second test, the function returned a non-nil value, which in CL is "as good as" returning true. CL has generalized booleans, which means that anything that is not nil counts as a true value, even though the symbol t is designated to be the "canonical" representation of truth—the standard type boolean, after all, is defined as (member nil t).)

If restart-case-signaling-form-p has returned true, then restart-case must rewrite the signaling form. Let us briefly analyze the possibilities here; we can see that the functions signal, warn, and error have the same lambda lists, which means that we are allowed to group them together. The fourth function, cerror, has one more required argument, and so we will treat it separately.

Let us start with the first case, in which we will expand a non-cerror form. It will be our first chance to use the coerce-to-condition helper function which we defined in the earlier chapters.

```
(defun restart-case-expand-non-cerror (expansion)
  (destructuring-bind (function-name datum . args) expansion
    (let* ((type (case function-name
                   (signal 'simple-condition)
                   (warn 'simple-warning)
                   (error 'simple-error)))
           (condition (gensym "CONDITION")))
      `(let ((,condition (coerce-to-condition ,datum (list ,@args) ',type ',function-name)))
         (with-condition-restarts ,condition (car *restart-clusters*)
           (,function-name ,condition))))))
```

We expand into a `let` form that binds a new variable and instantiates a condition object via `coerce-to-condition`, based on the arguments that were passed into the function and the name of the function. This condition is then associated with all the restarts from the most recent restart cluster, bound by the `restart-case` form into which this expression shall be spliced. Once that association is done, the original function is used to signal the newly created condition object.

We can test this function in the REPL to verify that it generates the expected output:

```
PCS> (restart-case-expand-non-cerror '(error "Failure"))
(LET ((#:CONDITION851 (COERCE-TO-CONDITION "Failure" (LIST) 'SIMPLE-ERROR 'ERROR)))
  (WITH-CONDITION-RESTARTS #:CONDITION851 (CAR *RESTART-CLUSTERS*)
    (ERROR #:CONDITION851)))
```

This one works; now let us dig into the `cerror` case, which has an optional format control for the `continue` restart that it establishes, but—at the same time—does not need to compute the resulting simple condition type.

```
(defun restart-case-expand-cerror (expansion)
  (destructuring-bind (function-name format-control datum . args) expansion
    (let* ((type 'simple-error)
           (condition (gensym "CONDITION")))
      `(let ((,condition (coerce-to-condition ,datum (list ,@args) ',type ',function-name)))
         (with-condition-restarts ,condition (car *restart-clusters*)
           (,function-name ,format-control ,condition))))))
```

We may test that it expands into something we want:

```
PCS> (restart-case-expand-cerror '(cerror "Continue from failure." "Failure"))
(LET ((#:CONDITION866 (COERCE-TO-CONDITION "Failure" 'NIL 'SIMPLE-ERROR 'CERROR)))
  (WITH-CONDITION-RESTARTS #:CONDITION866 (CAR *RESTART-CLUSTERS*)
    (CERROR "Continue from failure." #:CONDITION866)))
```

With both branches of our code now available, we may finally define the function `restart-case-expand-signaling-form` that decides which branch to take based on the first element of the macroexpanded expression:

```
(defun restart-case-expand-signaling-form (expression env)
  (let ((expansion (macroexpand expression env)))
    (case (car expansion)
      ((signal warn error) (restart-case-expand-non-cerror expansion))
      (cerror (restart-case-expand-cerror expansion)))))
```

And we may go ahead and test it:

```
PCS> (restart-case-expand-signaling-form '(error "Failure") nil)
(LET ((#:CONDITION868 (COERCE-TO-CONDITION "Failure" (LIST) 'SIMPLE-ERROR 'ERROR)))
  (WITH-CONDITION-RESTARTS #:CONDITION868 (CAR *RESTART-CLUSTERS*)
    (ERROR #:CONDITION868)))

PCS> (restart-case-expand-signaling-form '(cerror "Continue from failure." "Failure") nil)
(LET ((#:CONDITION867 (COERCE-TO-CONDITION "Failure" 'NIL 'SIMPLE-ERROR 'CERROR)))
  (WITH-CONDITION-RESTARTS #:CONDITION867 (CAR *RESTART-CLUSTERS*)
    (CERROR "Continue from failure." #:CONDITION867)))
```

(The preceding code expands into a call of cerror, which we have not yet defined; we will do that in the next sections and test it there.)

Finally, let us look at the example expansion of restart-case with error to see that the error expression indeed expands into a with-condition-restarts-wrapped form.

```
(restart-case (error "Failure!")
  (return-42 ()
    :test (lambda (condition) (typep condition 'error))
    :report report-return-42
    42))

(LET ((#:RESTART-CASE-VAR940 NIL))
  (DECLARE (IGNORABLE #:RESTART-CASE-VAR940))
  (BLOCK #:RESTART-CASE-BLOCK939
    (TAGBODY
      (RESTART-BIND ((RETURN-42
                      (LAMBDA (&REST #:RESTART-ARGS942)
                        (SETF #:RESTART-CASE-VAR940 #:RESTART-ARGS942)
                        (GO #:RETURN-42-RESTART-BINDING941))
                      :TEST-FUNCTION #'(LAMBDA (CONDITION) (TYPEP CONDITION 'ERROR))
                      :REPORT-FUNCTION #'REPORT-RETURN-42))
        (RETURN-FROM #:RESTART-CASE-BLOCK939
          (LET ((#:CONDITION943 (COERCE-TO-CONDITION "Failure!" (LIST) 'SIMPLE-ERROR 'ERROR)))
            (WITH-CONDITION-RESTARTS #:CONDITION943 (CAR *RESTART-CLUSTERS*)
              (ERROR #:CONDITION943)))))
      #:RETURN-42-RESTART-BINDING941
      (RETURN-FROM #:RESTART-CASE-BLOCK939
        (APPLY (LAMBDA () 42) #:RESTART-CASE-VAR940)))))
```

It is not yet possible to test this expansion, even though we have defined a dummy implementation of error—we would need a handler to route the condition over to the established restart. We will test this behavior in the next sections, after our handler-binding mechanism is implemented.

This concludes the implementation of a portable and ANSI-conforming restart-case—the most complex macro in the Common Lisp condition system.

## 3.6.5  Implementing simple restarts

Thankfully, the only remaining restart-related macro is a simple one. with-simple-restarts expands into a restart-case with a :report option based on the format control and optional format arguments. If the restart case is invoked, it returns nil and t as *multiple values*.

```
(defmacro with-simple-restart ((name format-control &rest args) &body forms)
  (let ((stream (gensym "STREAM")))
    `(restart-case ,(if (= 1 (length forms)) (car forms) `(progn ,@forms))
       (,name ()
         :report (lambda (,stream) (format ,stream ,format-control ,@args))
         (values nil t)))))
```

(In most cases, only the first value returned by an expression, named the *primary value*, is taken into account; however, some CL operators return more than one value, which some other operators, such as nth-value or multiple-value-bind, are able to accept.)

(Additionally, the (if (= 1 (length forms)) ...) check is used to ensure that a singular standard signaling form (signal, error, etc.) will be spliced in without a progn, so restart-case may perform its implicit condition-restart association properly.)

The macroexpansion is readable without much effort; we can expand the with-simple-restart form and read the resulting restart-case to verify that it does, indeed, work as intended:

```
(with-simple-restart (fail "Fail the computation.")
  (compute-something))

(RESTART-CASE (COMPUTE-SOMETHING)
  (FAIL NIL :REPORT
  (LAMBDA (#:STREAM846) (FORMAT #:STREAM846 "Fail the computation."))
  (VALUES NIL T)))
```

# 3.7 System-defined restarts

The CL standard defines five standard restarts that may (or even should) be bound by standard CL operators. They are abort, continue, muffle-warning, store-value, and use-value.

Each of these restarts also has its associated restart-invoking function with the same name. We will implement these now, starting with the least complicated ones—continue, store-value, and use-value.

```
(defun continue (&optional condition)
  (let ((restart (find-restart 'continue condition)))
    (when restart (invoke-restart restart))))

(defun store-value (value &optional condition)
  (let ((restart (find-restart 'store-value condition)))
    (when restart (invoke-restart restart value))))

(defun use-value (value &optional condition)
  (let ((restart (find-restart 'use-value condition)))
    (when restart (invoke-restart restart value))))
```

These functions are the least complicated ones because they are not required to signal any kind of errors if the restart they need to invoke is not active; in such a case they simply return nil. This is in contrast to muffle-warning and abort, which require that a control-error be signaled in such a case. For our convenience (and for more meaningful reports), we will define a custom subtype of control-error and signal it from within abort and muffle-warning.

```
(defun report-restart-not-found (condition stream)
  (format stream "Restart ~S is not active."
          (restart-not-found-restart-name condition)))

(define-condition restart-not-found (control-error)
  ((restart-name :reader restart-not-found-restart-name :initarg :restart-name))
  (:report report-restart-not-found))
```

Thanks to these definitions, we may now implement abort and muffle-warning, which—again—are similar to each other.

```
(defun abort (&optional condition)
  (let ((restart (find-restart 'abort condition)))
    (if restart
        (invoke-restart restart)
        (error 'restart-not-found :restart-name 'abort))))
```

175

```
(defun muffle-warning (&optional condition)
  (let ((restart (find-restart 'muffle-warning condition)))
    (if restart
        (invoke-restart restart)
        (error 'restart-not-found :restart-name 'muffle-warning))))
```

(Some Common Lisp implementations put additional error calls at the ends of abort and muffle-warning to implement the part of the specification that states that these two functions may *never* return; this might happen, e.g., if the abort or muffle-warning restart function fails to transfer control. For simplicity, we leave this functionality out of this book.)

We may additionally factor all the common code from the preceding restart-invoking functions into a single function, maybe-invoke-restart, which can then be called by all standard restart-invoking functions. This common function will accept the restart name, a condition object, and an optional parameter that states whether an error should be signaled if the restart is not found.

```
(defun maybe-invoke-restart (restart-name &optional condition errorp &rest arguments)
  (let ((restart (find-restart restart-name condition)))
    (cond (restart (apply #'invoke-restart restart arguments))
          (errorp (error 'restart-not-found :restart-name restart-name)))))

(defun abort (&optional condition)
  (maybe-invoke-restart 'abort condition t))

(defun muffle-warning (&optional condition)
  (maybe-invoke-restart 'muffle-warning condition t))

(defun continue (&optional condition)
  (maybe-invoke-restart 'continue condition))

(defun store-value (value &optional condition)
  (maybe-invoke-restart 'store-value condition nil value))

(defun use-value (value &optional condition)
  (maybe-invoke-restart 'use-value condition nil value))
```

Simple REPL tests of the negative cases follow:

```
PCS> (catch :error (abort))
;; Error: RESTART-NOT-FOUND
NIL
```

```
PCS> (catch :error (muffle-warning))
;; Error: RESTART-NOT-FOUND
NIL
```

# 3.8  Assertions

We have established enough restart-related macrology to be able to implement CL assertion operators now. These operators can be grouped into three pairs: non-correctable case assertions (ecase and etypecase), correctable case assertions (ccase and ctypecase), and general assertions (assert and check-type).

## 3.8.1  Case failures

Implementing case assertions will be easier if we notice that the errors signaled by these assertions are going to be similar to each other. They are all type errors that have three variables to them: the value that failed the assertion, the kind of assertion that was failed (which could be defined to be the name of that assertion), and a set of possibilities that was not matched.

Let us therefore abstract this into one common condition type, case-failure, along with one function that shall expand into an error case-failure for us.

```
(defun report-case-failure (condition stream)
  (format stream "~S fell through ~S expression. Wanted one of ~:S."
          (type-error-datum condition)
          (case-failure-name condition)
          (case-failure-possibilities condition)))

(define-condition case-failure (type-error)
  ((name :reader case-failure-name :initarg :name)
   (possibilities :reader case-failure-possibilities :initarg :possibilities))
  (:report report-case-failure))

(defun case-failure (datum complex-type operator-name keys)
  (error 'case-failure :datum datum
                       :expected-type `(,complex-type ,@keys)
                       :name operator-name
                       :possibilities keys))
```

Since case-failure is a type-error, we should provide it, upon instantiation, with values for its :datum and :expected-type keyword arguments. (Due to inheritance, signaling a case-failure will nonetheless activate all handlers that are looking for a type-error.) For constructing the type for :expected-type, we use the complex-type argument. For case variants, this complex type will contain the symbol member; for typecase, it will contain or.

## 3.8.2  Case utilities

Before we begin implementing our case assertions, we need to make a certain decision about our approach. We may implement them fully from scratch, expanding them into a cond with series of eql checks (for ecase and ccase) or a cond with a series of typep checks (for etypecase and ctypecase). However, we may also piggyback on our implementations' existing case and typecase operators, adapting them for our purpose. For simplicity, we will use the latter option.

There is an important difference between case and ecase/ccase, however, which we must account for. The pair of symbols t and otherwise have special meaning in case—they allow fall-through and catch-all cases that do not match any earlier case. These symbols carry no such special meanings in ecase or ccase, however; there, they are expected to be matched by eql just like any other keys.

Therefore, in order to implement ecase and ccase, we need a means of translating the t/otherwise cases from ecase/ccase into (t)/(otherwise) cases for case. Indeed, wrapping each of these two symbols in a list is, thankfully, enough to disable their special meaning inside case while preserving their ability to be matched by eql. With this trick in hand, our first utility function for case assertions is now ready to be implemented:

```
(defun case-transform-t-otherwise-cases (cases)
  (loop for (key . forms) in cases
        if (member key '(t otherwise)) collect `((,key) ,@forms)
        else collect `(,key ,@forms)))
```

We can immediately test it in the REPL to see if it gives us the expected results:

```
PCS> (case-transform-t-otherwise-cases
      '((24 :foo)
        (:forty-two :bar)
        ((nil) :baz)
        (t :fallthrough)))
```

```
((24 :FOO)
 (:FORTY-TWO :BAR)
 ((NIL) :BAZ)
 ((T) :FALLTHROUGH))

PCS> (case-transform-t-otherwise-cases
      '((24 :foo)
        (:forty-two :bar)
        ((nil) :baz)
        (otherwise :fallthrough)))
((24 :FOO)
 (:FORTY-TWO :BAR)
 ((NIL) :BAZ)
 ((OTHERWISE) :FALLTHROUGH))
```

That works well. Another utility that we will need is a way to collect all keys from a list of ecase/ccase cases, so that we will have something appropriate to pass along to our case-failure function:

```
(defun case-accumulate-keys (cases)
  (loop for case in cases
        for key-or-keys = (first case)
        if (listp key-or-keys) append key-or-keys
        else collect key-or-keys))
```

This function iterates through the cases, checking the first element of each. When it's a list, its contents are appended to the collection; otherwise, the singular key is collected. We can verify that this approach works:

```
PCS> (case-accumulate-keys
      '(((24 25 26) :foo)
        (:forty-two :bar)
        ((nil) :baz)
        (t :fallthrough)))
(24 25 26 :FORTY-TWO NIL T)
```

case-accumulate-keys will be useful for ecase/ccase, where keys are allowed to come in lists or as atoms; we will not use it for etypecase/ctypecase, since type specifiers are allowed to be lists.

# 3.8.3 Non-correctable case assertions

With the preceding helper functions, we are now ready to implement ecase and etypecase.
Let us start with the first one. ecase accepts a form (keyform) evaluated at runtime
to produce the key to be tested and a list of cases. We will implement ecase via case,
remembering to transform the cases to get rid of the special meaning of any t/otherwise
keys.

```
(defun expand-ecase (keyform cases)
  (let ((keys (case-accumulate-keys cases))
        (variable (gensym "ECASE-VARIABLE")))
    `(let ((,variable ,keyform))
       (case ,variable ,@(case-transform-t-otherwise-cases cases)
         (t (case-failure ,variable 'member 'ecase ',keys))))))

(defmacro ecase (keyform &rest cases)
  (expand-ecase keyform cases))
```

We can see that we add our own t case to the body of case in order always to signal
an error in case of matching failure. In addition, we see that the keyform is bound to a
temporary variable that we create around the form; this is to prevent multiple evaluation
when we need to pass the value to the case-failure form. We can test the expansion of our
macro

```
PCS> (expand-ecase 'nil
                   '(((24 25 26) :foo)
                     (:forty-two :bar)
                     ((nil) :baz)
                     (t :no-fallthrough)))
(LET ((#:ECASE-VARIABLE970 NIL))
  (CASE NIL
    ((24 25 26) :FOO)
    (:FORTY-TWO :BAR)
    ((NIL) :BAZ)
    ((T) :NO-FALLTHROUGH)
    (T (CASE-FAILURE #:ECASE-VARIABLE970 'MEMBER 'ECASE '(24 25 26 :FORTY-TWO NIL T)))))
```

and verify that it indeed works as expected:

```
PCS> (ecase nil
       ((24 25 26) :foo)
       (:forty-two :bar)
       ((nil) :baz)
       (t :no-fallthrough))
:BAZ

PCS> (catch :error
       (ecase :twenty-four
         ((24 25 26) :foo)
         (:forty-two :bar)
         ((nil) :baz)
         (t :no-fallthrough)))
;; Error: CASE-FAILURE
NIL
```

The implementation of etypecase is going to be similar, except that we will use mapcar #'first instead of case-accumulate-keys, we do not need to do anything about t, and otherwise is a valid type specifier and therefore we do not need to care about it at all either.

```
(defun expand-etypecase (keyform cases)
  (let ((keys (mapcar #'first cases))
        (variable (gensym "ETYPECASE-VARIABLE")))
    `(let ((,variable ,keyform))
       (typecase ,keyform ,@cases
         (t (case-failure ,variable 'or 'etypecase ',keys))))))

(defmacro etypecase (keyform &rest cases)
  (expand-etypecase keyform cases))
```

We can test the expansion of expand-etypecase in the REPL and then check the macro itself:

```
PCS> (expand-etypecase '"forty-two"
                       '(((or integer rational float) :foo)
                         (keyword :bar)
                         (string :baz)))
(LET ((#:ETYPECASE-VARIABLE978 "forty-two"))
  (TYPECASE "forty-two"
```

```
    ((OR INTEGER RATIONAL FLOAT) :FOO)
    (KEYWORD :BAR)
    (STRING :BAZ)
    (T (ERROR 'CASE-FAILURE :DATUM #:ETYPECASE-VARIABLE978
                            :EXPECTED-TYPE '(OR (OR INTEGER RATIONAL FLOAT) KEYWORD STRING)
                            :NAME 'ETYPECASE
                            :POSSIBILITIES '((OR INTEGER RATIONAL FLOAT) KEYWORD STRING)))))

PCS> (etypecase "forty-two"
       ((or integer rational float) :foo)
       (keyword :bar)
       (string :baz))
:BAZ

PCS> (catch :error
       (etypecase 'forty-two
         ((or integer rational float) :foo)
         (keyword :bar)
         (string :baz)))
;; Error: CASE-FAILURE
NIL
```

## 3.8.4  Correctable case assertions

With the first pair of correctable assertions implemented, we may move on to the second one. The correctable case assertions work similarly to the non-correctable ones, except that they additionally bind a store-value restart that allows the programmer to retry the whole assertion with the keyform place set to a new value. This additional binding, in turn, can be implemented with a macro that accepts a place to set, a tag to transfer control to, and a set of body forms to execute in an environment where the store-value restart is bound.

This abstraction is worth separating into a separate macro, because it can be shared between ccase and ctypecase.

```
(defun store-value-read-evaluated-form ()
  (format *query-io* "~&;; Type a form to be evaluated:~%")
  (list (eval (read *query-io*))))

(defun expand-with-store-value-restart (temp-var place tag forms)
  (let ((report-var (gensym "STORE-VALUE-REPORT"))
        (new-value-var (gensym "NEW-VALUE"))
        (form-or-forms (if (= 1 (length forms)) (first forms) `(progn ,@forms))))
```

```
`(flet ((,report-var (stream)
           (format stream "Supply a new value of ~S." ',place)))
   (restart-case ,form-or-forms
     (store-value (,new-value-var)
       :report ,report-var
       :interactive store-value-read-evaluated-form
       (setf ,temp-var ,new-value-var
             ,place ,new-value-var)
       (go ,tag))))))
(defmacro with-store-value-restart ((temp-var place tag) &body forms)
  (expand-with-store-value-restart temp-var place tag forms))
```

The macro expands into a restart-case form, with a local function defined for reporting the restart. The function store-value-read-evaluated-form is used to query the user for a form to set the place to; this is the interactive function of the store-value restart established within with-store-value-restart.

The established store-value restart case utilizes all three arguments that it is given: the temporary variable and the place passed to it are set with the provided value, and control is then transferred to the appropriate go tag.

Let us see the expansion of that form on sample data:

```
PCS> (expand-with-store-value-restart 'temp-var 'place 'tag '((frobnicate)))
(FLET ((#:STORE-VALUE-REPORT980 (STREAM) (FORMAT STREAM "Supply a new value of ~S." 'PLACE)))
  (RESTART-CASE (FROBNICATE)
    (STORE-VALUE (#:NEW-VALUE981)
      :REPORT #:STORE-VALUE-REPORT980
      :INTERACTIVE STORE-VALUE-READ-EVALUATED-FORM
      (SETF TEMP-VAR #:NEW-VALUE981
            PLACE #:NEW-VALUE981)
      (GO TAG))))
```

We can use this macro to implement our correctable case assertions. Let us start with ccase:

```
(defun expand-ccase (keyform cases)
  (let ((keys (case-accumulate-keys cases))
        (variable (gensym "CCASE-VARIABLE"))
        (block-name (gensym "CCASE-BLOCK"))
        (tag (gensym "CCASE-TAG")))
```

```
`(block ,block-name
   (let ((,variable ,keyform))
     (tagbody ,tag
       (return-from ,block-name
         (case ,variable ,@(case-transform-t-otherwise-cases cases)
             (t (with-store-value-restart (,variable ,keyform ,tag)
                 (case-failure ,variable 'member 'ccase ',keys)))))))))))

(defmacro ccase (keyform &rest cases)
  (expand-ccase keyform cases))
```

We can see that the structure of special forms is more complex this time. We establish a block from which to return our value, a lexical variable that will hold the value of the keyform, and a tagbody with a single tag in the beginning. Immediately inside, we attempt to return a value via return-from; this returning is meant to succeed if the case succeeds, and otherwise, control is transferred back to the tagbody tag, and return-from is entered again.

(The lexical variable is bound before tagbody and its name is passed to with-store-value-restart in order to prevent the keyform being evaluated on each entry into tagbody.)

Let us attempt to expand ccase for place x and a single case in which the value 42 returns :foo.

```
PCS> (expand-ccase 'x '((42 :foo)))
(BLOCK #:CCASE-BLOCK1025
  (LET ((#:CCASE-VARIABLE1024 X))
    (TAGBODY
     #:CCASE-TAG1026
      (RETURN-FROM #:CCASE-BLOCK1025
        (CASE #:CCASE-VARIABLE1024
          (42 :FOO)
          (T (WITH-STORE-VALUE-RESTART (#:CCASE-VARIABLE1024 X #:CCASE-TAG1026)
              (CASE-FAILURE #:CCASE-VARIABLE1024 'MEMBER 'CCASE '(42)))))))))
```

Let us test our macro for both positive and negative outcomes:

```
PCS> (let ((x 42))
       (ccase x (42 :foo)))
:FOO
```

```
PCS> (catch :error
        (let ((x 24))
          (ccase x (42 :foo))))
;; Error: 24 fell through CCASE expression. Wanted one of (42).
NIL
```

Our typecase implementation is going to be similar in structure:

```
(defun expand-ctypecase (keyform cases)
  (let ((keys (case-accumulate-keys cases))
        (variable (gensym "CTYPECASE-VARIABLE"))
        (block-name (gensym "CTYPECASE-BLOCK"))
        (tag (gensym "CTYPECASE-TAG")))
    `(block ,block-name
       (let ((,variable ,keyform))
         (tagbody ,tag
           (return-from ,block-name
             (typecase ,keyform ,@cases
                       (t (with-store-value-restart (,variable ,keyform ,tag)
                            (case-failure ,variable 'or 'ctypecase ',keys)))))))))

(defmacro ctypecase (keyform &rest cases)
  (expand-ctypecase keyform cases))
```

We can likewise verify its expansion and positive result in the REPL.

```
PCS> (expand-ctypecase 'x '((integer :foo)))
(BLOCK #:CTYPECASE-BLOCK1031
  (LET ((#:CTYPECASE-VARIABLE1030 X))
    (TAGBODY
     #:CTYPECASE-TAG1032
       (RETURN-FROM #:CTYPECASE-BLOCK1031
         (TYPECASE X
           (INTEGER :FOO)
           (T (WITH-STORE-VALUE-RESTART (#:CTYPECASE-VARIABLE1030 X #:CTYPECASE-TAG1032)
                (CASE-FAILURE #:CTYPECASE-VARIABLE1030 'OR 'CTYPECASE '(INTEGER)))))))))

PCS> (let ((x 42))
        (ctypecase x (integer :foo)))
:FOO
```

```
PCS> (catch :error
       (let ((x 42))
         (ctypecase x (keyword :foo))))
;; Error: 42 fell through CTYPECASE expression. Wanted one of (KEYWORD).
NIL
```

## 3.8.5  General assertions

With our case assertions ready, we can now focus on the remaining two assertions: assert itself and check-type. The former is the most general CL assertion operator: not only does it allow arbitrary forms to be evaluated, but it is also the only CL assertion operator capable of allowing the programmer interactively to set multiple places at once. The two support functions that we will write for assert will be used exactly for that purpose: one of them will report the continue report bound by assert, and the other will be responsible for querying the user for whether they would like to supply a new value for a single place.

```
(defun assert-restart-report (names stream)
  (format stream "Retry assertion")
  (if names
      (format stream " with new value~P for ~{~S~^, ~}." (length names) names)
      (format stream ".")))

(defun assert-prompt (place-name value)
  (cond ((y-or-n-p "~&;; The old value of ~S is ~S.~%~
                    ;; Do you want to supply a new value?"
                   place-name value)
         (format *query-io* "~&;; Type a form to be evaluated:~%")
         (flet ((read-it ()
                  (format *query-io* "> ")
                  (eval (read *query-io*))))
           (cond ((symbolp place-name)
                  (format *query-io*
                          "~&;; (The old value is bound to the symbol ~S.)~%"
                          place-name)
                  (progv (list place-name) (list value) (read-it)))
                 (t (read-it)))))
        (t value)))
```

Let us focus on the second function for a moment. It contains a conditional expression that first calls a function y-or-n-p. That function prints the prompt to *query-io* and waits for the user to answer either with a y or an n. In case of n, the function returns false, and value is returned; in case of y, the function returns true, and the conditional branch is entered.

Once inside, the function checks whether place-name is a symbol; if that is true, that symbol is dynamically bound *at runtime* using the special operator progv. Then, an expression is read and evaluated at runtime to provide the value to be returned from assert-prompt. If the place is not a symbol, then the progv binding is skipped, but an expression is still read and evaluated.

It is best to see this function in action in order to understand how it works:

```
PCS> (assert-prompt 'x 42)
;; The old value of X is 42.
;; Do you want to supply a new value? (y or n) y          ; user input here
;; Type a form to be evaluated:
;; (The old value is bound to the symbol X.)
> (* x x)                                                 ; user input here
1764

PCS> (assert-prompt '(car some-cons) 42)
;; The old value of (CAR SOME-CONS) is 42.
;; Do you want to supply a new value? (y or n) y          ; user input here
;; Type a form to be evaluated:
> 84                                                      ; user input here
84

PCS> (assert-prompt 'x 42)
;; The old value of X is 42.
;; Do you want to supply a new value? (y or n) n          ; user input here
42
```

We can see that, in the first example, we can use the symbol x inside the query made by assert-prompt, even though x was never bound as a global dynamic variable. This is allowed by the fact that the eval call is executed inside progv, and therefore a new dynamic binding for x is established. This means that, even if x was originally a lexical variable, it is re-created as a dynamic variable that we can use in the form read and evaluated by assert.

In addition, we can see that assert-prompt always returns a value—either the new one or the old one. This means that we can use the return value of that function as an argument to setf in order to assign values to the place.

We may now work on our implementation of assert. It will be somewhat similar to the earlier assertion operators: we will need a tagbody to which we will transfer control to in order to retry the assertion, and a place-setting continue restart will be established. The main differences are that the only value it returns is nil, which will save us from establishing a block; in addition, assert can set multiple places, which we will need to account for.

```
(defmacro assert (test-form &optional places datum &rest arguments)
  (flet ((make-place-setter (place) `(setf ,place (assert-prompt ',place ,place))))
    (let ((tag (gensym "ASSERT-TAG")))
      `(tagbody ,tag
         (unless ,test-form
           (restart-case ,(if datum
                              `(error ,datum ,@arguments)
                              `(error "The assertion ~S failed." ',test-form))
             (continue ()
               :report (lambda (stream) (assert-restart-report ',places stream))
               ,@(mapcar #'make-place-setter places)
               (go ,tag)))))))
```

The main structure of our assert operator is lightweight: we have a tagbody wrapping an unless. This setup means that, first, the test form is evaluated, and if it returns true, then the rest of the form is not entered. Only when an assertion fails, and test-form returns true, do we get to see the rest of assert's functionality.

Immediately after establishing a continue restart, an error is signaled, based on the datum and arguments that are passed to assert. A continue restart is available, with its report calling our helper function assert-restart-report.

We can see that setting multiple places is taken care of by the local function make-place-setter; this function turns the list of places into a list of setf forms. The value for each such setf form is returned by the interactive function assert-prompt which we defined earlier. Immediately after setting the places, control is transferred back to the unless test, retrying the assertion with possibly new values given to our places (if any).

```
PCS> (assert t)
NIL

PCS> (catch :error
       (assert nil))
;; Error: The assertion NIL failed.
NIL
```

(More intricate tests of the full assert will come when we are capable of handling the signaled error, for which we need to implement handlers.)

The sixth—and final—assertion macro, check-type, has a somewhat similar, if simpler, structure. We have a tagbody over an unless typep check; if the check fails, then a store-value restart is established, and an error is immediately signaled. The actual condition is created in a separate helper function, extracted from the main body of the macro.

```
(defun check-type-error (place value type type-string)
  (error
    'simple-type-error
    :datum value
    :expected-type type
    :format-control (if type-string
                        "The value of ~S is ~S, which is not ~A."
                        "The value of ~S is ~S, which is not of type ~S.")
    :format-arguments (list place value (or type-string type))))

(defun expand-check-type (place type type-string)
  (let ((variable (gensym "CHECK-TYPE-VARIABLE"))
        (tag (gensym "CHECK-TYPE-TAG")))
    `(let ((,variable ,place))
       (tagbody ,tag
          (unless (typep ,variable ',type)
            (with-store-value-restart (,variable ,place ,tag)
              (check-type-error ',place ,variable ',type ,type-string)))))))

(defmacro check-type (place type &optional type-string)
  (expand-check-type place type type-string))
```

By now, the author hopes that the reader has gained enough confidence in reading macros to be able to read this one themselves; we shall simply expand it in the REPL and verify that a positive-outcome example works well:

```
PCS> (expand-check-type 'x 'integer nil)
(LET ((#:CHECK-TYPE-VARIABLE1034 X))
  (TAGBODY #:CHECK-TYPE-TAG1035
    (UNLESS (TYPEP #:CHECK-TYPE-VARIABLE1034 'INTEGER)
      (WITH-STORE-VALUE-RESTART (#:CHECK-TYPE-VARIABLE1034 X #:CHECK-TYPE-TAG1035)
        (CHECK-TYPE-ERROR 'X #:CHECK-TYPE-VARIABLE1034 'INTEGER NIL)))))

PCS> (let ((x 42))
       (check-type x integer))
NIL

PCS> (catch :error
       (let ((x 42))
         (check-type x keyword)))
;; Error: The value of X is 42, which is not of type KEYWORD.
NIL
```

As mentioned earlier, testing the restarts established by the correctable and general assertions will be performed after we implement handlers, and we will therefore be able to handle the errors signaled by these operators by invoking a proper restart.

# 3.9  Signaling

Our assertions are now done, but they are not yet functional or testable. This is because we have not yet defined the signaling functions used within them: signal, warn, error, and cerror. We will do this now.

The first and the most basic signaling function, signal, requires us to build some infrastructure for two future parts of the condition system. In order to be able to process all currently active handlers, we need to declare a variable to hold these handlers; in addition, signal is allowed to call break when the variable *break-on-signals* is non-nil. These two variables need to be defined:

```
(defvar *break-on-signals* nil)

(defvar *handler-clusters* '())
```

We are now allowed to define signal. It makes use of coerce-to-condition to ensure that it is dealing with a condition object; it then checks whether or not break should be called before signaling the condition, and finally, it walks the list of handler clusters and invokes any matching handlers found there in order.

```
(defun signal (datum &rest arguments)
  (let ((condition (coerce-to-condition datum arguments 'simple-condition 'signal)))
    (if (typep condition *break-on-signals*)
        (break "~A~%Break entered because of *BREAK-ON-SIGNALS*." condition))
    (loop for (cluster . remaining-clusters) on *handler-clusters*
          do (let ((*handler-clusters* remaining-clusters))
               (dolist (handler cluster)
                 (when (typep condition (car handler))
                   (funcall (cdr handler) condition)))))))
```

It is interesting to note that *handler-clusters* is being rebound as the loop inside signal progresses. This rebinding is required in order to implement the clustering mechanism required by handlers: a handler invoked from a given cluster may only see handlers that are "older" than itself, and this behavior is implemented by dynamically binding *handler-clusters* to the list of all handler clusters "older" than the cluster that the currently invoked handler belongs to.

Even though we do not have any defined standard means of binding handlers, we may nonetheless bind *handler-clusters* manually in order to test our signal implementation. We will perform this now.

```
PCS> (flet ((handler-1 (condition) (format t ";; Got a ~S.~%" condition))
            (handler-2 (condition) (format t ";; Also got a ~S.~%" condition))
            (handler-3 (condition) (format t ";; I too got a ~S.~%" condition)))
       (let ((*handler-clusters* `(((condition . ,#'handler-1)
                                    (error . ,#'handler-2))
                                   ((condition . ,#'handler-3)))))
         (signal (make-condition 'condition))))
;; Got a #<CONDITION {100E885C63}>.
;; I too got a #<CONDITION {100E885C63}>.
NIL

PCS> (flet ((handler-1 (condition) (format t ";; Got a ~S.~%" condition))
            (handler-2 (condition) (format t ";; Also got a ~S.~%" condition))
            (handler-3 (condition) (format t ";; I too got a ~S.~%" condition)))
```

```
        (let ((*handler-clusters* `(((condition . ,#'handler-1)
                                     (error . ,#'handler-2))
                                    ((condition . ,#'handler-3)))))
          (signal (make-condition 'error))))
;; Got a #<ERROR {100E9455D3}>.
;; Also got a #<ERROR {100E9455D3}>.
;; I too got a #<ERROR {100E9455D3}>.
NIL
```

We can now define warn, which will call signal as a part of its operation. It utilizes check-type to ensure that the condition passed to the function is a warning condition, as mandated by the standard: then, it establishes its muffle-warning restart, signals the condition, and reports the condition if the signaling did not cause a transfer of control.

```
(defun warn (datum &rest arguments)
  (let ((condition (coerce-to-condition datum arguments 'simple-warning 'warn)))
    (check-type condition warning)
    (with-simple-restart (muffle-warning "Muffle the warning.")
      (signal condition)
      (format *error-output* "~&;; Warning: ~A~%" condition))
    nil))
```

(The nil at the end is required by the standard, since warn must return nil as its only value if it returns normally; with-simple-restart will return an additional t as the secondary value if its restart was invoked.)

Let us now test the three basic cases: when the warning is not muffled, when muffle-warning is called, and when control is transferred outside the handler function (as if in handler-case).

```
PCS> (flet ((handler-1 (condition) (format t ";; Got a ~S.~%" condition))
            (handler-2 (condition) (format t ";; Also got a ~S.~%" condition)))
       (let ((*handler-clusters* `(((condition . ,#'handler-1))
                                   ((warning . ,#'handler-2)))))
         (warn (make-condition 'warning))))
;; Got a #<WARNING {100F669063}>.
;; Also got a #<WARNING {100F669063}>.
;; Warning: Condition WARNING was signaled.
NIL
```

```
PCS> (flet ((handler-1 (condition) (format t ";; Got a ~S.~%" condition))
            (handler-2 (condition) (declare (ignore condition)) (muffle-warning)))
       (let ((*handler-clusters* `(((condition . ,#'handler-1))
                                    ((warning . ,#'handler-2)))))
         (warn (make-condition 'warning))))
;; Got a #<WARNING {100F78B153}>.
NIL

PCS> (block nil
       (flet ((handler-1 (condition) (format t ";; Got a ~S.~%" condition))
              (handler-2 (condition) (declare (ignore condition)) (return 42)))
         (let ((*handler-clusters* `(((condition . ,#'handler-1))
                                      ((warning . ,#'handler-2)))))
           (warn (make-condition 'warning)))))
;; Got a #<WARNING {100F5CDB63}>.
42
```

Finally, we may implement error (which redefines the earlier stub definition of same) and cerror. error signals the condition object before entering the debugger, and cerror calls error with an established simple restart named continue.

```
(defun error (datum &rest arguments)
  (let ((condition (coerce-to-condition datum arguments 'simple-error 'error)))
    (signal condition)
    (invoke-debugger condition)))

(defun cerror (continue-string datum &rest arguments)
  (with-simple-restart (continue "~A" (apply #'format nil continue-string arguments))
    (apply #'error datum arguments))
  nil)
```

Once again, we have run into bootstrapping issues: we have not yet defined the debugger, so we are unable to invoke it. We will work around the issue in a similar way: we shall stub the debugger out and have it transfer control via throw.

```
(defun invoke-debugger (condition)
  (format *error-output* ";; Debugger entered: ~A~%" condition)
  (throw :error nil))
```

A proper implementation of the debugger will come in the next sections. Until then, we can test it with a `catch` tag and by manually binding condition handlers:

```
PCS> (catch :error
        (flet ((handler-1 (condition) (format t ";; Got a ~S.~%" condition))
               (handler-2 (condition) (format t ";; Also got a ~S.~%" condition))
               (handler-3 (condition) (format t ";; I too got a ~S.~%" condition)))
          (let ((*handler-clusters* `(((condition . ,#'handler-1)
                                       (error . ,#'handler-2)
                                       (condition . ,#'handler-3)))))
            (error (make-condition 'error)))))
;; Got a #<ERROR {10100CE1F3}>.
;; Also got a #<ERROR {10100CE1F3}>.
;; I too got a #<ERROR {10100CE1F3}>.
;; Debugger entered: Condition ERROR was signaled.
NIL

PCS> (block nil
        (flet ((handler-1 (condition) (format t ";; Got a ~S.~%" condition))
               (handler-2 (condition) (declare (ignore condition)) (return)))
          (let ((*handler-clusters* `(((condition . ,#'handler-1))
                                      ((error . ,#'handler-2)))))
            (error (make-condition 'error)))))
;; Got a #<ERROR {1012A78233}>.
NIL
```

Now that we can manually bind handlers, we may also begin testing our restarts—starting with the `continue` restart established by `cerror` and then performing a tiny test of `restart-bind`:

```
PCS> (flet ((handler-1 (condition) (format t ";; Got a ~S.~%" condition))
            (handler-2 (condition) (continue condition)))
       (let ((*handler-clusters* `(((condition . ,#'handler-1))
                                   ((error . ,#'handler-2)))))
         (cerror "Continue." (make-condition 'error))
         42))
;; Got a #<ERROR {1012DAD8B3}>.
42
```

```
PCS> (restart-bind ((foo (lambda () (format t ";; Restart FOO was invoked.~%"))))
       (flet ((handler-1 (condition) (declare (ignore condition)) (invoke-restart 'foo)))
         (let ((*handler-clusters* `(((condition . ,#'handler-1)))))
           (signal (make-condition 'condition)))))
;; Restart FOO was invoked.
NIL
```

# 3.10  Handlers

We defined our variable for handler clusters while implementing signal, and our testing with manually binding *handler-clusters* showed that our signaling infrastructure is working well. We can therefore immediately proceed with writing the handler-bind macro, which is—maybe unsurprisingly—similar to our previous implementation of restart-bind.

## 3.10.1  Binding handlers

```
(defun handler-bind-make-binding (binding)
  (destructuring-bind (condition-type function) binding
    `(cons ',condition-type ,function)))

(defun expand-handler-bind (bindings forms)
  (let ((cluster (mapcar #'handler-bind-make-binding bindings)))
    `(let ((*handler-clusters* (cons (list ,@cluster) *handler-clusters*)))
       ,@forms)))

(defmacro handler-bind (bindings &body forms)
  (expand-handler-bind bindings forms))
```

Other than the function and macro names, the only distinct things are the form of a handler binding (which must have exactly two elements: the condition type and the handler function) and the fact that handlers themselves are not structures, but conses.

We can immediately put this macro to use by rewriting some of the signaling test cases from earlier to use handler-bind—and to test the restarts of restart-case, as we promised in the earlier chapters.

```
PCS> (flet ((handler-1 (condition) (format t ";; Got a ~S.~%" condition))
            (handler-2 (condition) (format t ";; Also got a ~S.~%" condition))
            (handler-3 (condition) (format t ";; I too got a ~S.~%" condition)))
```

```
          (handler-bind ((condition #'handler-3))
            (handler-bind ((condition #'handler-1)
                           (error #'handler-2))
              (signal (make-condition 'error)))))
;; Got a #<ERROR {1013AFF0C3}>.
;; Also got a #<ERROR {1013AFF0C3}>.
;; I too got a #<ERROR {1013AFF0C3}>.
NIL

PCS> (flet ((handler-1 (condition) (format t ";; Got a ~S.~%" condition))
            (handler-2 (condition) (declare (ignore condition)) (muffle-warning)))
       (handler-bind ((condition #'handler-1)
                      (warning #'handler-2))
         (warn (make-condition 'warning))))
;; Got a #<WARNING {1013BB1E23}>.
NIL

PCS> (block nil
       (flet ((handler-1 (condition) (format t ";; Got a ~S.~%" condition))
              (handler-2 (condition) (declare (ignore condition)) (return)))
         (handler-bind ((condition #'handler-1)
                        (error #'handler-2))
           (error (make-condition 'error)))))
;; Got a #<ERROR {1013E3C563}>.
NIL

PCS> (handler-bind ((error (lambda (condition)
                             (let ((restart (find-restart 'return-42 condition)))
                               (invoke-restart restart)))))
       (restart-case (error "Failure!")
         (return-42 ()
           :test (lambda (condition) (typep condition 'error))
           :report report-return-42
           42)))
42
```

## 3.10.2  Handler cases

With a working handler-bind, we can begin working on getting a working handler-case. This operator is, thankfully, simpler than restart-case, but it nonetheless introduces one piece of functionality that is completely new: the :no-error case, which is called when the expression passed to handler-case returns normally. Our handler-case implementation will therefore be split into two parts: one which implements the normal, non-:no-error behavior and another which handles the :no-error case.

The :no-error case is only run if the expression from handler-case returns normally, and therefore no handlers are triggered. Therefore, it is possible to separate the :no-error case and express it via additional code that calls the "standard" handler-case which does not contain a :no-error case.

```
(defun expand-handler-case-with-no-error-case (form cases)
  (let* ((no-error-case (assoc :no-error cases))
         (other-cases (remove no-error-case cases))
         (normal-return (gensym "NORMAL-RETURN"))
         (case-return  (gensym "CASE-RETURN")))
    `(block ,case-return
       (multiple-value-call (lambda ,@(cdr no-error-case))
         (block ,normal-return
           (return-from ,case-return
             (handler-case (return-from ,normal-return ,form)
               ,@other-cases)))))))
```

First of all, we separate the :no-error case from all other cases, and we generate a pair of block names for the two blocks that we establish. The two blocks are nested and intersect with each other: the form that was originally passed to handler-case is wrapped in a return-from that triggers a return from the normal-return block, and the values of that form are then passed as arguments to the function created from the :no-error case. The recursive handler-case call is wrapped in a return-from that triggers a return to the outermost case-return; this utilizes the fact that the full handler-case is now going to return a value if and only if any of the handler cases have been triggered and control has been routed out of the original expression.

```
PCS> (expand-handler-case-with-no-error-case
       '(+ 2 2)
       '((error () (format t ";; Oops~%"))
         (:no-error (x) (format t ";; Got ~A~%" x))))
(BLOCK #:CASE-RETURN1082
  (MULTIPLE-VALUE-CALL (LAMBDA (X) (FORMAT T ";; Got ~A~%" X))
    (BLOCK #:NORMAL-RETURN1081
      (RETURN-FROM #:CASE-RETURN1082
        (HANDLER-CASE (RETURN-FROM #:NORMAL-RETURN1081 (+ 2 2))
          (ERROR NIL (FORMAT T ";; Oops~%")))))))
```

This function will be called if and only if a :no-error case is present among the cases passed to handler-case, which means that now we may focus on implementing the "standard" situation—where all the cases have condition types for which control shall be transferred and a case should be executed.

The internal structure for our handler-case macro is going to be similar to our first iteration of restart-case. We will want to annotate our cases with a unique tag; we will want to generate handler bindings and handler cases; finally, we will want the main body of our macroexpansion to have a block for returning values from, a temporary variable for passing arguments around, and a tagbody that will allow transferring control to the handler cases.

```
(defun handler-case-parse-case (case)
  (destructuring-bind (type lambda-list . forms) case
    (let ((tag (gensym "HANDLER-TAG")))
      (list tag type lambda-list forms))))

(defun handler-case-make-handler-binding (case temp-var)
  (destructuring-bind (tag type lambda-list forms) case
    (declare (ignore forms))
    (let ((condition (gensym "CONDITION")))
      `(,type (lambda (,condition)
                (declare (ignorable ,condition))
                ,@(when lambda-list `((setf ,temp-var ,condition)))
                (go ,tag))))))

(defun handler-case-make-handler-case (case temp-var block-name)
  (destructuring-bind (tag type lambda-list body) case
    (declare (ignore type))
    `(,tag (return-from ,block-name
             ,(if lambda-list
                  `(let ((,(first lambda-list) ,temp-var)) ,@body)
                  `(locally ,@body))))))
```

One thing that is different in the functions that generate bindings and cases is the fact that the lambda list is simpler in handler-case; the only permitted values are an empty list (if we do not want to use the signaled condition) and a list containing one symbol (if we do want to use it). In the former case, no binding for the condition object is made, and in the latter, a let is introduced to bind the variable. Because of this simpler structure, the handler case expands into a locally or let instead of into a lambda form.

Let us briefly test these functions to ensure that they return values that we would expect them to return.

```
PCS> (handler-case-parse-case '(error (c) (format t ";; Error: ~A" c)))
(#:HANDLER-TAG1143 ERROR (C) ((FORMAT T ";; Error: ~A" C)))

PCS> (let ((case (handler-case-parse-case '(error (c) (format t ";; Error: ~A" c)))))
       (handler-case-make-handler-binding case 'temp-var))
(ERROR (LAMBDA (#:CONDITION1145)
         (DECLARE (IGNORABLE #:CONDITION1145))
         (SETF TEMP-VAR #:CONDITION1145)
         (GO #:HANDLER-TAG1144)))

PCS> (let ((case (handler-case-parse-case '(error (c) (format t ";; Error: ~A" c)))))
       (handler-case-make-handler-case case 'temp-var 'block-name))
(#:HANDLER-TAG1146
 (RETURN-FROM BLOCK-NAME
   (LET ((C TEMP-VAR))
     (FORMAT T ";; Error: ~A" C))))
```

We can now write a function that expands into the full handler-case body.

```
(defun expand-handler-case-without-no-error-case (form cases)
  (let ((block-name (gensym "HANDLER-CASE-BLOCK"))
        (temp-var (gensym "HANDLER-CASE-VAR"))
        (data (mapcar #'handler-case-parse-case cases)))
    (flet ((make-handler-binding (case)
             (handler-case-make-handler-binding case temp-var))
           (make-handler-case (case)
             (handler-case-make-handler-case case temp-var block-name)))
      `(let ((,temp-var nil))
         (declare (ignorable ,temp-var))
         (block ,block-name
           (tagbody
             (handler-bind ,(mapcar #'make-handler-binding data)
               (return-from ,block-name ,form))
             ,@(apply #'append (mapcar #'make-handler-case data))))))))
```

The similarities between expand-handler-case-without-no-error-case and expand-restart-case should be visible almost immediately; because of this similarity, we will not comment on this expansion function any further and instead skip straight to testing its expansion in the REPL:

```
PCS> (expand-handler-case-without-no-error-case
       '(signal 'warning)
       '((error (c) (format t ";; Error: ~A~%" c))
         (warning (c) (format t ";; Warning: ~A~%" c))
         (condition () (format t ";; Condition!~%"))))
(LET ((#:HANDLER-CASE-VAR1153 NIL))
  (DECLARE (IGNORABLE #:HANDLER-CASE-VAR1153))
  (BLOCK #:HANDLER-CASE-BLOCK1152
    (TAGBODY
      (HANDLER-BIND ((ERROR (LAMBDA (#:CONDITION1157)
                              (DECLARE (IGNORABLE #:CONDITION1157))
                              (SETF #:HANDLER-CASE-VAR1153 #:CONDITION1157)
                              (GO #:HANDLER-TAG1154)))
                     (WARNING (LAMBDA (#:CONDITION1158)
                                (DECLARE (IGNORABLE #:CONDITION1158))
                                (SETF #:HANDLER-CASE-VAR1153 #:CONDITION1158)
                                (GO #:HANDLER-TAG1155)))
                     (CONDITION (LAMBDA (#:CONDITION1159)
                                  (DECLARE (IGNORABLE #:CONDITION1159))
                                  (GO #:HANDLER-TAG1156))))
        (RETURN-FROM #:HANDLER-CASE-BLOCK1152 (SIGNAL 'WARNING)))
      #:HANDLER-TAG1154
       (RETURN-FROM #:HANDLER-CASE-BLOCK1152
         (LET ((C #:HANDLER-CASE-VAR1153))
           (FORMAT T ";; Error: ~A~%" C)))
      #:HANDLER-TAG1155
       (RETURN-FROM #:HANDLER-CASE-BLOCK1152
         (LET ((C #:HANDLER-CASE-VAR1153))
           (FORMAT T ";; Warning: ~A~%" C)))
      #:HANDLER-TAG1156
       (RETURN-FROM #:HANDLER-CASE-BLOCK1152
         (LOCALLY (FORMAT T ";; Condition!~%"))))))
```

We have a pair of functions that expand handler-case in the presence of a :no-error case and in its absence. We now need a function that will detect which case to use and choose one expanding function or the other. Since this is going to be the ultimate expanding function of handler-case, we may also define our macro at the same time:

```
(defun expand-handler-case (form cases)
  (if (member :no-error cases :key #'car)
      (expand-handler-case-with-no-error-case form cases)
      (expand-handler-case-without-no-error-case form cases)))

(defmacro handler-case (form &rest cases)
  (expand-handler-case form cases))
```

Now that we have these, we may check our macroexpansions one final time and then run basic tests in our REPL:

```
PCS> (expand-handler-case
      '(signal 'warning)
      '((warning () (format t ";; Warning!~%"))))
(LET ((#:HANDLER-CASE-VAR1104 NIL))
  (DECLARE (IGNORABLE #:HANDLER-CASE-VAR1104))
  (BLOCK #:HANDLER-CASE-BLOCK1103
    (TAGBODY
      (HANDLER-BIND ((WARNING (LAMBDA (#:CONDITION1106)
                               (DECLARE (IGNORABLE #:CONDITION1106))
                               (GO #:HANDLER-TAG1105))))
        (RETURN-FROM #:HANDLER-CASE-BLOCK1103 (SIGNAL 'WARNING)))
      #:HANDLER-TAG1105
      (RETURN-FROM #:HANDLER-CASE-BLOCK1103 (LOCALLY (FORMAT T ";; Warning!~%"))))))

PCS> (expand-handler-case
      '(signal 'condition)
      '((warning () (format t ";; Warning!~%"))
        (:no-error (&rest args) (declare (ignore args)) (format t ";; No error!~%"))))
(BLOCK #:CASE-RETURN1116
  (MULTIPLE-VALUE-CALL
    (LAMBDA (&REST ARGS) (DECLARE (IGNORE ARGS)) (FORMAT T ";; No error!~%"))
    (BLOCK #:NORMAL-RETURN1115
      (RETURN-FROM #:CASE-RETURN1116
        (HANDLER-CASE (RETURN-FROM #:NORMAL-RETURN1115 (SIGNAL 'CONDITION))
          (WARNING NIL (FORMAT T ";; Warning!~%")))))))

PCS> (handler-case (signal 'warning)
      (warning () (format t ";; Warning!~%")))
;; Warning!
NIL
```

```
PCS> (handler-case (signal 'condition)
       (warning () (format t ";; Warning!~%"))
       (:no-error (&rest args) (declare (ignore args)) (format t ";; No error!~%")))
;; No error!
NIL
```

Expanding and testing the final handling macro—ignore-errors—is left as an exercise for the reader.

```
(defmacro ignore-errors (&rest forms)
  `(handler-case (progn ,@forms)
     (error (condition) (values nil condition))))
```

## 3.10.3  Testing assertions

Now that we are nearing the end of this chapter, it is time to fulfill an old promise. In the earlier chapters, we were unable to test our restart-binding assertions properly, since we were missing a vital component used to connect conditions and restarts. That component—handlers—is available now, which means that we are capable of testing all four of these assertions.

```
PCS> (handler-bind ((error (lambda (condition) (store-value 42 condition))))
       (let ((x 24))
         (ccase x (42 :ok))))
:OK

PCS> (handler-bind ((error (lambda (condition) (store-value 42 condition))))
       (let ((x :forty-two))
         (ctypecase x (integer :ok))))
:OK

PCS> (handler-bind ((error (lambda (condition) (store-value 42 condition))))
       (let ((x :forty-two))
         (check-type x integer)))
NIL

PCS> (handler-bind ((error (lambda (condition) (continue condition))))
       (let ((x :forty-two))
         (assert (typep x 'integer) (x))))
```

```
;; The old value of X is :FORTY-TWO.
;; Do you want to supply a new value? (y or n) y          ; user input here

;; Type a form to be evaluated:
;; (The old value is bound to the symbol X.)
42                                                         ; user input here
NIL
```

# 3.11  A featureful debugger

Our condition system is, at this point, more or less complete: we have fully working conditions, handlers, and restarts. The only missing piece that we have stubbed out is the function invoke-debugger that is supposed to call the system debugger to help the programmer handle an otherwise unhandled condition. We will now implement our debugger function and test it piece by piece, finishing our implementation by writing invoke-debugger along with *debugger-hook* and break as soon as we are done.

We will define our debugger in terms of actions that should be possible to perform within the debugger. For example, it should be possible to evaluate arbitrary Lisp forms, to report and return the condition with which the debugger has been entered, and to list and invoke available restarts. We can notice that these commands are fully driven by input from the programmer—the debugger should first receive a *command* that informs the debugger what kind of action it should take, and then, after accepting any additional data, it should perform that command.

The reader may note that we have already implemented a simple debugger in the first part of the book. This chapter will build on the knowledge from there, implementing a more complex and well-structured debugger system than the one we produced earlier.

## 3.11.1  Debugger commands

Let us model our commands via CL methods. In order to remain modular, each command should receive a possibly full set of information accessible to our debugger, that is, the command name itself, a debug stream from which it should receive input and to which it should print, the condition object that was invoked, and an optional list of additional arguments for which the command would otherwise need to prompt the user.

Let us define the `run-debugger-command` generic function along with its base case—a command that has not been recognized by the debugger.

```
(defgeneric run-debugger-command (command stream condition &rest arguments))

(defmethod run-debugger-command (command stream condition &rest arguments)
  (declare (ignore arguments))
  (format stream "~&;; ~S is not a recognized command.
;; Type :HELP for available commands.~%" command))
```

A brief test in the REPL shows us how this function is going to be used:

```
PCS> (run-debugger-command :foo *debug-io* (make-condition 'condition))
;; :FOO is not a recognized command.
;; Type :HELP for available commands.
NIL
```

In order to have the function recognize individual commands, which are going to be Lisp keywords, we are going to use a mechanism called *eql specializers*; they make it possible to create methods that specialize on individual Lisp objects and are allowed to be called when the argument to the generic function is `eql` to the object that is `eql`-specialized on. Lisp keywords are comparable via `eql`; therefore, they are a suitable fit for such a mechanism.

We are free to define commands by using `defmethod` and manually parsing the optional argument list, but for multiple commands, this might become unwieldy. It will be beneficial for us to introduce a more declarative way of defining new debugger commands that hides the implementation details from us; it would accept the command name, the stream and condition arguments and an optional list of arguments in its lambda list, and a set of forms to be executed.

Let us therefore define a macro that abstracts away this syntax; we will name it `define-command`.

```
(defmacro define-command (name (stream condition &rest arguments) &body body)
  (let ((command-var (gensym "COMMAND"))
        (arguments-var (gensym "ARGUMENTS")))
    `(defmethod run-debugger-command
         ((,command-var (eql ,name)) ,stream ,condition &rest ,arguments-var)
       (destructuring-bind ,arguments ,arguments-var ,@body))))
```

We can see that this macro is a wrapper around `defmethod` that creates a new method with an `eql` specializer on the `name` that we provide. In addition, it automatically destructures `arguments-var` into `arguments`, meaning that we will be able to provide arbitrary optional arguments inside `define-command`'s lambda list.

## 3.11.2  Evaluating Lisp forms

Let us demonstrate the preceding macrology on the first command that the user should encounter upon merely entering the debugger:

```
(defvar *debug-level* 0)

(define-command :eval (stream condition &optional form)
  (let ((level *debug-level*))
    (with-simple-restart (abort "Return to debugger level ~D." level)
      (let* ((real-form (or form (read stream)))
             (- real-form)
             (values (multiple-value-list (eval real-form))))
        (format stream "~&~{~S~^~%~}" values)
        (values values real-form)))))
```

We have defined a new dynamic variable that will be rebound by the main debugger function to state the current debugger level. Inside our `define-command` `:eval` form, we immediately use the current value of that variable to define a simple restart that will allow the programmer to return immediately to the current level of the debugger. Once inside, we either use the Lisp form that was passed via the optional argument or read it from the stream. We bind the *REPL variable* - to the form that we are processing (we will define later what a REPL variable is), and we evaluate that form, memorizing all values returned by it onto a list. We then print all the values to the stream and return these values and the form which we have *actually* evaluated, the reason for which will be explained at the end of the debugger chapter.

```
PCS> (let ((*debug-level* 3))
       (run-debugger-command :eval *debug-io* (make-condition 'error)
                             '(+ 2 2)))
4                                                    ; printed
(4)                                                  ; returned
(+ 2 2)                                              ; returned
```

```
PCS> (let ((*debug-level* 3))
      (run-debugger-command :eval *debug-io* (make-condition 'error)
                            '(values 1 2 3)))
1                                             ; printed
2                                             ; printed
3                                             ; printed
(1 2 3)                                       ; returned
(VALUES 1 2 3)                                ; returned

PCS> (let ((*debug-level* 3))
      (run-debugger-command :eval *debug-io* (make-condition 'error)))
(* 42 42)                                     ; user input here
1764                                          ; printed
(1764)                                        ; returned
(* 42 42)                                     ; returned
```

(Previously, we have been taking care to prepend all output printed by our code with `;;`. In the preceding example, that is not the case; we have therefore introduced additional comments that show which values were printed by the `:eval` command, which values were returned by the function call, and which values were manually input by the user.)

## 3.11.3  Reporting and returning conditions

Another important thing inside the debugger is having the user realize that a debugger has been entered and informing them why it was entered: therefore, we need to report the condition to the user.

```
(defun split (string)
  (loop for start = 0 then (1+ end)
        for end = (position #\Newline string :start start)
        collect (subseq string start end)
        while end))

(define-command :report (stream condition &optional (level *debug-level*))
  (format stream "~&;; Debugger level ~D entered on ~S:~%" level (type-of condition))
  (handler-case (let* ((report (princ-to-string condition)))
                  (format stream "~&~{;; ~A~%~}" (split report)))
    (error () (format stream "~&;; #<error while reporting condition>~%"))))
```

We have defined a small helper function to split a string by newline characters that will help us report multi-line conditions. Finally, inside the method, we inform the programmer that the debugger has been entered, and either report the condition to the stream, or—in case an error has been signaled while reporting the condition—we inform the programmer about that fact.

Seeing the macroexpansion of that define-command form may help to understand how it works under the hood:

```
(DEFMETHOD RUN-DEBUGGER-COMMAND
    ((#:COMMAND1216 (EQL :REPORT)) STREAM CONDITION &REST #:ARGUMENTS1217)
  (DESTRUCTURING-BIND (&OPTIONAL (LEVEL *DEBUG-LEVEL*)) #:ARGUMENTS1217
    (FORMAT STREAM "~&;; Debugger level ~D entered on ~S:~%" LEVEL (TYPE-OF CONDITION))
    (HANDLER-CASE (LET* ((REPORT (PRINC-TO-STRING CONDITION)))
                    (FORMAT STREAM "~&~{;; ~A~%~}" (SPLIT REPORT)))
      (ERROR NIL (FORMAT STREAM "~&;; #<error while reporting condition>~%")))))
```

We can now test this command in the REPL to simulate entering the level 3 debugger with an error condition.

```
PCS> (let ((*debug-level* 3))
       (run-debugger-command :report *debug-io* (make-condition 'error)))
;; Debugger level 3 entered on ERROR:
;; Condition ERROR was signaled.
NIL
```

Since our debugger is going to have a REPL, it will be beneficial to be able to pass the condition object with which the debugger was entered into the REPL, so the programmer may interact with it.

```
(define-command :condition (stream condition)
  (run-debugger-command :eval stream condition condition))
```

Here, we invoke one command from another command. This is to reuse existing code that we have written moments ago: we utilize the fact that condition objects are *self-evaluating* and therefore evaluating them again is a no-op and that the :eval command prints its value to the REPL before returning.

```
PCS> (let ((condition (make-condition 'error)))
       (run-debugger-command :condition *debug-io* condition))
#<ERROR {1011E31A23}>                              ; printed
(#<ERROR {1011E31A23}>)                            ; returned
#<ERROR {1011E31A23}>                              ; returned
```

(The condition object will be accessible in the REPL after invoking this command, since it will immediately be bound to the REPL variable * by the function that implements the REPL; we will explain this mechanism later in the book.)

## 3.11.4  Listing and invoking restarts

We have now implemented the basic interaction with the condition object with which the debugger has been entered. We may move to the next important part of the debugger: allowing the programmer to list and invoke individual restarts.

```
(defun restart-max-name-length (restarts)
  (flet ((name-length (restart) (length (string (restart-name restart)))))
    (if restarts (reduce #'max (mapcar #'name-length restarts)) 0)))

(define-command :restarts (stream condition)
  (let ((restarts (compute-restarts condition)))
    (cond (restarts
            (format stream "~&;; Available restarts:~%")
            (loop with max-name-length = (restart-max-name-length restarts)
                  for i from 0
                  for restart in restarts
                  for report = (handler-case (princ-to-string restart)
                                 (error () "#<error while reporting restart>"))
                  for restart-name = (or (restart-name restart) "")
                  do (format stream ";; ~2,' D: [~vA] ~A~%"
                             i max-name-length restart-name report)))
          (t (format stream "~&;; No available restarts.~%")))))
```

The preceding command implements printing the list of all restarts. The big loop form is used to print the number, name, and report of each restart. The helper function restart-max-name-length is used for computing the maximum length of restart names; it is used along with the complex format form in order to provide an aesthetically pleasing list of restarts. If no restarts whatsoever are available, then we also inform the programmer of this.

```
PCS> (run-debugger-command :restarts *debug-io* (make-condition 'error))
;; No available restarts.
NIL
```

```
PCS> (restart-case (run-debugger-command :restarts *debug-io* (make-condition 'error))
       (abort () :report "Abort the operation." :abort)
       (retry () :report "Retry the operation." :retry)
       (refrobnicate () :report "Refrobnicate the operands." :refrobnicate))
;; Available restarts:
;;  0: [ABORT      ] Abort the operation.
;;  1: [RETRY      ] Retry the operation.
;;  2: [REFROBNICATE] Refrobnicate the operands.
NIL
```

The restarts have assigned numbers, which will be used to invoke the restarts in question. Let us define a debugger command that will invoke a restart with the given number.

```
(define-command :restart (stream condition &optional n)
  (let* ((n (or n (read stream)))
         (restart (nth n (compute-restarts condition))))
    (if restart
        (invoke-restart-interactively restart)
        (format stream "~&;; There is no restart with number ~D.~%" n))))
```

We can test it in both its interactive and non-interactive forms:

```
PCS> (restart-case (run-debugger-command :restart *debug-io* (make-condition 'error) 0)
       (abort () :report "Abort the operation." :abort)
       (retry () :report "Retry the operation." :retry)
       (refrobnicate () :report "Refrobnicate the operands." :refrobnicate))
:ABORT

PCS> (restart-case (run-debugger-command :restart *debug-io* (make-condition 'error))
       (abort () :report "Abort the operation." :abort)
       (retry () :report "Retry the operation." :retry)
       (refrobnicate () :report "Refrobnicate the operands." :refrobnicate))
2                                                   ; user input here
:REFROBNICATE

PCS> (restart-case (run-debugger-command :restart *debug-io* (make-condition 'error) 42)
       (abort () :report "Abort the operation." :abort)
       (retry () :report "Retry the operation." :retry)
       (refrobnicate () :report "Refrobnicate the operands." :refrobnicate))
;; There is no restart with number 42.
NIL
```

In addition, we will provide four commands for the most commonly used standard restarts: abort and continue. In order to abort, the programmer can use :abort or :q; in order to continue, the programmer can use :continue or :c.

```
(defun debugger-invoke-restart (name stream condition)
  (let ((restart (find-restart name condition)))
    (if restart
        (invoke-restart-interactively restart)
        (format stream "~&;; There is no active ~A restart.~%" name))))

(define-command :abort (stream condition)
  (debugger-invoke-restart 'abort stream condition))

(define-command :q (stream condition)
  (debugger-invoke-restart 'continue stream condition))

(define-command :continue (stream condition)
  (debugger-invoke-restart 'continue stream condition))

(define-command :c (stream condition)
  (debugger-invoke-restart 'continue stream condition))
```

A series of very brief REPL tests follows in order to verify that these commands work correctly.

```
PCS> (restart-case (run-debugger-command :abort *debug-io* (make-condition 'error))
       (abort () :report "Abort the operation." :abort)
       (continue () :report "Continue the operation." :continue))
:ABORT

PCS> (restart-case (run-debugger-command :q *debug-io* (make-condition 'error))
       (abort () :report "Abort the operation." :abort)
       (continue () :report "Continue the operation." :continue))
:ABORT

PCS> (restart-case (run-debugger-command :continue *debug-io* (make-condition 'error))
       (abort () :report "Abort the operation." :abort)
       (continue () :report "Continue the operation." :continue))
:CONTINUE

PCS> (restart-case (run-debugger-command :c *debug-io* (make-condition 'error))
       (abort () :report "Abort the operation." :abort)
       (continue () :report "Continue the operation." :continue))
:CONTINUE
```

# 3.11.5  Debugger help and REPL

The preceding commands will not be helpful for the programmer if the programmer does not know about them. Therefore, we need a help command that will list all the available commands.

```
(define-command :help (stream condition)
  (format stream "~&~
;; This is the standard debugger of the Common Lisp Condition System.
;; The debugger read-eval-print loop supports the standard REPL variables:
;;   *   **   ***   +   ++   +++   /   //   ///   -
;;
;; Available debugger commands:
;;   :HELP            Show this text.
;;   :EVAL <form>     Evaluate a form typed after the :EVAL command.
;;   :REPORT          Report the condition the debugger was invoked with.
;;   :CONDITION       Return the condition the debugger was invoked with.
;;   :RESTARTS        Print available restarts.
;;   :RESTART <n>, <n>  Invoke a restart with the given number.")
  (when (find-restart 'abort condition)
    (format stream "~&;;   :ABORT, :Q          Invoke an ABORT restart.~%"))
  (when (find-restart 'continue condition)
    (format stream "~&;;   :CONTINUE, :C       Invoke a CONTINUE restart.~%"))
  (format stream "~&~
;;
;; Any non-keyword non-integer form is evaluated.~%"))
```

Other than being very output-heavy, the only interesting thing about this function is that it checks for the visibility of any abort and continue restarts and only lists the respective commands if these restarts are available for invocation. We may verify if that last part is true.

```
PCS> (run-debugger-command :help *debug-io* (make-condition 'error))
;; This is the standard debugger of the Common Lisp Condition System.
;; The debugger read-eval-print loop supports the standard REPL variables:
;;   *   **   ***   +   ++   +++   /   //   ///   -
;;
;; Available debugger commands:
;;   :HELP            Show this text.
;;   :EVAL <form>     Evaluate a form typed after the :EVAL command.
```

```
;;   :REPORT              Report the condition the debugger was invoked with.
;;   :CONDITION           Return the condition the debugger was invoked with.
;;   :RESTARTS            Print available restarts.
;;   :RESTART <n>, <n>    Invoke a restart with the given number.
;;
;; Any non-keyword non-integer form is evaluated.
NIL

PCS> (restart-case (run-debugger-command :help *debug-io* (make-condition 'error))
       (abort () :report "Abort the operation." :abort)
       (continue () :report "Continue the operation." :continue))
;; This is the standard debugger of the Common Lisp Condition System.
;; The debugger read-eval-print loop supports the standard REPL variables:
;;   *   **   ***   +   ++   +++   /   //   ///   -
;;
;; Available debugger commands:
;;   :HELP                Show this text.
;;   :EVAL <form>         Evaluate a form typed after the :EVAL command.
;;   :REPORT              Report the condition the debugger was invoked with.
;;   :CONDITION           Return the condition the debugger was invoked with.
;;   :RESTARTS            Print available restarts.
;;   :RESTART <n>, <n>    Invoke a restart with the given number.
;;   :ABORT, :Q           Invoke an ABORT restart.
;;   :CONTINUE, :C        Invoke a CONTINUE restart.
;;
;; Any non-keyword non-integer form is evaluated.
NIL
```

## 3.11.5.1  REPL variables

The help screen mentions *REPL variables,* a term which we have used before. Let us make a very quick introduction to them, since we will want our REPL to implement that functionality.

The REPL variables are a set of ten symbols: *, **, ***, +, ++, +++, /, //, ///, and -. They are bound by the CL REPL for utility purposes. The *-variables contain the results of evaluating the last three expressions, the +-variables contain the expressions themselves, the /-variables contain lists of all values returned by the three expressions, and - contains the expression that is being evaluated right now. If there were no previous REPL expressions, these variables are bound to nil.

Let us demonstrate this in the REPL:

```
PCS> (+ 2 2)
4

PCS> (let ((x 42)) (check-type x integer))
NIL

PCS> (values :foo :bar :baz)
:FOO
:BAR
:BAZ

PCS> (list (list * / +) (list ** // ++) (list *** /// +++) -)
((:FOO                      ; *
  (:FOO :BAR :BAZ)          ; /
  (VALUES :FOO :BAR :BAZ)) ; +
 (NIL                       ; **
  (NIL)                     ; //
  (LET ((X 42)) (CHECK-TYPE X INTEGER))) ; ++
 (4         ; ***
  (4)       ; ///
  (+ 2 2)) ; +++
 (LIST (LIST * / +) (LIST ** // ++) (LIST *** /// +++) -) ; -
 )
```

In order to provide the programmer with a pleasant REPL experience, we will need to account for setting these variables in our REPL. Since our debugger is meant to be used interactively, we will assume that the host's REPL has already established its bindings for these REPL values; therefore, we will only set them and not create new bindings for them.

## 3.11.5.2 Debugger read-eval-print step

Once the debugger has started and is ready to accept input from the programmer, we will want to print a prompt that will inform the user (i.e., the programmer) that we are ready to accept input from them. Afterward, we will read a form provided by them and check its type. If it is a keyword, it shall denote a debugger command to be invoked; if it is an integer, it shall denote the restart that should be invoked. If it is any other kind of form, it shall be equivalent to invoking the :eval command on that form.

```lisp
(defun read-eval-print-command (stream condition)
  (format stream "~&[~D] Debug> "*debug-level*)
  (let* ((thing (read stream)))
    (multiple-value-bind (values actual-thing)
        (typecase thing
          (keyword (run-debugger-command thing stream condition))
          (integer (run-debugger-command :restart stream condition thing))
          (t (run-debugger-command :eval stream condition thing)))
      (unless actual-thing (setf actual-thing thing))
      (prog1 values
        (shiftf /// // / values)
        (shiftf *** ** * (first values))
        (shiftf +++ ++ + actual-thing)))))
```

We can see that we bind the two values returned by run-debugger-command. While
the role of values is clear in the preceding code, the role of actual-thing needs a bit of
comment. This value is returned only from certain commands, and when it is returned, it
*supersedes* the form that was input into the REPL. This is, for example, so the user, upon
typing :eval (+ 2 2) in the debugger, receives a more friendly (+ 2 2) form bound to the +
value, rather than the less useful symbol :eval.

We can call this function in the REPL to test a single iteration of our debugger
read-eval-print cycle.

```
PCS> (read-eval-print-command *debug-io* (make-condition 'condition))
[0] Debug> (+ 2 2)                                  ; user input here
4                                                   ; printed
(4)                                                 ; returned

PCS> (read-eval-print-command *debug-io* (make-condition 'condition))
[0] Debug> :eval :foo                               ; user input here
:FOO                                                ; printed
(:FOO)                                              ; returned

PCS> (read-eval-print-command *debug-io* (make-condition 'condition))
[0] Debug> :report                                  ; user input here
;; Debugger level 0 entered on CONDITION:
;; Condition CONDITION was signaled.
NIL                                                 ; returned
```

With the single step of our REPL available and tested, we may now implement the standard debugger proper. Upon entry, we will bind the debug level to one more than what it was before (effectively increasing it by one), report the condition, inform the programmer about the existence of the :help command, and call read-eval-print-command in a loop.

```
(defun standard-debugger (condition &optional (stream *debug-io*))
  (let ((*debug-level* (1+ *debug-level*)))
    (run-debugger-command :report stream condition)
    (format stream "~&;; Type :HELP for available commands.~%")
    (loop (read-eval-print-command stream condition))))
```

We can test this function in the REPL, but we need to be cautious about it: this function never returns normally, which is intended and mandated by the CL standard. Therefore, we will need some way out of the debugger—for which we will establish a simple restart around the call to the debugger.

```
PCS> (with-simple-restart (abort "Leave the debugger.")
       (standard-debugger (make-condition 'condition)))
;; Debugger level 1 entered on CONDITION:
;; Condition CONDITION was signaled.
;; Type :HELP for available commands.
[1] Debug> (+ 2 2)                                ; user input here

4
[1] Debug> (list * / +)                           ; user input here

(4 (4) (+ 2 2))
[1] Debug> :restarts

;; Available restarts:
;;  0: [ABORT] Leave the debugger.
[1] Debug> :restart 0                             ; user input here

NIL
T
```

(The final two values are returned from the "outer" REPL by with-simple-restart.)

# 3.11.6  Debugger interface

Now that our debugger is more or less usable and useful for the programmer, we need to integrate it into the rest of our condition system by implementing the standard functionality related to the debugger: *debugger-hook*, break, and invoke-debugger.

So far, we have used a stub implementation of invoke-debugger that was good enough for our use cases; now it is time to replace that stub with a fully standard-compliant function that first queries the debugger hook and calls it and only then calls the standard debugger.

```
(defvar *debugger-hook* nil)

(defun invoke-debugger (condition)
  (when *debugger-hook*
    (let ((hook *debugger-hook*)
          (*debugger-hook* nil))
      (funcall hook condition hook)))
  (standard-debugger condition))
```

Having this definition means that now we can use invoke-debugger instead of our custom standard-debugger function.

```
PCS> (with-simple-restart (abort "Leave the debugger.")
       (invoke-debugger (make-condition 'condition)))
;; Debugger level 1 entered on CONDITION:
;; Condition CONDITION was signaled.
;; Type :HELP for available commands.
[1] Debug> :abort                                    ; user input here

NIL
T
```

The only remaining function is break, which establishes a continue restart and directly calls the debugger with the provided format control and arguments, returning nil.

```
(defun break (&optional (format-control "Break") &rest format-arguments)
  (let ((*debugger-hook* nil)
        (condition (make-condition 'simple-condition
                                   :format-control format-control
                                   :format-arguments format-arguments)))
    (with-simple-restart (continue "Return from BREAK.")
      (invoke-debugger condition))
    nil))
```

216

Finally, we may perform one final REPL test to complete the testing process of our Portable Condition System.

```
PCS> (break)
;; Debugger level 1 entered on SIMPLE-CONDITION:
;; Break
;; Type :HELP for available commands.
[1] Debug> :continue                                    ; user input here

NIL
```

# 3.12  Finishing touches

Our condition system is now complete. If we are using this condition system in an implementation that does not have a condition system, we can, for example, use the condition types we defined, along with our error function, inside the implementation's arithmetic operations. This will ensure that our division-by-zero condition is signaled when we attempt to evaluate, for example, (/ 2 0).

It is, however, more likely that the reader following the code in this book already has a fully conforming Common Lisp implementation that has a condition system of its own; therefore, this Portable Condition System which we have defined is, in a way, a piece of *guest* code that has no full control over the *host's* condition system; therefore, if the host Lisp system signals its own division-by-zero error, it is fully independent from our guest condition system and therefore will not be captured by our debugger or even recognized as an object of the condition type that we have defined ourselves.

## 3.12.1  Integration

The authors of this book have prepared an ASDF system named portable-condition-system.integration that provides a means of integrating the host's condition system with PCS. While we will not go into details of its inner functioning, we will nonetheless show an example debugger session where the host's condition object is wrapped in a condition object of our own and where the host's restarts are available for calling as if they were restarts defined with our own mechanism.

```
;;; (ql:quickload :portable-condition-system.integration)
;;; (in-package :portable-condition-system.integration)

INTEGRATION> (restart-case (with-debugger (#'debugger) (/ 2 0))
               (return-42 () :report "Return 42 instead." 42))
;; Debugger level 1 entered on FOREIGN-ERROR:
;; Foreign condition FOREIGN-ERROR was signaled:
;; arithmetic error COMMON-LISP:DIVISION-BY-ZERO signaled
;; Operation was (/ 2 0).
;; Type :HELP for available commands.
[1] Debug> :restarts                              ; user input here

;; Available restarts:
;;  0: [RETURN-42] Return 42 instead.
;;  1: [RETRY    ] (*) Retry SLIME REPL evaluation request.
;;  2: [ABORT    ] (*) Return to SLIME's top level.
;;  3: [ABORT    ] (*) abort thread (#<THREAD "repl-thread" RUNNING {100CC01DE3}>)
[1] Debug> 0                                      ; user input here
42                                                ; returned

INTEGRATION> (restart-case (with-debugger (#'debugger) (/ 2 0))
               (return-42 () :report "Return 42 instead." 42))
;; Debugger level 1 entered on FOREIGN-ERROR:
;; Foreign condition FOREIGN-ERROR was signaled:
;; arithmetic error COMMON-LISP:DIVISION-BY-ZERO signaled
;; Operation was (/ 2 0).
;; Type :HELP for available commands.
[1] Debug> :abort                                 ; user input here
; Evaluation aborted on #<DIVISION-BY-ZERO {1010F04FD3}>.
```

Please see the manual of the `portable-condition-system.integration` system for more details.

## 3.12.2 Additional work

The condition system we have created in this book passes the series of tests from the ANSI-TEST suite related to the condition system and assertion operators. While it is compliant, it is not very robust when it comes to undefined behavior; it is, for example, possible to pass some duplicate keyword arguments to `restart-bind` and `define-condition`, which, in turn, would trigger undefined behavior. For brevity and educational reasons, we have omitted multiple places where argument validation and type checks could be introduced; the reader is welcome to look at the GitHub version of Portable Condition System and inspect the safety measures already present in the code, as well as suggest new ones to be added.

This concludes our work on implementing a complete Common Lisp condition system.

# CHAPTER 4

# Wrapping up

During the first half of this book, we have introduced the concept of dynamic variables and showed how they can be used to implement new kinds of functionality: subsystems of hooks and choices whose behavior depends on the dynamic context in which they are executed. We have drawn direct parallels between these two subsystems and the existing standard systems of Common Lisp condition handlers and restarts. We have shown how these subsystems tie in with the existing standard mechanisms of transferring control in CL programs. Finally, we have described the interactive means by which the condition system and the Lisp debugger are allowed to interact with the programmer.

The second half has led us through the non-trivial task of implementing a complete, ANSI-compliant Common Lisp condition system, from the very definition of the first condition type to implementing the interactive debugger function. To accomplish that, we have drawn parallels and gathered inspiration from the individual mechanisms that we devised during our work through the first half of the book.

It is notable that we have written a Lisp condition system in Lisp itself. Multiple parts of CL—the condition system, Common Lisp Object System, `loop`, `format`, `print-object`, and `documentation`—have historically been implemented this way, layered as separate modules upon a smaller language core.

This accomplishment demonstrates that it is easy to introduce new modules and paradigms into Lisp in a way that forms seamless integration with the rest of Lisp. We owe that to the nature of Lisp, which is a dynamic, image-based language with a powerful macro system; while this last trait is certainly the predominant one allowing such modifications, the first two are also important contributors, because they allow one to develop and test naturally in an incremental manner and to redefine already existing parts of the language.

A particularly curious reader might want to compare the systems of hooks and choices implemented in this book with a description of the original implementation of the condition system written by Kent M. Pitman in 1988 for *Common Lisp the Language version 1*. (For posterity, the code of that implementation has also been copied into the code repository for Portable Condition System.)

© Michał "phoe" Herda 2020
M. "phoe" Herda, *The Common Lisp Condition System*, https://doi.org/10.1007/978-1-4842-6134-7_4

The rest of this chapter is meant to explain a few more aspects of the condition system that might seem more related to philosophy and design than to concrete implementation. We will describe the difference between the binding and casing operators that are related to handlers and restarts; and finally, we will criticize the approach we have taken in the first part of our book and describe the pitfalls, inconsistencies, and pain points of the condition system.

# 4.1  The purpose of the condition system

In the first part of the book, we have made parallels that connected the CL handler subsystem with the system of hooks that we have created. While what we have said is technically correct at the detail level, one could consider it to be misleading when we analyze the condition system from a different, more ideological point of view. It can be said that the action of invoking the hooks is, in fact, the activity of seeking *advice* about how to handle a particular situation that is implemented by calling a series of relevant hook functions in order from most to least specific. Advice, in this context, is understood as externally provided pieces of code that augment and supplement chunks of an already existing program.

The actual purpose of a condition system, including its handler and restart subsystems if present, is not to call hooks, to invoke choices, or even to execute code whenever some condition is signaled or a restart is invoked; the actual purpose is to maximize the possibilities and means by which a body of code can be externally instructed, or *advised*, to treat situations encountered during its execution. The technical details, such as executing hooks, invoking choices, or even entering the debugger, are only means to achieving an ideological goal of having a system that seeks and utilizes advice supplied to it by any available means—be it via programmatically supplying a handler function, via interactively choosing and invoking one of the predefined restarts, or by resolving the situation manually by means of using a REPL inside an interactive Lisp debugger.

Advice can be therefore provided fully programmatically via a handler when a programmer expects some situation to happen, semi-manually via a restart that is invokable from a debugger and automates some process that a programmer may want to utilize, or fully manually by means of using a Lisp REPL to debug the situation—even if the other end of that REPL is hundreds of millions of miles away from the programmer. In the end, the program does not care about how *exactly* its execution has been resumed after an error. Therefore, it is wise to make the process of resuming the program's execution as efficient and informing as possible for the programmer. Preserving the dynamic environment and the wound stack and making these available inside the Lisp debugger are merely means of fulfilling that goal.

# 4.2  Binding vs. casing

The logical distinction between the `*-bind` macros (`handler-bind` and `restart-bind`) and the `*-case` macros (`handler-case` and `restart-case`) can be understood as an analogy between binding operators—such as `let`, `let*`, `flet`, `labels`, `macrolet`, `symbol-macrolet`, and so on— and the Lisp macro `case`, along with its standard siblings `ccase`, `ecase`, and `typecase`. By this distinction, `with-simple-restart` naturally falls into the bag of `*-case` macros, since it manifests as a wrapper around `restart-case`; the same goes for the `handler-bind-case` macro which we define ourselves in an appendix to this book.

The role of a binding operator is to modify the environment in which other forms are run. In case of `let` and `let*`, the change in the environment is effective by means of introducing new variables. `flet` and `labels` introduce local function bindings, while `macrolet` and `symbol-macrolet` introduce bindings for local macros and local symbol macros. It can be said that these operators affect the variable and function *namespaces* by introducing new bindings into it. (For clarity, binding new macros counts as adding new bindings to the function namespace, while binding new symbol macros counts as adding new bindings to the variable namespace.)

In this context, `handler-bind` can be considered to add new bindings to the *handler* namespace. This handler namespace is a somewhat curious one, since handlers do not have names of their own; they instead use the condition types that the handler functions are bound to. On the other hand, the restart namespace is a fully fledged one: each restart bound by `restart-bind` has a name (even if this name is `nil`) that is bound—in the restart namespace—to the restart object that we can invoke.

Theoretically, the act of binding is essentially a no-op until our code actually utilizes the bindings in some way—regardless of the namespace we bind in. For variables and symbol macros, such utilization effectively occurs upon accessing the value cells of the symbols that name these variables and symbol macros. For functions and macros, it occurs upon the act of trying to call them. For handlers, it counts as "utilization" when a condition gets signaled whose type matches one of these handlers. Finally, for restarts, "utilization" occurs upon the act of calling `compute-restarts` or `find-restart` in order to access the restart objects or upon invoking these restart objects through any means.

The `case`-like operators, on the other hand, follow a different programming idiom. The standard use of `case` in CL is to pass it a Lisp form, which is evaluated to produce a value called a *test key*. The list of all cases is then checked in order to see if the test key is `eql` to any of the objects specified for the individual cases. If a match is found, then the forms associated with that particular case are executed, and their return value is the effective returned value of the `case` form.

`handler-case` and `restart-case` follow the same idiom as `case`, except that they search for matches more deeply than just at the point where their form returns a value. These operators await, respectively, `signal` and `invoke-restart` calls issued within their dynamic scope, at which point they check their lists of handler cases or restart cases. For handlers, the type of condition is matched against the type of each handler, whereas restart names are matched via `eql`, unless a restart object is invoked directly by retrieving it via `compute-restarts`. For both operators, if a match is found, control is immediately transferred out of the signaling or invoking form and into the matching case, whose forms are then executed and whose return value becomes the return value of the given macro.

## 4.3  Separation of concerns

In the first half of the book, we have translated the approach we used with the hook and choice subsystems into the handler and restart subsystems. While that approach was (hopefully) suitable for teaching the basics of these two CL subsystems, it might be surprising to hear from the book's author that it would not be the best choice for use in actual, real code.

The main argument for not using handlers and restarts in such a way is separation of concerns. The handler and restart systems have an already well-established meaning in CL. While condition handlers are known to *decline* to handle a condition sometimes, by not transferring control (an option which is explicitly mentioned in the ANSI standard), restarts in CL are most commonly known as "means of leaving the debugger," completely ignoring the fact that they can also be used in the way for which we originally used our choice system.

To elaborate, using `handler-bind` to evaluate code for signaled conditions is common in real-life code, but `restart-bind` is pretty much unused to establish restarts. This stands in direct contrast to our initial implementation of the choice subsystem, which was a system of hooks that we could call selectively without transferring control. (In fact, we explicitly mentioned that using choices to transfer control was changing the structure of our code and creating tighter coupling between the place where our choices are bound and the place where they are computed and invoked.)

This potential perceived disconnect means that using restarts for purpose of *not* restarting some abstract process in the program might violate the principle of least astonishment. Programmers reading our code might thus not expect to see `restart-bind` used in a non-restarting way, and they might become confused by it.

Another question is whether such restarts should show up in the debugger at all. It is possible to avoid their appearance there by setting up a test function that returns `nil` if the condition argument passed to the test function is non-`nil`. But this in turn might lead to confusion if the programmer mistakenly calls `compute-restarts` or `find-restarts` without any condition object whatsoever and then sees some "means of leaving the debugger" which does not actually transfer control anywhere.

Summing up, one could argue that it might be preferable to leave the original, CL-provided handler and restart subsystems to their original roles and instead create or use independent mechanisms for hooks and choices. Such mechanisms are easy enough to construct, as we have demonstrated in the earlier chapters; in fact, multiple implementations of hooks and events in CL have already been created and are available to be fetched from Quicklisp. These systems also feature better introspection for individual hook objects and the ability to declare hooks with indefinite scope. Some examples are `cl-events`, `cl-hooks`, and `modularize-hooks`.

# 4.4  Algebraic effects

There is an idea that has been gaining popularity as of late, going by the name of *algebraic effects* and *algebraic effect handlers*. Its first widely known implementations have been done in strictly statically typed strictly functional programming languages, such as Haskell and Eff; from there, it has trickled back into dynamically typed languages with weak typing, such as JavaScript.

The ideas behind algebraic effects are surprisingly similar to the ones by Common Lisp condition system: they separate the act of signaling a given situation in the program from the act of handling it, and they make it possible to provide a set of handlers for these situations dynamically, at the call site of that piece of code. Many parallels between the Common Lisp condition system and the system of algebraic effects have been drawn, but it seems that the two ideas have developed independently from one another.

Only recently has the work been done to provide enough mathematical and logical scaffolding to be able to bring these ideas into the world of languages such as Haskell, which explains the surge of popularity as of late. An important implication of this spread is that a condition system—or, if we decide to use that terminology, a system of algebraic effects—can be implemented even in languages which do not follow the imperative paradigm and therefore have no mutable variable bindings, through which dynamic scoping could be implemented the same way we did it in C.

## 4.5  Downsides of the condition system

As we mentioned before, the Common Lisp condition system is, like all of CL, a product of a standardization committee; the people who have designed, discussed, and agreed on CL over 25 years ago were, to some extent, solving problems that we do not need to consider nowadays. That fact causes some aspects of the language—in our case, of the condition system—to appear today as weird, unusual, and inconsistent or otherwise "should have been done differently."

## 4.5.1  Separation from CLOS

`define-condition` and `defclass` are similar to each other, yet they are distinct in the Common Lisp standard. This disparity is caused by a long history of the condition system; the original `define-condition` had been created in the times of *Common Lisp the Language version 1*, when CLOS did not yet exist and therefore `defclass` was not yet available. During the time of CL standardization, the proposal to merge the condition system fully into CLOS was rejected, resulting in a condition-defining system that behaves like `defclass`, looks like `defclass`, is supposed to work like `defclass`, but is not `defclass`. A similar situation arises around the inheritance model of condition types—a multiple inheritance model identical to the one used by CLOS, but explicitly mentioned not to be necessarily CLOS-based.

In many CL implementations, conditions are indeed instances of the CLOS-defined `standard-class` and are therefore `standard-object`s themselves; this consistency, however, is not mandated by the standard and in fact not followed by a least one popular CL implementation. One could daydream of the standard stating that condition classes could have a *metaclass* named `condition-class`; no such thing is required by the standard, however.

Because of that disparity, it is impossible to, among other things, use the general statement "condition class" instead of "condition type" when referring to standard CL code, portably access slot values of a condition object by means of `slot-value`, create mixin classes that can be added to standard classes and condition classes alike, and define constructor functions for condition objects by defining `initialize-instance:after` methods on condition types. (The last fact can be worked around by using `make-instance` instead of `make-condition` for creating condition instances, which seems to work on that particular implementation; the author of this book cheekily suggests that this behavior could become standard in the implementation in question, to bridge that gap.)

### 4.5.1.1 Making conditions of complex condition types

An unfortunate consequence of the divergence of `define-condition` from `defclass` is that the specification for `make-condition` requires its datum to be a specifier for a condition type. Given that the Common Lisp condition type is based on set theory, the form (`or condition integer`) could be argued to be a valid condition type (since any condition is of type (`or condition integer`)), and therefore that form should be a valid argument to `make-condition`. An even more eyebrow-raising consequence: it should be possible to instantiate condition types such as (`or program-error file-error`) or (`and warning condition`), although the mental gymnastics required to adapt `make-condition` to accept such condition type designators are left as an exercise for no one in particular.

## 4.5.2 Dynamic extent of restart objects

It is "not a bug" in a sense that it is a feature; however, the fact that restarts are defined to have dynamic extent in CL may generate confusion for newcomers and experienced Lisp programmers alike. While it is undefined behavior to access any objects of dynamic extent outside the scope in which they're valid, it is nonetheless trivial to invoke that undefined behavior for restarts—for example, by evaluating (`compute-restarts`) in the REPL and allowing the resulting list to be printed. At the time of writing this book, evaluating the following one-liner causes at least one commonly used CL implementation to "halt and catch fire" by means of signaling memory corruption errors.

```
((lambda () (print (restart-bind ((x (lambda ()))) (compute-restarts)))))
```

## 4.5.3  Speed

While it is possible to use the Common Lisp condition system as a control transfer mechanism for algorithms that perform backtracking, it might not be the best fit for instances where performance of such a solution is a priority. Compared to the primitive CL operators for transfer of control, such as `tagbody/go`, `block/return-from`, or `catch/throw`, the condition system needs to perform more work in addition to using one of these primitives: a condition object needs to be constructed with the provided arguments; the list of handlers needs to be walked, with a runtime type check being done for each handler; and all applicable handler functions need to be called, until a transfer of control occurs. Therefore, heavily relying on the condition system in hot loops, and places that require optimization for speed, may be a poor choice as compared to simply using the CL primitives for performing non-local exits. Profiling such code is often the best way to confirm such suspicions of poor performance choices: when profiling code that uses the condition system in this way shows that significant time is spent in `signal` and handler functions, then that result could serve as a strong clue that preferring simpler primitives would be more appropriate in that instance.

## 4.5.4  Optimization settings

The Common Lisp standard permits the condition system to be partially disabled for certain optimization settings. In particular, setting a high `speed` and low `safety` quality at the same time allows the compiler to generate code that omits all safety checks. Such code may exhibit undefined behavior instead of signaling errors if it contains any sort of bugs. This might lead to memory corruption, crashes, infinite loops, or—in the worst case—silent corruption of data. In such cases, Lisp does not need to signal errors in case of accessing unbound variables, undefined functions, arrays outside of their bounds, and so on.

It is not exactly a downside of the condition system, but rather the fact that the programmer has purposely chosen no longer to depend on Lisp safety checks, by explicitly disabling such checks.

## 4.5.5  Introspection

The introspection facility for the condition system is arguably poor. There is no portable way of inspecting the full lists of handlers; that lack is compounded by the fact that handlers are only defined in terms of matching handler types and their handler functions and therefore were never meant to have distinct types of their own, like restarts do. While it is possible to compute a list of restarts applicable for a given situation, it is not possible to get a list of *all* established restarts and manually inspect their report, interactive, or test functions.

In addition, the CL standard specifies nothing regarding backtrace information. Libraries such as Dissect have to resort to implementation-defined mechanisms in order to be able to fetch stack information across different CL implementations.

One more pain point is the fact that the debugger itself is not programmable. There does exist the *debugger-hook* variable that is respected by all functions which invoke the debugger—except for break, which binds this variable to nil before entering the debugger. Because of this lack of programmability, again, libraries such as Swank, Slynk, or trivial-custom-debugger, which implement their own debuggers, are required to hook into implementation-specific code.

One more issue related to signaling introspection is the fact that there is no indication of which operator has signaled a particular condition nor any reason given for why a debugger has been invoked. This prevents code from acting differently depending on whether a particular condition has been signaled using signal, warn, error, or cerror, as well as prevents a portable debugger from acting differently based on whether it has been entered due to an unhandled error or, for example, due to break.

## 4.5.6  Concrete condition types

The tree of standard condition types is not very detailed. On one hand, we are missing some specific condition types that are more targeted, such as a serious condition stack-overflow that represents hitting a hardware limitation of the current platform, or more elaborate variants of file-error that go into more details of what is amiss: the file is missing, the file is being edited by another user, the file is read-only, and so on; on the other hand, Common Lisp misses some useful variants of already existing types, such as variants of simple conditions including simple-program-error which would be directly useful for CL programmers.

This apparent incompleteness, again, is the result of the Common Lisp committee deciding on what would be the best for the language being standardized: defining too few condition types would cripple the condition functionality on which the programmers could rely, but defining too many would increase the burden on implementers and on people adapting existing programs into CL—forcing them to ensure that the errors signaled by their code were of proper standard type. In fact, one of the authors of the standard mentioned that it was already a success to have fit the existing set of condition types inside the CL standard!

## 4.5.7 Warning conditions and #'WARN

While it is possible to signal any kind of condition object via `signal`, `error`, or `cerror`, the function `warn` is required to signal a `type-error` if the condition object supplied to it is not of type `warning`. This requirement means that it is illegal to `warn` on conditions that are not warnings—even though the reasons for such a requirement are not clear.

## 4.5.8 Implementing custom SIGNAL-like operators

The function `coerce-to-condition` is not directly exposed nor programmable. This has two unfortunate consequences: firstly, it makes it impossible to provide to the signaling operators any data which is not a condition, a string, a function, or a symbol; secondly, it prevents the possibility of writing new signaling functions which hook into this functionality portably—functions such as `signal`.

One example of the preceding limitation which is exhibited by many CL implementations is signaling *compiler notes*, which are conditions of lesser relevance than `warning` or even `style-warning`. Compiler notes are information for the programmer that are related to valid CL code, but inform the programmer, for example, about dead code branches which are never reachable or about the fact that the compiler was unable to perform some requested optimizations. Not only are compiler note condition types not a part of the standard, but it is also impossible to write a portable `compiler-notify` function that first coerces its data to a condition of type `compiler-note`, then signals it, and finally performs some additional reporting in cases where the condition was not handled.

## 4.5.9 Lack of functional interfaces to handlers and restarts

Since the CL operators `handler-bind` and `restart-bind` are macros rather than functions, the condition type and restart name inside them are not evaluated. This makes it impossible to provide new handlers and restarts in a functional way, such as in this hypothetical example:

```
;;; Calls function FOO in an environment with a new handler for condition type MY-CONDITION
(call-with-handler #'foo 'my-condition (lambda (c) (print 42)))

;;; Calls function FOO in an environment with a new restart named MY-RESTART
(call-with-restart #'foo 'my-restart (lambda () (print 42))
```

It is possible to work around this limitation in a portable way, but not without invoking the compiler at runtime; the example implementations of the preceding functions are described in an appendix to this book.

## 4.5.10 Smaller issues

The condition system also has smaller issues and pet peeves which are only relevant in particular contexts:

- One such issue is the fact that the `:no-error` clause in `handler-case` should be named differently, due to the fact that `handler-case` may handle conditions that are not in fact errors.

- Another one is the fact that the clustering behavior is not consistent between handlers and restarts: a handler may only invoke handlers that are "older" than it, while a restart has access to all restarts that have ever been bound in its dynamic environment.

- Yet another issue, previously mentioned, is the difference in syntax between `handler-bind`/`restart-bind` (`:report-function`, `:interactive-function`, `:test-function`) and `handler-case`/`restart-case` (`:report`, `:interactive`, `:test`) and, in some cases, `define-condition` (which also accepts a `:report` option that is consistent with the `-case` operators). One set of keywords accepts a function object, and the other accepts forms suitable for passing to the `function` special operator. This issue is related to the old feud, which dates back to the times when older Lisp dialects were still alive, between the proponents of (`lambda` ...) and the proponents of #'(`lambda` ...). #'(`lambda` ...) was used as a means to be compatible with those dialects, and CL ended up defining the macro (`lambda` ...), which expands into #'(`lambda` ...), for this exact reason. Note in this connection that the #'-less form (`lambda` ...) is the only function designator suitable for use both in `:report-function`/`:interactive-function`/`:test-function` and in `:repor t`/`:interactive`/`:test`.

- While it is not an issue with the Common Lisp condition system, some readers might be interested in the fact that early versions of the Rust programming language had a simple condition system of its own. It has been removed, though: the commit that removed them said that the introduction of conditions had "some unforeseen shortcomings," listed in detail in the commit, and mentioned that condition-based input/output has been abandoned in favor of a result-based solution with a lesser "cognitive burden."

## 4.5.11  Summary: Downsides of the Common Lisp condition system

We have listed a series of downsides and pitfalls in the Common Lisp condition system.

On one hand, ending this chapter on such a negative note might appear off-putting, especially in the context of a programming language which has been described as "dead" for decades in some places; on the other hand, the author considers it important to collect all these issues in one place, both for completeness in describing the condition system as it is currently standardized within ANSI CL and for spreading awareness of practical issues which programmers may face while utilizing the condition system in real-world applications. The author hopes that the above list will comprise a generally useful compilation of issues found through thirty years of practice with the Common Lisp condition system, which itself was built upon thirty previous years of practice with error handling in general. It should be valuable for designers and implementers of future condition systems, either in eventual future revisions of CL itself, or in other programming languages.

In addition, it is important to remark that the condition system remains unique, even with its flaws: it is one of the few aspects of Lisp which have *not* yet been adopted by other languages which are nowadays considered mainstream. This is in contrast to features such as if/then/else conditionals, first-class function objects, recursion, dynamic typing, garbage collection, syntax trees composed of expressions rather than statements, symbol types, image-based programming, and, most recently, symbolic code notation for non-S-expression-based languages. (The reader may want to see Paul Graham's "What Made Lisp Different" for details.)

Importantly, even though the condition system has not made it into the core of other languages, it should be noted that the author is aware of multiple implementations of condition systems available as libraries for Python, Clojure, Ruby, and Perl (conditions and restarts). There is also an article named *Condition Systems in an Exceptional Language* by Chris Houser that describes the means of implementing a simplified (as in, with error conditions only) condition system in Clojure.

# 4.6  Condition system in practice

To sweeten the slight bitterness left by the last chapter, and to end the book on a proper positive note, we shall now show several use cases for the condition system for exception handling *and beyond exception handling* that are directly usable in practical applications. The examples listed here are small, so they can be understood easily; they are meant to be a source of inspiration, and they may be used as individual building blocks and techniques for creating more intricate program flow control structures.

Do note that this list is incomplete in covering the potential types of use cases; dear reader, you are encouraged to expand on it with your own real-world examples.

## 4.6.1  Unit test library: Collecting results

The testing library should-test by Vsevolod Dyomkin utilizes the condition system as a basis. A unit test in this framework consists of a number of assertions stated with should, should-signal, or should-print-to; these forms are allowed to be placed arbitrarily within the test code or even nested. An example from this library's self-test module is:

```
(deftest test ()
  (should signal should-test-error
        (let ((*test-output* (make-broadcast-stream)))
          (test :test (gensym))))
  ;; some assertions skipped ...
  (should be true
        (let ((*test-output* (make-broadcast-stream)))
          (deftest foo2 ()
            (let ((bar t))
              (+ 1 2)
              (should be true bar)))
          (prog1 (test :test 'foo2)
            (undeftest 'foo2)))))
```

The macro should, after checking the assertion et al., signals conditions of appropriate types; these conditions contain the test results of each assertion. The handlers for these condition types, invoked via signaling, are then capable of recording the test results appropriately. Without a condition system and consequently without the capability to signal conditions, the testing framework would need to work with some predefined structures to capture the test results; such approach is widespread in other testing frameworks, both in the CL world and in other programming variables.

A similar effect may be used for collecting other kinds of data from within dynamically nested code. For example, we may consider code that performs elaborate string matching in order to capture the spans that match predefined values. Using signaling in such applications allows the information about results to be passed to code many levels above the concrete matching operations without disrupting the flow of the matching process itself.

Similar effects may be achieved with raw dynamic variables or lexical closures. However, Vsevolod argues that using conditions and signaling allows the resulting code to be more semantic and modular, as handlers can be fully decoupled from the signaling points; in addition, using signals avoids the need to define dynamic variables or pass lexical closures deeper into the call stack.

## 4.6.2  Web framework: Sending results over the network

The preceding technique may be adapted in a way where results are not explicitly collected as Lisp data, but are instead sent over a network socket; this allows for creation of web frameworks based around the ways in which the condition system works:

- Defining a given condition type may mean creating a particular way of outputting an object to the network.

- Signaling may mean that a particular Lisp object should be output.

- Condition handlers may implement the actual logic for sending data to network sockets.

- Restarts established around the signaling sites may be used as a means of control flow that are invoked by handlers in order to tell the framework that the current object has been processed and the framework may continue processing new ones (in a way similar to the muffle-warning restart established by the warn function).

## 4.6.3  GUI applications: Interactive querying

Another possibility is utilizing the fact that restarts may be invoked directly by the Lisp program instead of by condition handlers or the debugger. Such restarts may perform operations as a part of program logic that is available from anywhere and either return values or transfer control to a defined point within a sub-procedure of the program.

A good example for that is utilizing restarts in a graphical client application. Let us assume that, in the middle of some complex process composed of multiple steps, a REST request made from the client fails due to, for example, invalid credentials. This can be detected in the application, which may then invoke a restart that brings up a dialog querying the user to provide more suitable credentials. Using restarts in this technique allows for decoupling the dialog from the error site. It is also a good way of programming a means to continue the whole complex procedure, along with the previous steps which have already been successfully executed.

## 4.6.4  Generating data: Python-like generators

The following code defines a primitive facility for iterating the data similar to how simple Python generators function:

```
(define-condition generated ()
  ((item :initarg :item :reader generated-item)))

(defun yield (item)
  (restart-case (signal 'generated :item item)
    (resume () item)))

(defmacro doing ((item generator-form &optional result) &body body)
  (with-gensyms (e)
    `(block nil
       (handler-bind ((generated (lambda (,e)
                                   (let ((,item (generated-item ,e)))
                                     (loop ,@body)
                                     (invoke-restart (find-restart 'resume))))))
         ,generator-form)
       ,result)))
```

Here is an example code using this facility:

```
CL-USER> (let ((foo '(1 2 3)))
           (doing (item (yield (pop foo)))
             (print item)
             (when (emptyp foo) (return))))
1
2
3
NIL

CL-USER> (doing (item (yield (random 10)))
           (when (= item 0) (return))
           (print item))
9
5
6
9
7
2
9
1
3
4
7
5
8
3
4
NIL
```

The preceding code is a pretty rough and quick implementation which can be improved, for example, by hiding the termination test and the explicit return; however, the idea behind this code and the way in which it functions should be clear for the reader. The demonstrated mechanism does not permit implementing full coroutines nor does it provide a way to utilize a Python-like yield-from, but it still demonstrates the potential uses for non-local return features of the Common Lisp condition system.

# CHAPTER 5

# Appendixes

## 5.1 Appendix A: Implementation of dynamic variables in C

The C language, just like Lisp, has a macro system that allows one to extend the language with new syntax. Unlike Lisp macros, however, C macros are not an integral part of the language; they are loaded and expanded before the actual compilation happens by the utility called the *preprocessor*, which parses C code before passing it to the further stages of the C toolchain.

As we mentioned earlier, the C programming language has no innate notion of dynamic variables. However, we can "bolt" dynamic variables onto the language; we can write macros for the C preprocessor that expand into C data and code that implement a more robust variant of the dynamic variable emulation shown in an earlier chapter of the book. In fact, this appendix will implement the `dynamic_var` and `dynamic_bind` constructs introduced earlier in that chapter.

Before we write the actual macro, let us first write out the code into which the macro should expand. We will want to implement a dynamic variable named x of type `int` with the initial value of 42.

First of all, let us introduce our global variable named x.

```
int x = 42;
```

Nothing out of the ordinary here just yet; it is a standard global variable so far. The actual magic for it is going to happen elsewhere. Our `dynamic_bind` operator is going to create temporary variables that hold information about previous bindings of that variable and restore them upon leaving the scope.

© Michał "phoe" Herda 2020
M. "phoe" Herda, *The Common Lisp Condition System*, https://doi.org/10.1007/978-1-4842-6134-7_5

Therefore, we need to define a function that will perform cleanup upon exiting a dynamic scope.

```
void __dynamic_int_x_cleanup__(int* arg) {
  x = *arg;
}
```

Upon calling the cleanup function, the variable x is set to the value pointed at by arg, therefore restoring the previous value of the variable.

We will also want a means of creating new dynamic bindings. We would like to retain the curly braces of our dynamic_bind operator, and therefore we will use a C macro technique known as the *run-once for loop*. An example code that creates a new binding for int x with the value 5 may look like the following:

```
for(int __dynamic_int_x_continue__ = 1; __dynamic_int_x_continue__;)
  for(int __dynamic_int_x_save__
        __attribute__((cleanup(__dynamic_int_x_cleanup__)))
      = x;
      __dynamic_int_x_continue__;)
    for (x = 5; __dynamic_int_x_continue__; __dynamic_int_x_continue__ = 0) {
      ...;
}
```

In order to use the C stack instead of an explicit one, we use a triple-nested for loop. Let us go through them in order:

- We would like the body within our braces to be executed only once. Therefore, in the outermost loop, we establish a local boolean variable named __dynamic_x_continue__ with an initial value of 1. This variable is checked in each of the for loops and is set to 0 in the innermost loop to ensure that all loops terminate after exactly one iteration.

- The second loop establishes a variable named __dynamic_x_save__ that holds cleanup information for our variable x. We annotate that variable with a cleanup *attribute* which ensures that our cleanup function is called when the variable goes out of scope. (cleanup is a C extension, supported by GCC and Clang compilers.)

- Once the cleanup information is saved, the third loop may assign a new value to the variable.

We can use the preceding technique to write a simple C program that demonstrates how dynamic bindings may be implemented.

```
include <stdio.h>

int x = 42;

void __dynamic_int_x_cleanup__(int* arg) {
  x = *arg;
}

int get_x() {
  return x;
}

void rebind() {
  for(int __dynamic_int_x_continue__ = 1; __dynamic_int_x_continue__;)
    for(int __dynamic_int_x_save__
         __attribute__((cleanup(__dynamic_int_x_cleanup__)))
         = x;
         __dynamic_int_x_continue__;)
      for (x = 5; __dynamic_int_x_continue__; __dynamic_int_x_continue__ = 0) {
        printf("dynamic binding, before assignment: %d\n", get_x());
        x = 222;
        printf("dynamic binding, after assignment: %d\n", get_x());
  }
}

int main(int argc, char** argv) {
  printf("top-level binding: %d\n", get_x());
  rebind();
  printf("top-level binding: %d\n", get_x());
  return 0;
}
```

Compiling and running this code gives us the results expected of a variable with dynamic binding:

```
$ gcc test.c -o test && ./test
top-level binding: 42
dynamic binding, before assignment: 5
dynamic binding, after assignment: 222
top-level binding(): 42
```

Our code works, even if it is somewhat bare-bones now. We need to cover its internals with a more pleasant interface and add syntax sugar which will hide the initial definitions and triple loop behind a dynamic_var and dynamic_bind.

The resulting code should look like the following:

```
#include <stdio.h>

dynamic_var(int, x, 5);

void rebind() {
  dynamic_bind(int, x, 42) {
    printf("before assignment: %d\n", x);
    x = 24;
    printf("after assignment: %d\n", x);
  }
}

int main(int argc, char** argv) {
  printf("toplevel binding: %d\n", x);
  rebind();
  printf("toplevel binding: %d\n", x);
  return 0;
}
```

If we count the internal (surrounded by double underscores) C symbols in the preceding code, we can count three of them:

- __dynamic_int_x_cleanup__ naming the cleanup function

- __dynamic_int_x_save__ naming the temporary variable that saves the original value

- __dynamic_int_x_continue__ naming the temporary iteration control variable

We will need C macros that generate such internal symbols for us. Luckily, the C preprocessor provides the required ## operation that concatenates symbols; we can use it to implement the macros generating our internal symbols.

```
#define dynamic_name(type, name, postfix)                \
  __dynamic_ ## type ## _ ## name ## _ ## postfix ## __  \
```

(In the body of dynamic_name, the symbols type, name, and postfix are replaced with the values passed to the macro, because they are passed to it as arguments. All remaining symbols are used verbatim.)

Once we have the symbols, we can proceed with implementing the expansion of dynamic_var. We will write a new macro that expands into the dynamic variable declaration.

```
#define dynamic_var_aux(type, name, cleanup) \
  void cleanup (type * arg) { name = *arg; } \

#define dynamic_var(type, name, value)            \
  type name = value;                              \
  dynamic_var_aux(type,                           \
                  name,                           \
                  dynamic_name(type, name, cleanup)) \
```

We could have written this as a single macro. For clarity, however, we have separated the part that expands into actual C code (dynamic_var_aux) from the part that retrieves symbols from external macro calls (dynamic_var).

The last remaining part is dynamic_bind that needs to expand into the triple single-iteration for loop. Once again, we will use an aux macro to separate the act of generating symbols from the act of expanding into code, especially because dynamic_bind needs three generated symbols inside its expansion.

```
#define dynamic_bind_aux(type, name, value, save, pop, var)   \
  for(int var = 1; var;)                                      \
    for(type save __attribute__((cleanup(pop))) = name; var;) \
      for(name = value; var; var = 0)                         \

#define dynamic_bind(type, name, value)           \
  dynamic_bind_aux(type,                          \
                   name,                          \
                   value,                         \
                   dynamic_name(type, name, save),    \
                   dynamic_name(type, name, cleanup), \
                   dynamic_name(type, name, continue)) \
```

And that's it. With the preceding C preprocessor magic that uses a single C extension, our dynamic bindings now work, and we can enjoy dynamic variables in a language that used not to have them.

The preceding example uses the C stack to contain the previous values of our dynamic variable. This will work well for single integers, but it might cause stack overflows if the rebound variable is, for example, a `double[256]` and it is rebound multiple times, as the data is copied on every binding of the dynamic variable. In addition, we generate a separate cleanup function for each variable, which is wasteful. The code repository for this book contains alternative implementations of dynamic variables in C that address these problems.

(Sidenote: the Rust programming language has an implementation of dynamic variables—or *fluid variables*, as they are called there—available in the `fluid-let` crate. This implementation utilizes a technique which is similar to the one described earlier, though it makes use of Rust's concepts of lifetimes and ownership that are unavailable in C.)

# 5.2 Appendix B: Additional utilities for working with Common Lisp conditions

## 5.2.1 CALL-WITH-HANDLER and CALL-WITH-RESTART

As described earlier, there is no functional variant to the CL macros `handler-bind` and `restart-bind`. This makes it impossible to specify condition types for newly bound handlers and restart names for newly bound restarts at runtime, if we want to limit ourselves to using only these two macros. Thanks to the image-based capabilities of CL, however, it is possible to specify functions which enable us to to provide condition types. Our approach will leverage the runtime availability of the compiler and the standard `coerce` function.

For a detailed explanation, `coerce` is specified to yield a function object when provided with a `lambda` form. Therefore, we can construct the `lambda` form using standard Lisp operators, such as backquote notation, pass the resulting form to `coerce` to receive a function object, and then `funcall` it.

This allows us to write the following Lisp functions:

```
(defun call-with-handler (thunk condition-type handler)
  (let ((lambda-form
          `(lambda ()
             (handler-bind ((,condition-type ,handler))
               (funcall ,thunk)))))
    (funcall (coerce lambda-form 'function))))
```

```
(defun call-with-restart (thunk restart-name restart-function
                          &key (interactive-function nil interactive-function-p)
                               (test-function nil test-function-p)
                               (report-function nil report-function-p))
  (let ((lambda-form
          `(lambda ()
             (restart-bind ((,restart-name ,restart-function
                             ,@(when interactive-function-p
                                 `(:interactive-function ,interactive-function))
                             ,@(when report-function-p
                                 `(:report-function ,report-function))
                             ,@(when test-function-p
                                 `(:test-function ,test-function))))
               (funcall ,thunk)))))
    (funcall (coerce lambda-form 'function))))
```

These two newly created functions allow us to specify condition types for handlers and restart names for restarts as variable arguments.

```
CL-USER> (block foo
           (call-with-handler
            (lambda () (error "bar"))
            'error
            (lambda (c) (return-from foo c))))
#<SIMPLE-ERROR "bar" {1003076FB3}>

CL-USER> (block foo
           (call-with-restart
            (lambda () (invoke-restart 'frob))
            'frob
            (lambda () (return-from foo 42))))
42
```

Using these functions at runtime might prove beneficial during interactive development. On the other hand, since each call to either of these functions does invoke the compiler, they might prove slower for production purposes, as compared to the standard macros handler-bind and restart-bind.

A workaround for this possible bottleneck would be to cache the compiled anonymous functions, which would require the compiler to be invoked only once per condition type or restart name. We can store the functions in a pair of hash tables: a hash table for condition types (which are allowed to be lists and must therefore be compared via `equal`) and a hash table for restarts (for which the keys need to be lists too; we will explain this later in this chapter).

```
(defvar *call-with-handler-cache* (make-hash-table :test #'equal))

(defvar *call-with-restart-cache* (make-hash-table :test #'equal))
```

(As a famous programming law states, there are only two hard problems in computer science: cache invalidation, naming things, and off-by-one errors. Now that we have a cache, we necessarily have an instance of that first of the hard problems: we must decide how and when entries should be removed from our cache. For this simple example, we will punt on removing entries from it, since it is unlikely that the size of this hash table will become significant during the lifetime of a single Lisp image.)

We will now write the code for the cached `call-with-handler`. One function will ensure the presence of a function object inside the cache, and the other will perform actual calling of that function.

```
(defun ensure-call-with-handler-function (condition-type)
  (multiple-value-bind (value foundp) (gethash condition-type *call-with-handler-cache*)
    (if foundp
        value
        (let ((lambda-form
                `(lambda (handler thunk)
                   (handler-bind ((,condition-type handler))
                     (funcall thunk)))))
          (setf (gethash condition-type *call-with-handler-cache*)
                (coerce lambda-form 'function))))))

(defun call-with-handler (thunk condition-type handler)
  (funcall (ensure-call-with-handler-function condition-type)
           handler thunk))
```

For handlers, there are no keyword arguments to be passed into `handler-bind`. The situation complicates itself, however, when it comes to `restart-bind`: for every restart name, there can be multiple combinations of `:interactive-function`, `:report-function`, and `:test-function` passed to the macro. We are unable to pass `nil` as arguments for any of these, since the values of these keyword arguments must evaluate to functions; therefore, we will generate a different function for each combination of the restart name and the three booleans which state whether report, interactive, and test functions have been provided. A list containing these four values will serve as a valid equal-matching key for *call-with-restart-cache*.

```
(defun ensure-call-with-restart-function (restart-name interactive-p report-p test-p)
  (let ((key (list restart-name interactive-p report-p test-p)))
    (multiple-value-bind (value foundp) (gethash key *call-with-restart-cache*)
      (if foundp
          value
          (let ((lambda-form
                  `(lambda (restart-function thunk interactive report test)
                     (declare (ignorable interactive report test))
                     (restart-bind
                         ((,restart-name
                           restart-function
                           ,@(when interactive-p `(:interactive-function interactive))
                           ,@(when report-p `(:report-function report))
                           ,@(when test-p `(:test-function test))))
                       (funcall thunk)))))
            (setf (gethash key *call-with-restart-cache*)
                  (coerce lambda-form 'function)))))))

(defun call-with-restart (thunk restart-name restart-function
                          &key (interactive-function nil interactive-p)
                               (report-function nil report-p)
                               (test-function nil test-p))
  (let ((function (ensure-call-with-restart-function
                    restart-name (and interactive-p t) (and report-p t) (and test-p t))))
    (funcall function restart-function thunk
             interactive-function report-function test-function)))
```

We can see that these three keyword arguments are included *conditionally* inside the handler binding in the generated function. In addition, call-with-restart checks whether or not the keyword arguments have been provided. The (and interactive-t t) construct is present to ensure that t is the symbol with which the cache key is constructed; note that the parameters which state whether or not a value has been supplied are allowed to be bound to any non-nil value—not necessarily t—when they are true.

With such a caching construction, the compiler will only be called once for each condition type and for each combination of restart name, interactive-p, report-p, and test-p, therefore, up to eight times for each restart name.

# 5.2.2 HANDLER-BIND* and HANDLER-CASE*

The clustering mechanism of `handler-bind` and `handler-case` might be unwanted in some cases where the condition system is used. In particular, in a situation where a single operator binds multiple handlers, the programmer may desire for a latter handler to signal a condition that triggers the handler function of a former handler.

We therefore propose `handler-bind*` and `handler-case*`, variants of `handler-bind` and `handler-case` that explicitly do not utilize clustering for the handlers that they bind. This implies that, within the same form, handlers bound earlier can be invoked by handlers bound later. We can say that `let` is to `let*` as `handler-bind` is to `handler-bind*` and as `handler-case` is to `handler-case*`.

In the following example, if `my-condition` is signaled, we would like the `error` call inside the handler function to trigger the `my-error` handler bound earlier within the same form.

```
(handler-bind* ((my-error ...)
                (my-condition (lambda (c) (error 'my-error :c c))))
  ...)
```

We can observe the difference between `handler-bind` and `handler-bind*` on the following example, where each handler formats a line to standard output and then re-signals the condition.

```
CL-USER> (handler-bind ((condition (lambda (c)
                                     (format t ";; A~%")
                                     (signal c)))
                        (condition (lambda (c)
                                     (format t ";; B~%")
                                     (signal c)))
                        (condition (lambda (c)
                                     (format t ";; C~%")
                                     (signal c))))
           (signal 'condition))
;; A
;; B
;; C
NIL

CL-USER> (handler-bind* ((condition (lambda (c)
                                      (format t ";; A~%")
                                      (signal c)))
```

```
                    (condition (lambda (c)
                               (format t ";; B~%")
                               (signal c)))
                    (condition (lambda (c)
                               (format t ";; C~%")
                               (signal c))))
        (signal 'condition))
;; C
;; B
;; A
;; A
;; B
;; A
;; A
NIL
```

A similar effect can be seen when comparing `handler-case` and `handler-case*`.

```
CL-USER> (handler-case (signal 'condition)
          (condition (c) (format t ";; A~%") (signal c))
          (condition (c) (format t ";; B~%") (signal c))
          (condition (c) (format t ";; C~%") (signal c)))
;; A
NIL

CL-USER> (handler-case* (signal 'condition)
          (condition (c) (format t ";; A~%") (signal c))
          (condition (c) (format t ";; B~%") (signal c))
          (condition (c) (format t ";; C~%") (signal c)))
;; C
;; B
;; A
NIL
```

An important side effect of that fact is that the order in which multiple handlers bound by `handler-bind*` and `handler-case*` is different. In `handler-bind` and `handler-case`, the handlers are invoked from first to last; in `handler-bind*` and `handler-case*`, they are invoked from last to first.

The implementation of `handler-bind*` is straightforward, since this operator has no edge cases.

```lisp
(defun expand-handler-bind* (bindings body)
  (if (null bindings)
      `(progn ,@body)
      `(handler-bind (,(car bindings))
         (handler-bind* ,(cdr bindings) ,@body))))

(defmacro handler-bind* (bindings &body body)
  (expand-handler-bind* bindings body))
```

On the other hand, `handler-case*` needs to account for the `:no-error` case, which must become the outermost one.

```lisp
(defun make-handler-case*-with-no-error-case (form cases)
  (let* ((no-error-case (assoc :no-error cases))
         (other-cases (remove no-error-case cases)))
    (let ((normal-return (gensym "NORMAL-RETURN"))
          (error-return  (gensym "ERROR-RETURN")))
      `(block ,error-return
         (multiple-value-call (lambda ,@(cdr no-error-case))
           (block ,normal-return
             (return-from ,error-return
               (handler-case* (return-from ,normal-return ,form)
                 ,@other-cases))))))))

(defun make-handler-case*-without-no-error-case (form cases)
  (if (null cases)
      form
      `(handler-case (handler-case* ,form ,@(cdr cases))
         ,(car cases))))

(defun expand-handler-case* (form cases)
  (let ((no-error-case-count (count :no-error cases :key #'car)))
    (case no-error-case-count
      (0 (make-handler-case*-without-no-error-case form cases))
      (1 (make-handler-case*-with-no-error-case form cases))
      (t (error "Multiple :NO-ERROR cases found in HANDLER-CASE*.")))))

(defmacro handler-case* (form &rest cases)
  (expand-handler-case* form cases))
```

# 5.2.3 HANDLER-BIND-CASE

Let us introduce one more utility into the condition system. Although not specified in the ANSI standard, this utility will prove useful for a certain class of problems, so we will go ahead and implement it ourselves here.

In the world of handlers, handler-bind is sometimes used as a building block to construct handler-bind-case, an operator with the same syntax as handler-case. The handler-bind-case name comes from the fact that this operator can be seen as a mixture of handler-bind and handler-case: the handler body is executed within the dynamic environment of signal like in handler-bind, but then control is transferred back outside like in handler-case. In other words, handler-bind-case, upon reacting to a signaled condition, evaluates the handler body first, allowing it to operate within the dynamic environment in which the condition was signaled. *Only then* does it unwind the stack by transferring control outside of the handler.

This approach is useful for, for example, allowing the handler to preserve the backtrace in case of an error; using handler-case for such situations would be useless, because the handler body needs to operate before the stack is unwound and therefore before the backtrace of the error site is destroyed.

An example implementation of handler-bind-case, adapted from the CMU CL source of handler-case and refactored for clarity, may look like the following:

```
(defun make-handler-bind-case-with-no-error-case (form cases)
  (let* ((no-error-case (assoc :no-error cases))
         (other-cases (remove no-error-case cases)))
    (let ((normal-return (gensym "NORMAL-RETURN"))
          (error-return  (gensym "ERROR-RETURN")))
      `(block ,error-return
         (multiple-value-call (lambda ,@(cdr no-error-case))
           (block ,normal-return
             (return-from ,error-return
               (handler-bind-case (return-from ,normal-return ,form)
                 ,@other-cases)))))))))

(defun make-handler-bind-case-without-no-error-case (form cases)
  (let ((block-name (gensym "HANDLER-BIND-CASE-BLOCK")))
    (flet ((make-handler-binding (case)
             (destructuring-bind (type lambda-list . body) case
               `(,type (lambda ,lambda-list
                         (return-from ,block-name (locally ,@body)))))))
```

```
      (let ((bindings (mapcar #'make-handler-binding cases)))
        `(block ,block-name (handler-bind ,bindings ,form))))))

(defun expand-handler-bind-case (form cases)
  (let ((no-error-case-count (count :no-error cases :key #'car)))
    (case no-error-case-count
      (0 (make-handler-bind-case-without-no-error-case form cases))
      (1 (make-handler-bind-case-with-no-error-case form cases))
      (t (error "Multiple :NO-ERROR cases found in HANDLER-BIND-CASE.")))))

(defmacro handler-bind-case (form &rest cases)
  (expand-handler-bind-case form cases))
```

We can see that the expansion can occur along one of two branches. One of them is utilized if a :no-error case is present; that case is treated specially. The implementation delegates other non-:no-error cases to be handled via a recursive macro call to handler-bind-case. The case of :no-error is handled identically in handler-bind-case as in handler-case, and the normal case is, thankfully, less complex in handler-bind-case than is its matching implementation in handler-case.

handler-bind-case needs to iterate through the cases provided to it and turn them into properly formatted bindings for handler-bind. The anonymous function within each binding needs to execute the body of each case and then return the resulting value to the outermost block. Once all cases are processed and the list of bindings is created, this list is spliced into handler-bind, and the resulting code is returned.

(For completeness, the locally form wrapped around the splicing of body is there to allow *local declarations* to work inside it. Describing declarations is, however, out of scope for this book.)

We may test a combination of handler-bind-case and unwind-protect and compare the resulting order in which forms are executed to the order that results from using the standard macro handler-case.

```
CL-USER> (handler-case (unwind-protect (signal 'condition)
                         (format t ";; Going out of dynamic scope~%"))
           (condition (c) (format t ";; Handling condition ~S~%" c)))
;; Going out of dynamic scope
;; Handling condition #<CONDITION {1001BC4FA3}>
NIL
```

```
CL-USER> (handler-bind-case (unwind-protect (signal 'condition)
                              (format t ";; Going out of dynamic scope~%"))
           (condition (c) (format t ";; Handling condition ~S~%" c)))
;; Handling condition #<CONDITION {1001C77553}>
;; Going out of dynamic scope
NIL
```

We may also check the macroexpansion of the sample handler-bind-case form, to see what the final expansion looks like and how it utilizes handler-bind internally. In addition to eyeballing it, we can also evaluate it live, for example, by copy-pasting it to the read-eval-print loop. Note that by default gensym'ed symbols are not readable by the Lisp reader subsystem (i.e., the first step of the read-eval-print loop); to sidestep this issue, such code has to be printed with *print-gensym* set or bound to nil—this will cause the Lisp printer subsystem to print gensym'ed symbols in a readable format.

```
CL-USER> (BLOCK HANDLER-BIND-CASE-BLOCK617
           (HANDLER-BIND ((CONDITION
                           (LAMBDA (C)
                             (RETURN-FROM HANDLER-BIND-CASE-BLOCK617
                               (LOCALLY (FORMAT T ";; Handling condition ~S~%" C)))))))
             (UNWIND-PROTECT (SIGNAL 'CONDITION)
               (FORMAT T ";; Going out of dynamic scope~%"))))
;; Handling condition #<CONDITION {100258ADF3}>
;; Going out of dynamic scope
NIL
```

For completeness, we also provide a sequential version of the operator, handler-bind-case*.

```
(defun make-handler-bind-case*-with-no-error-case (form cases)
  (let* ((no-error-case (assoc :no-error cases))
         (other-cases (remove no-error-case cases)))
    (let ((normal-return (gensym "NORMAL-RETURN"))
          (error-return  (gensym "ERROR-RETURN")))
      `(block ,error-return
         (multiple-value-call (lambda ,@(cdr no-error-case))
           (block ,normal-return
             (return-from ,error-return
               (handler-bind-case* (return-from ,normal-return ,form)
                 ,@other-cases))))))))
```

```
(defun make-handler-bind-case*-without-no-error-case (form cases)
  (if (null cases)
      form
      `(handler-bind-case (handler-bind-case* ,form ,@(cdr cases))
         ,(car cases))))

(defun expand-handler-bind-case* (form cases)
  (let ((no-error-case-count (count :no-error cases :key #'car)))
    (case no-error-case-count
      (0 (make-handler-bind-case*-without-no-error-case form cases))
      (1 (make-handler-bind-case*-with-no-error-case form cases))
      (t (error "Multiple :NO-ERROR cases found in HANDLER-BIND-CASE*.")))))

(defmacro handler-bind-case* (form &rest cases)
  (expand-handler-bind-case* form cases))
```

# 5.3  Appendix C: Lisp macros 101

A Common Lisp *macro* is a peculiar kind of function which transforms Lisp data into Lisp code. Wherever a function cannot be used to achieve a particular task within Lisp syntax, usually a macro can be employed in its place; this fact stems from two basic differences between how functions and macros are treated in Lisp.

The first basic difference from the outer point of view is that functions receive their arguments as the values which result after evaluating their forms; macros receive the unevaluated forms verbatim. This gives macros the option of skipping the normal evaluation rules of Lisp forms and then either evaluating them selectively or inventing completely new syntax rules to process those verbatim forms.

The second basic difference is while return values of functions are returned to a caller, return values of macros are *inserted in place* of the macro call and evaluated again. When a macro is called, the macro call site is "replaced" with the code that it "returns"; this is why a macro is always meant to yield a piece of valid Lisp code.

While ordinary functions are usually called at *execution time*, macros are usually called at *compilation time*. This is because the Lisp compiler, as it processes Lisp forms during compilation, is required to expand all macros completely before proceeding with compilations; it is not required to do the same with functions.

# 5.3.1  Basics of macro writing

Let us write an example form that uses the standard macro and, which evaluates its arguments in turn until one of them returns false.

```
(and (= 0 (random 6)) (error "Bang!"))
```

This simple implementation of Russian roulette contains a macro call. When the compiler parses this form, it expands the and call and replaces the whole form with the result of the *macroexpansion function*. The concrete implementation of and depends on the Lisp implementation; an example expansion is shown as follows:

```
(IF (= 0 (RANDOM 6)) (ERROR "Bang!"))
```

This simple example is perhaps not very impressive. But, we can chain arguments passed to it arbitrarily. Let us modify the game a bit and only make a bang when we hit the roulette three times in a row.

```
(and (= 0 (random 6)) (= 0 (random 6)) (= 0 (random 6)) (error "Bang!"))
```

An example *recursive* expansion of this can be seen here:

```
(IF (= 0 (RANDOM 6))
    (AND (= 0 (RANDOM 6)) (= 0 (RANDOM 6)) (ERROR "Bang!")))
```

Using recursive macroexpansion, it is possible to generate the final, fully macroexpanded form:

```
(IF (= 0 (RANDOM 6))
    (IF (= 0 (RANDOM 6))
        (IF (= 0 (RANDOM 6))
            (ERROR "Bang!"))))
```

Let us define our version of that macro, named my-and, which will implement the following scheme:

```
(defmacro my-and (&rest forms)
  (cond ((null forms) 'nil)
        ((null (rest forms)) (first forms))
        (t (list 'if (first forms) (cons 'my-and (rest forms))))))
```

We can see that our macro has a conditional with three possible branches. If the list of forms is empty (which means that the macro was called like (my-and)), it returns nil; if the list of forms contains only one element, then that element is returned. Otherwise (when the list of forms contains more than one element), a compound form is returned: a three-element list with the symbol if as its first element, the first form as its second element, and another compound form, a cons of the symbol my-and and the rest of the forms—those which remain after removing the first form. The form returned by the macro is then treated as Lisp code by the compiler.

## 5.3.2  Backquote

The explicit list-and-literal-symbols syntax in the macro will produce the correct result, but Common Lisp exposes another kind of notation that allows us to make macro bodies better resemble the final output of the macro. This is called *backquote notation* or *quasiquote*. Backquote notation consists of four (or, in practice, three) syntactic operators:

- `` ` `` *quasiquotes* an expression.
- , *unquotes* an expression.
- ,@ *splicing-unquotes* an expression.
- ,. is a variant of ,@ that has generally fallen out of use, since it offers no benefits and many more pitfalls than ,@.

Backquoting is similar to the quoting (') operator of CL, as it preserves a form in its verbatim state; if we simply use a backquote in place of a normal quote with no further backquote notation, then the two resulting forms will be equivalent. The main difference is that backquote allows subforms of the backquoted expression to be *unquoted selectively*. Let us demonstrate this:

```
CL-USER> (let ((values '(1 2 3)))
           '(funcall function values))
(FUNCALL FUNCTION VALUES)

CL-USER> (let ((values '(1 2 3)))
           `(funcall function values))
(FUNCALL FUNCTION VALUES)
```

```
CL-USER> (let ((values '(1 2 3)))
           `(funcall function ,values))
(FUNCALL FUNCTION (1 2 3))

CL-USER> (let ((values '(1 2 3)))
           `(funcall function ,@values))
(FUNCALL FUNCTION 1 2 3)
```

In the first two cases, the whole funcall form has been quoted verbatim. In the third case, we can see that the variable body has been replaced with its value, the list (1 2 3). In the fourth case, we can see that the variable body has been replaced with *multiple values*; these values required body to be bound to a list, and the elements of this list have been spliced into the outer form.

In other words, in a backquoted expression, Lisp data which are not unquoted (with , or ,@) end up effectively quoted under normal quoting rules and therefore come through verbatim; Lisp data which are unquoted with , or ,@ are evaluated as usual to yield a value, and then this value is inserted or spliced into the resulting form.

(It is possible to nest backquotes into so-called *double* or *triple backquote* notation; describing this technique is out of scope of this book.)

## 5.3.3  Symbol capture

One of the common pitfalls when writing macros is the risk of introducing *symbol capture*, which is a typically adverse or unexpected effect that occurs when a symbol used in the macroexpansion shares its name with a symbol already present in the lexical scope of the macro call site.

Let us consider a modified version of the for macro that Paul Graham introduces in chapter 9.6 of *On Lisp*.

```
(defmacro for ((var start stop) &body body)
  `(do ((,var ,start (1+ ,var))
        (limit ,stop))
       ((> ,var limit))
     ,@body))
```

The macro seems to work correctly

```
CL-USER> (for (i 0 3)
           (format t ";; ~D~%" i))
;; 0
;; 1
;; 2
;; 3
NIL
```

until it interacts with a variable named in a particular way—in our case, limit.

```
CL-USER> (let ((limit 10))
           (for (i 0 3)
             (format t ";; ~D ~D~%" i limit)))
;; 0 3
;; 1 3
;; 2 3
;; 3 3
NIL
```

We have clearly defined limit to be 10, and yet, the format call prints 3 instead. We can see why this happens by using macroexpand-1 on our for form:

```
(let ((limit 10))
  (for (i 0 3)
    (format t ";; ~D ~D~%" i limit)))

(let ((limit 10))
  (DO ((I 0 (1+ I))
       (LIMIT 3))
      ((> I LIMIT))
    (FORMAT T ";; ~D ~D~%" I LIMIT)))
```

We can see that the outer limit binding is *shadowed* by an internal binding of the same symbol that is made inside do. In effect, the outer binding goes unused, and the inner binding interferes with the format form that we want to execute.

A solution is to use *gensyms* inside our macroexpansion. Gensyms, short for "generated symbols," are freshly generated symbols that are completely unique: they have no relationship to any package and are distinct from all other symbols. Because of that, they are printed with a #: prefix.

(Providing detailed information about symbols, packages, and the relationship between the two is not in scope of this book. The reader may want to consult *The Complete Idiot's Guide to Common Lisp Packages* by Erann Gat/Ron Garret, after disregarding the somewhat crude name of that article.)

A corrected version of our `for` macro may look like this:

```
(defmacro for ((var start stop) &body body)
  (let ((limit (gensym "LIMIT")))
    `(do ((,var ,start (1+ ,var))
          (,limit ,stop))
         ((> ,var ,limit))
       ,@body)))
```

We can now expand our example from earlier to see the difference:

```
(let ((limit 10))
  (for (i 0 3)
    (format t ";; ~D ~D~%" i limit)))

(let ((limit 10))
  (DO ((I 0 (1+ I))
       (#:LIMIT737 3))
      ((> I #:LIMIT737))
    (FORMAT T ";; ~D ~D~%" I LIMIT)))
```

The former `limit` variable has been replaced with a gensym that is guaranteed not to collide with any existing symbols, no matter where in our Lisp world they might come from. We can also verify that our new form works:

```
CL-USER> (let ((limit 10))
           (for (i 0 3)
             (format t ";; ~D ~D~%" i limit)))
;; 0 10
;; 1 10
;; 2 10
;; 3 10
NIL
```

This symbol capture problem is not limited to variable names; in certain situations, it is also possible to capture function names and to interact with symbols in other Lisp namespaces. Using gensyms is a solution for the majority of all these cases.

## 5.3.4 Order of evaluation

Macros are generally responsible to ensure that their arguments are evaluated in the proper order. Let us consider a small variation of the preceding for macro:

```
(defmacro for ((var start stop) &body body)
  (let ((limit (gensym "LIMIT")))
    `(do ((,limit ,stop)
          (,var ,start (1+ ,var)))
         ((> ,var ,limit))
       ,@body)))
```

In this example, the bindings established by the expansion of for are in inverse order: first, we establish the limit, and only then do we establish the iteration variable. Such behavior might violate the programmer's expectations, especially when *side effects* are involved in computing the forms in question; such a side effect might be, for example, printing to the screen. For the following example, the programmer may expect ;; Returning 0! to be printed *before* ;; Returning 3!; the preceding version of the macro will violate this expectation.

```
CL-USER> (flet ((return-0 () (format t ";; Returning 0!~%") 0)
                (return-3 () (format t ";; Returning 3!~%") 3))
           (for (i (return-0) (return-3))
             (format t ";; ~D~%" i)))
;; Returning 3!
;; Returning 0!
;; 0
;; 1
;; 2
;; 3
NIL
```

The solution in this case is once again to invert the order in which variables are bound; for different macros, the required solutions will depend on the order in which the forms passed to the macro are expected to be evaluated.

# 5.3.5  Multiple evaluation

Another mistake that is possible when writing the for macro is failing to introduce a limit variable at all and passing the stop parameter directly into the body of do.

```
(defmacro for ((var start stop) &body body)
  `(do ((,var ,start (1+ ,var)))
       ((> ,var ,stop))
     ,@body))
```

This causes the (return-3) form to be evaluated anew on every iteration, which might or might not be what we want a particular macro to do. In our case, the effect will be printing the ;; Returning 3! message on each iteration of the do macro, which plainly would be undesired.

```
CL-USER> (flet ((return-0 () (format t ";; Returning 0!~%") 0)
                (return-3 () (format t ";; Returning 3!~%") 3))
           (for (i (return-0) (return-3))
             (format t ";; ~D~%" i)))
;; Returning 0!
;; Returning 3!
;; 0
;; Returning 3!
;; 1
;; Returning 3!
;; 2
;; Returning 3!
;; 3
;; Returning 3!
NIL
```

The typical solution here is to create lexical variables within the macroexpansion and use the name of the variable instead of inserting the full form everywhere. This will ensure that the form is evaluated only once and that the resulting value is then used throughout the body of our macro. In this case, we need—once again—to step back and re-introduce our limit variable, also creating a gensym for it in order to avoid variable capture.

## 5.3.6 When not to write macros

In short, only use macros if a function won't do. If a function is enough, you should write a function.

There are two groups of situations for which macros are the proper tool. These are evaluation control and syntactic abstraction. An example of evaluation control is the and macro that we demonstrated earlier and re-implemented as my-and; an example of syntactic abstraction is the for macro, also demonstrated earlier.

In other words, a macro should be used only when the syntax rules for functions are not enough—namely, when evaluating all forms before passing their values to the called function is *not* what we want.

This is because a macro receives its arguments unevaluated and is capable of performing arbitrary transformations on them. The earlier example of for cannot be written as a function—the (i 0 3) form would have been misinterpreted as a call of an unknown function named i, instead of being processed as a binding for an iteration variable.

However, macros also have their downsides: it is impossible to use the #' notation with them; for example, #'and is invalid syntax. Therefore, it is impossible to pass macro functions directly as values to, for example, mapcar. In addition, macro calls are invisible in debug traces, since they no longer exist in compiled code (only their expansions do).

## 5.3.7 Reference

For more information and detail on basics of macro writing, the reader should consult the "Macros: Defining Your Own" chapter of *Practical Common Lisp* by Peter Seibel, as well as Chapters 9 and 10 of *On Lisp* by Paul Graham.

# 5.4 Appendix D: Condition system reference

## 5.4.1 Restarts and related functions

### 5.4.1.1 Class RESTART

- Class precedence list: restart, t

Represents a restart available in a given dynamic environment. A restart can be *named* with a symbol; an anonymous restart has nil as its name.

A restart always has a *restart function*, which is called when the restart is *invoked*.

A restart may be *active* or not. For a restart to be active, its *test function* must return true, and it must either not be *associated* with any condition or it must be associated with the condition that is used to compute the active restarts.

A restart may have a *report function* associated with it; that function describes how a restart is *reported*, meaning how the restart object is printed with *print-escape* being bound to nil.

A restart may have an *interactive function* that may be called to query the user interactively for arguments for that restart. If no interactive function is provided, that list is always assumed to be '().

All restarts have dynamic extent relative to the scope of the form that established them.

## 5.4.1.2  Function RESTART-NAME

- (restart-name restart) → name

  - restart – a restart.

  - name – a symbol.

Returns the name of a restart, or nil in case of anonymous restarts.

## 5.4.1.3  Function COMPUTE-RESTARTS

- (compute-restarts &optional condition) → restarts

  - condition – a condition, or nil.

  - restarts – a list of restarts.

Returns an immutable list of all restarts which are active in the dynamic environment where compute-restarts is called, sorted with most recently established restarts first.

If condition is non-nil, then compute-restarts skips restarts associated with conditions other than condition.

## 5.4.1.4  Function FIND-RESTART

- (find-restart designator &optional condition) → maybe-restart

  - designator – a restart object or a non-nil symbol.

  - condition – a condition.

  - maybe-restart – a restart or nil.

If designator is a restart, find-restart checks whether or not it is active. If yes, the restart is returned; otherwise, nil is returned.

If designator is a symbol, find-restart returns the newest established active restart named with that symbol.

If condition is non-nil, then find-restarts skips restarts associated with conditions other than condition.

## 5.4.1.5  Function INVOKE-RESTART

- (invoke-restart designator &optional arguments) → result*

  - designator – a restart object or a non-nil symbol.

  - arguments – arbitrary Lisp data.

  - result* – arbitrary Lisp data.

If designator is a restart, then its restart function is called with the provided arguments.

If designator is a symbol, then invoke-restart finds the newest established active restart named with that symbol and then invokes it with the provided arguments.

If the restart function returns normally, then results are the values returned from that function.

## 5.4.1.6  Function INVOKE-RESTART-INTERACTIVELY

- (invoke-restart-interactively designator) → result*

  - designator – a restart object or a non-nil symbol.

  - result – arbitrary Lisp data.

If designator is a restart, then its interactive function is called to retrieve a list of arguments for that restart. Then, the restart function is called with these arguments.

If designator is a symbol, then invoke-restart finds the newest established active restart named with that symbol and then invokes it interactively.

If the restart function returns normally, then results are the values returned from that function.

## Examples

```
CL-USER> (type-of (first (compute-restarts)))
RESTART

CL-USER> (restart-name (first (compute-restarts)))
ABORT                           ; may differ across implementations

CL-USER> (progn (format t "~&;; ~S~%" (compute-restarts)) nil)
;; (#<RESTART ABORT {7FFAE3DAEAB3}>)    ; may differ across implementations
NIL

CL-USER> (find-restart 'abort)
#<RESTART ABORT {7FFAE3DADC03}>

CL-USER> (restart-bind ((return-42 (lambda () 42)))
           (invoke-restart 'return-42))
42

CL-USER> (restart-bind ((always-visible (lambda ())))
           (format t "~&;; ~S~%" (find-restart 'always-visible)) nil)
;; #<RESTART ALWAYS-VISIBLE {7FFAE3DAD213}>
NIL

CL-USER> (flet ((report-always-visible (stream)
                 (write-string "Invoke the always visible restart." stream)))
           (restart-bind ((always-visible (lambda ()) :report-function #'report-always-
visible))
             (format t "~&;; ~A~%" (find-restart 'always-visible)) nil))
;; Invoke the always visible restart.
NIL

CL-USER> (restart-bind ((never-visible (lambda ()) :test-function (constantly nil)))
           (format t "~&;; ~S~%" (find-restart 'never-visible)) nil)
;; NIL
NIL

CL-USER> (flet ((query ()
                 (format *query-io* "~&;; Type a number: ")
                 (list (read *query-io*))))
           (restart-bind ((return-a-number #'identity :interactive-function #'query))
             (invoke-restart-interactively 'return-a-number)))
;; Type a number: 42                          ; user input here
42
```

# 5.4.2  Condition-restart association

## 5.4.2.1  Macro WITH-CONDITION-RESTARTS

- (with-condition-restarts condition restarts &body body) → result*

  - condition – a form, evaluated to produce a condition.

  - restarts – a form, evaluated to produce a list of restarts.

  - body – an implicit progn, evaluated to produce result*.

  - result – arbitrary Lisp data.

Evaluates body in a dynamic environment where the provided condition is associated with each of the provided restarts.

If the body forms return normally, results are the values returned from these forms.

**Examples**

```
CL-USER> (let ((toplevel-restarts (compute-restarts))
               (condition-1 (make-instance 'condition))
               (condition-2 (make-instance 'condition)))
           (restart-bind ((restart-1 (lambda ()))
                          (restart-2 (lambda ())))
             (with-condition-restarts condition-1 (list (find-restart 'restart-1))
             (with-condition-restarts condition-2 (list (find-restart 'restart-2))
               (format t ";; All restarts:~%")
               (format t ";; ~S~%" (mapcar #'restart-name
                                           (set-difference (compute-restarts)
                                                           toplevel-restarts)))
               (format t ";; Restarts applicable for condition-1:~%")
               (format t ";; ~S~%" (mapcar #'restart-name
                                           (set-difference (compute-restarts condition-1)
                                                           toplevel-restarts)))
               (format t ";; Restarts applicable for condition-2:~%")
               (format t ";; ~S~%" (mapcar #'restart-name
                                           (set-difference (compute-restarts condition-2)
                                                           toplevel-restarts)))))))
;; All restarts:
;; (RESTART-2 RESTART-1)
;; Restarts applicable for condition-1:
;; (RESTART-1)
```

```
;; Restarts applicable for condition-2:
;; (RESTART-2)
NIL
```

## 5.4.3  Restart macros

### 5.4.3.1  Macro RESTART-BIND

- (restart-bind (&rest bindings) &body body) → result*

    - bindings – a list of restart bindings.

    - body – an implicit progn, evaluated to produce result*.

    - result – arbitrary Lisp data.

- A restart binding: (name restart-function . options)

    - name – a symbol, not evaluated.

    - function – a form, evaluated to produce a restart function.

    - options – a property list.

Evaluates body in a dynamic environment where new restarts are established. The restarts are constructed based on the provided restart bindings. Each restart is given a name and a restart function based on the symbol and function passed to the restart binding.

The keys allowed for options are :interactive-function, :report-function, and test-function. Their values are evaluated to produce an interactive function, a report function, and a test function for the established restart:

- The interactive function must be a function of zero arguments that returns a list of arguments suitable to apply the restart function to. If not supplied, it is equivalent to (constantly '()).

- The test function must be a function that accepts a condition argument and returns a generalized boolean. If not supplied, it is equivalent to (constantly t).

- The report function must be a function that accepts a stream argument and writes the restart's report to that stream. If not supplied, the restart report is implementation-dependent.

If the body forms return normally, results are the values returned from these forms.

## 5.4.3.2 Macro RESTART-CASE

- `(restart-case form &rest cases)` → `result*`

    - `form` – a form, evaluated to produce `result*`.

    - `cases` – a list of restart cases.

    - `result` – arbitrary Lisp data.

- A restart case: `(name lambda-list &rest keywords-and-body)`

    - `name` – a symbol, not evaluated.

    - `lambda-list` – an ordinary lambda-list, not evaluated.

    - `keywords-and-body` – a list of keyword-value option pairs, followed by a list of body forms; the body forms are evaluated.

- Keyword-value option pairs: `&key interactive report test`

    - `interactive` – a symbol or a `lambda` form. May be supplied at most once.

    - `report` – a symbol, a string, or a `lambda` form. May be supplied at most once.

    - `test` – a symbol or a `lambda` form. May be supplied at most once.

Evaluates `body` in a dynamic environment where new restarts are established. The restarts are constructed based on the provided restart cases. Each restart is given a name based on the symbol passed to the restart case.

The restart function for each bound restart, upon being called, immediately transfers control to the restart case that is constructed based on the data passed to the macro; the arguments passed to the restart function are passed to the restart case, and the body of that restart case then produces the `results` that are returned from `restart-case`.

The values of keyword-value option pairs are used to produce an interactive function, a report function, and a test function for the established restart:

- The interactive function must be a function of zero arguments that returns a list of arguments suitable to apply the restart function to. If not supplied, it is equivalent to `(constantly '())`.

- The test function must be a function that accepts a condition argument and returns a generalized boolean. If not supplied, it is equivalent to (constantly t).

- The report function must be a function that accepts a stream argument and writes the restart's report to that stream. If not supplied, the restart report is implementation-dependent.

If form returns normally, results are the values returned from these forms.

## 5.4.3.3 Macro WITH-SIMPLE-RESTART

- (with-simple-restart (name format-control &rest format-arguments) &body body) → result*

  - name – a symbol.

  - format-control – a format control.

  - format-arguments – a list of arbitrary Lisp data.

  - result – arbitrary Lisp data.

Evaluates body in a dynamic environment where a new restart is established. The restart is constructed based on the provided name, and its report is constructed based on the provided format control and arguments.

If the restart is invoked, control is immediately transferred outside the body of with-simple-restart, returning two values: nil and t. Otherwise, if the body forms return normally, results are the values returned from these forms.

### Examples

```
CL-USER> (restart-bind ((new-restart (lambda () (format t "~&;;
New restart!~%")))) 
         (format t "~&;; ~S~%" (find-restart 'new-restart)))
;; #<RESTART NEW-RESTART {7FFAE3DAD213}>
NIL

CL-USER> (restart-bind ((new-restart (lambda () (format t "~&;;
New restart!~%")))) 
         (invoke-restart 'new-restart)
         42)
;; New restart!
42
```

```
CL-USER> (restart-case (progn (format t "~&;; ~S~%" (find-restart
'new-restart)) 42)
          (new-restart () (format t "~&;; New restart!~%") 24))
;; #<RESTART NEW-RESTART {7FFAE3DAD1D3}>
42

CL-USER> (restart-case (progn (invoke-restart 'new-restart) 42)
          (new-restart () (format t "~&;; New restart!~%") 24))
;; New restart!
24

CL-USER> (with-simple-restart (new-restart "Invoke the new restart.")
          (format t "~&;; ~S~%" (find-restart 'new-restart)))
;; #<RESTART NEW-RESTART {7FFAE3DAD1D3}>
NIL

CL-USER> (with-simple-restart (new-restart "Invoke the new restart.")
          (format t "~&;; ~A~%" (find-restart 'new-restart)))
;; Invoke the new restart.
NIL

CL-USER> (with-simple-restart (new-restart "Invoke the new restart.")
          (invoke-restart 'new-restart))
NIL
T
```

# 5.4.4  Standard restarts

## 5.4.4.1  Restart ABORT

- Arguments: ()

Aborts the currently executing action by means of transferring control.

An abort restart of some kind should always be established by the Lisp environment.

## 5.4.4.2  Restart MUFFLE-WARNING

- Arguments: ()

Transfers control back into warn in order to inform it that the warning condition has been accounted for and no further handling is needed.

## 5.4.4.3  Restart CONTINUE

- Arguments: ()

Continues the action in case of situations where a single defined way to continue exists, such as in case of cerror or break.

## 5.4.4.4  Restart STORE-VALUE

- Arguments: (value)

  - value – arbitrary Lisp data.

Uses the provided value to recover from an error. The value is then stored for permanent use.

## 5.4.4.5  Restart USE-VALUE

- Arguments: (value)

  - value – arbitrary Lisp data.

Uses the provided value to recover from an error. The value is not stored for any kind of permanent use afterward.

## 5.4.4.6  Function ABORT, CONTINUE, MUFFLE-WARNING, USE-VALUE, STORE-VALUE

- (abort &optional condition) → |

- (muffle-warning &optional condition) → |

- (continue &optional condition) → nil

- (store-value value &optional condition) → nil

- (use-value value &optional condition) → nil

  - condition – a condition.

  - value – arbitrary Lisp datum.

Finds the newest established active restart with the same name as the function, as if via `find-restart`. If no such restart is found, `abort` and `muffle-warning` signal a `control-error`, while `continue`, `store-value`, and `use-value` return `nil`. If such a restart exists, it is invoked— in case of `store-value` and `use-value`, with the provided `value` argument.

If `condition` is non-`nil`, then the restart search skip restarts associated with conditions other than `condition`.

**Examples**

```
CL-USER> (handler-bind ((error #'abort))
           (+ 2 :two))
;; Evaluation aborted on TYPE-ERROR: The value :TWO is not of type NUMBER.

CL-USER> (handler-bind ((warning #'muffle-warning))
           (warn "Example warning."))
NIL

CL-USER> (handler-bind ((error #'continue))
           (cerror "Continue." "Example error."))
NIL

CL-USER> (handler-bind ((type-error (lambda (c) (declare (ignore c)) (store-value 42))))
           (let ((x "42")) (check-type x integer)))
NIL
```

# 5.4.5  Defining and instantiating conditions

## 5.4.5.1  Macro DEFINE-CONDITION

- (define-condition name (&rest parent-types) (&rest slot-specifiers) &key default-initargs documentation report) → name

  - `name` – a symbol, not evaluated.

  - `parent-types` – a list of symbols naming condition types, not evaluated. If empty, defaults to a list containing `condition`.

  - `slot-specifiers` – a list of slot specifiers.

  - `default-initargs` – a list of default initialization arguments, whose elements are evaluated when the condition object is instantiated. May be supplied at most once.

- documentation – a string, not evaluated. May be supplied at most once.

- report – a symbol, a string, or a `lambda` form. May be supplied at most once.

- A slot specifier: `slot-name` or (`slot-name &key reader writer accessor allocation initarg initform type`)

  - reader – a symbol, not evaluated. May be supplied multiple times.

  - writer – a symbol or a `setf` function name, not evaluated. May be supplied multiple times.

  - accessor – a symbol, not evaluated. May be supplied multiple times.

  - allocation – either `:instance` or `:class`, not evaluated. May be supplied at most once.

  - initarg – a symbol, not evaluated. May be supplied multiple times.

  - initform – a form, evaluated when the condition object is instantiated. May be supplied at most once.

  - type – a type specifier, not evaluated. May be supplied at most once.

Defines a new condition type named `name` with `parent-types` as its supertypes, slots described by `slot-specifiers`, and optional `default-initargs`, `documentation`, and `report`. Works like `defclass`, with the exception of the additional `:report` option and a lack of `:metaclass` option.

Each slot specified in `slot-specifiers` gets one reader function for each provided `:reader`, each writer function for each provided `:writer`, and a reader function and a `setf` writer function for each provided `:accessor`. The slot may be allocated on the `:instance` (separate values for each condition; default) or on the `:class` (single shared value across all objects). The slot may have multiple `:initargs` which are usable in `make-condition` and a single `:initform` that is used when no `:initarg` is used its value is evaluated and used for initializing the slot. Optionally, `:type` can be provided to declare the type of the slot.

It is possible to specify a list of default initialization arguments for the condition type via `:default-initargs`, a documentation string via `:documentation`, and a condition report via `:report`.

## 5.4.5.2  Function MAKE-CONDITION

- (make-condition condition-type &rest arguments) → condition

    - condition-type – a symbol naming a condition type.

    - arguments – a list of keyword-value pairs suitable for initializing the condition object.

    - condition – a condition.

Creates and returns an instance of condition type condition, initialized with arguments.

**Examples**

```
CL-USER> (define-condition foo-condition () ())
FOO-CONDITION

CL-USER> (make-condition 'foo-condition)
#<FOO-CONDITION {1018A1FED3}>

CL-USER> (typep (make-condition 'foo-condition) 'condition)
T
```

Readers, writers, accessors:

```
CL-USER> (define-condition bar-condition ()
           ((bar-slot :reader bar-slot-reader
                      :writer bar-slot-writer
                      :accessor bar-slot-accessor)))
BAR-CONDITION

CL-USER> (defvar *bar-condition* (make-condition 'bar-condition))
*BAR-CONDITION*

CL-USER> (bar-slot-writer 42 *bar-condition*)
42

CL-USER> (bar-slot-reader *bar-condition*)
42

CL-USER> (setf (bar-slot-accessor *bar-condition*) :forty-two)
:FORTY-TWO

CL-USER> (bar-slot-accessor *bar-condition*)
:FORTY-TWO
```

Slot inheritance:

```
CL-USER> (define-condition also-bar-condition (bar-condition) ())
ALSO-BAR-CONDITION

CL-USER> (defvar *also-bar-condition* (make-condition 'also-bar-condition))
*ALSO-BAR-CONDITION*

CL-USER> (setf (bar-slot-accessor *also-bar-condition*) :also-42)
:ALSO-42

CL-USER> (bar-slot-accessor *also-bar-condition*)
:ALSO-42
```

Initialization arguments, initialization forms, and default initialization arguments:

```
CL-USER> (define-condition baz-condition ()
          ((baz-slot :accessor baz-slot :initarg :baz-slot :initform :nothing)))
BAZ-CONDITION

CL-USER> (baz-slot (make-condition 'baz-condition))
:NOTHING

CL-USER> (baz-slot (make-condition 'baz-condition :baz-slot :something))
:SOMETHING

CL-USER> (define-condition fred-condition ()
          ((fred-slot :initarg :fred-slot :reader fred-slot))
          (:default-initargs :fred-slot "Roses are red"))
FRED-CONDITION

CL-USER> (fred-slot (make-condition 'fred-condition))
"Roses are red"

CL-USER> (fred-slot (make-condition 'fred-condition :fred-slot "Violets are blue"))
"Violets are blue"
```

Class-allocated slots:

```
CL-USER> (define-condition quux-condition (foo-condition)
          ((quux-slot :accessor quux-slot :allocation :class)))
QUUX-CONDITION

CL-USER> (defvar *quux-condition-1* (make-condition 'quux-condition))
*QUUX-CONDITION-1*
```

```
CL-USER> (defvar *quux-condition-2* (make-condition 'quux-condition))
*QUUX-CONDITION-2*

CL-USER> (setf (quux-slot *quux-condition-1*) :something)
:SOMETHING

CL-USER> (quux-slot *quux-condition-2*)
:SOMETHING
```

Reports and documentation strings:

```
CL-USER> (define-condition yiip-condition () ()
          (:report "A YIIP-CONDITION was signaled. Yiip!")
          (:documentation "A condition type representing yiips. Yiip!"))
YIIP-CONDITION

CL-USER> (princ-to-string (make-condition 'yiip-condition))
"A YIIP-CONDITION was signaled. Yiip!"

CL-USER> (documentation 'yiip-condition 'type)
"A condition type representing yiips. Yiip!"
```

# 5.4.6  Assertions

## 5.4.6.1  Macro ASSERT

- (assert test-form &optional places datum &rest arguments) → nil

  - test-form – a form, evaluated each time the assertion is tried and
    retried.

  - places – a list of places. Subforms of each place may be evaluated
    multiple times when assert signals an error.

  - datum, arguments – condition designators suitable for passing to
    error.

Evaluates test-form and checks whether it returned a true value. If not, an error is
signaled; if datum and arguments are passed to assert, they are used to construct the error
condition.

In addition to signaling an error, assert establishes a continue restart that allows the
user to set new values to the provided places before the assertion is retried.

## 5.4.6.2 Macro CHECK-TYPE

- `(check-type place type &optional type-string)`

  - `place` – a place. Its subforms may be evaluated multiple times when `check-type` signals an error.

  - `type` – a type specifier, not evaluated.

  - `type-string` – a string, evaluated.

Evaluates `place` and checks whether the value it returned is of type `type`. If not, a `type-error` is signaled; if `type-string` is provided, it is used to report the error.

In addition to signaling an error, `check-type` establishes a `store-value` restart that allows the user to set new values to the provided place before the assertion is retried.

## 5.4.6.3 Macro ECASE, ETYPECASE, CCASE, CTYPECASE

- `(ecase keyplace &rest cases)` → `result*`

- `(etypecase keyplace &rest cases)` → `result*`

- `(ccase keyplace &rest cases)` → `result*`

- `(ctypecase keyplace &rest cases)` → `result*`

  - `keyplace` – a form, evaluated once. In case of `ccase` and `ctypecase`, used as a place if the `store-value` restart is invoked, and its subforms may be evaluated multiple times when an error is signaled by the assertion.

  - `cases` – a list of cases.

- An `ecase`/`ccase` case: `(key-or-keys &rest forms)`

  - `key-or-keys` – a list of keys, or an atom that denotes a one-element list containing that atom as a key.

  - `forms` – an implicit progn, evaluated to produce `result*` if the given case matches.

275

- An etypecase/ctypecase case: (type &rest forms)

    - type – a type specifier.

    - forms – an implicit progn, evaluated to produce result* if the given case matches.

Evaluates keyplace and checks whether or not its value matches any of the provided cases. For ecase and ccase, the value needs to be eql to any of the provided keys; for etypecase and ctypecase, the value needs to be of one of the provided types. If no match is found, a type-error is signaled.

Additionally, ccase and ctypecase establish a store-value restart which allows the user to correct the error by providing a value to be stored in place before the assertion is retried.

**Examples**

General assertions:

```
CL-USER> (let ((x 42)) (assert (= x 42)))
NIL

CL-USER> (let ((x 24)) (assert (= x 42) (x) "X is ~A, not 42." 42))
;; Debugger level 1 entered on SIMPLE-ERROR:
;; X is 24, not 42.
;; Type :HELP for available commands.
[1] Debug> (continue)                              ; user input here
;; The old value of X is 24.
;; Do you want to supply a new value?  (y or n) y   ; user input here
;; Type a form to be evaluated:
42                                                 ; user input here
NIL

CL-USER> (let ((x 42)) (check-type x integer))
NIL

CL-USER> (let ((x :forty-two)) (check-type x integer) x)
;; Debugger level 1 entered on SIMPLE-TYPE-ERROR:
;; The value of X is :FORTY-TWO, which is not of type INTEGER.
;; Type :HELP for available commands.
[1] Debug> (store-value 42)                        ; user input here
42
```

Non-correctable case assertions:

```
CL-USER> (ecase 42 (42 :ok))
:OK

CL-USER> (ecase 24 (42 :ok))
;; Debugger level 1 entered on SB-KERNEL:CASE-FAILURE:
;; 24 fell through ECASE expression. Wanted one of (42).
;; Type :HELP for available commands.
[1] Debug> (abort)                                       ; user input here
;; Evaluation aborted on TYPE-ERROR: The value 24 is not of type (MEMBER 42).

CL-USER> (etypecase 42 (number :ok))
:OK

CL-USER> (etypecase 42 (keyword :ok))
;; Debugger level 1 entered on SB-KERNEL:CASE-FAILURE:
;; 42 fell through ETYPECASE expression. Wanted one of (KEYWORD).
;; Type :HELP for available commands.
[1] Debug> (abort)                                       ; user input here
;; Evaluation aborted on TYPE-ERROR: The value 42 is not of type (OR KEYWORD).
```

Correctable case assertions:

```
CL-USER> (let ((x 42)) (ccase x (42 :ok)))
:OK

CL-USER> (let ((x 24)) (ccase x (42 :ok)))
;; Debugger level 1 entered on SB-KERNEL:CASE-FAILURE:
;; 24 fell through CCASE expression. Wanted one of (42).
;; Type :HELP for available commands.
[1] Debug> (store-value 42)                              ; user input here
:OK

CL-USER> (let ((x 24)) (ctypecase x (number :ok)))
:OK

CL-USER> (let ((x 24)) (ctypecase x (keyword :ok)))
;; Debugger level 1 entered on SB-KERNEL:CASE-FAILURE:
;; 24 fell through CTYPECASE expression. Wanted one of (KEYWORD).
;; Type :HELP for available commands.
[1] Debug> (store-value :forty-two)                      ; user input here
:OK
```

# 5.4.7  Condition signaling

## 5.4.7.1  Function SIGNAL

- (signal datum &rest arguments) → nil

  - datum, arguments – condition designators:

    - If datum is a condition object, arguments must be nil.

    - If datum is a symbol naming a condition type, arguments must be a list of keyword-value pairs suitable for initializing the condition object.

    - If datum is a format control or a formatter function, arguments must be a list of format arguments matching the format control or formatter function.

Signals the condition resulting from coercing datum and arguments to a condition. Returns nil if control was not transferred by any handler.

The handlers are searched sequentially from most recent binding form to last and within a single binding form from first handler to last.

## 5.4.7.2  Function WARN

- (warn datum &rest arguments) → nil

  - datum, arguments – condition designators for a warning condition:

    - If datum is a condition object, arguments must be nil.

    - If datum is a symbol naming a condition type, arguments must be a list of keyword-value pairs suitable for initializing the condition object.

    - If datum is a format control or a formatter function, arguments must be a list of format arguments matching the format control or formatter function.

Establishes a muffle-warning restart and signals the condition resulting from coercing datum and arguments to a condition. If the muffle-warning restart is invoked, returns nil. Otherwise, reports the condition to *error-output* and returns nil if control was not transferred by any handler.

## 5.4.7.3 Function ERROR

- (error datum &rest arguments) → |

  - datum, arguments – condition designators:

    - If datum is a condition object, arguments must be nil.

    - If datum is a symbol naming a condition type, arguments must be a list of keyword-value pairs suitable for initializing the condition object.

    - If datum is a format control or a formatter function, arguments must be a list of format arguments matching the format control or formatter function.

Signals the condition resulting from coercing datum and arguments to a condition. Invokes the debugger if control was not transferred by any handler.

## 5.4.7.4 Function CERROR

- (cerror format-control datum &rest arguments) → nil

  - format-control – a format control.

  - datum, arguments – condition designators:

    - If datum is a condition object, arguments must be nil.

    - If datum is a symbol naming a condition type, arguments must be a list of keyword-value pairs suitable for initializing the condition object.

    - If datum is a format control or a formatter function, arguments must be a list of format arguments matching the format control or formatter function.

Signals the condition resulting from coercing datum and arguments to a condition. Establishes a continue restart and invokes the debugger if control was not transferred by any handler. arguments is additionally passed with format-control as a list of format arguments to report the established continue restart.

## Examples

Signaling:

```
CL-USER> (signal 'condition)
NIL

CL-USER> (warn 'warning)
;; WARNING: Condition WARNING was signaled.
NIL

CL-USER> (error 'error)
;; Debugger level 1 entered on ERROR:
;; Condition ERROR was signaled.
;; Type :HELP for available commands.
[1] Debug> (abort)                                ; user input here
;; Evaluation aborted on ERROR: Condition ERROR was signaled.

CL-USER> (cerror "Continue." 'error)
;; Debugger level 1 entered on ERROR:
;; Condition ERROR was signaled.
;; Type :HELP for available commands.
[1] Debug> (continue)                             ; user input here
NIL
```

Different data coercible to conditions:

```
CL-USER> (warn 'warning)
;; WARNING: Condition WARNING was signaled.
NIL

CL-USER> (warn (make-condition 'warning))
;; WARNING: Condition WARNING was signaled.
NIL

CL-USER> (warn "Warning: ~A." :something-scary)
;; WARNING: Warning: SOMETHING-SCARY.
NIL

CL-USER> (warn (lambda (stream argument) (format stream "Warning: ~A." argument))
:something-scary)
;; WARNING: Warning: SOMETHING-SCARY.
NIL
```

# 5.4.8  Handler macros

## 5.4.8.1  Macro HANDLER-BIND

- `(handler-bind (&rest bindings) &body body)` → result*
  - `bindings` – a list of handler bindings.
  - `body` – an implicit `progn`, evaluated to produce `result*`.
  - `result` – arbitrary Lisp data.
- A restart binding: `(type function)`
  - `type` – a type designator, not evaluated.
  - `function` – a form, evaluated to produce a handler function.

Evaluates `body` in a dynamic environment where new handlers are established. The handlers are provided based on the provided handler bindings. Each handler is created based on the provided type designator and handler function.

Any conditions signaled from within a handler body will only be able to invoke handlers established outside the `handler-bind` form that bound it.

If the `body` forms return normally, `results` are the values returned from these forms.

## 5.4.8.2  Macro HANDLER-CASE

- `(handler-case form &rest cases)` → result*
  - `form` – a form, evaluated to produce `result*`.
  - `cases` – a list of handler cases.
  - `result` – arbitrary Lisp data.
- A handler case: `(name lambda-list &rest body)`
  - `name` – a symbol, not evaluated.
  - `lambda-list` – an ordinary lambda-list, not evaluated. Must be either empty or contain a single required argument.
  - `body` – a list of body forms, evaluated.

Evaluates body in a dynamic environment where new handlers are established. The handlers are provided based on the provided handler bindings. Each handler is created based on the provided type designator and handler function.

The handler function for each bound handler, upon being called, immediately transfers control to the handler case that is constructed based on the data passed to the macro. If the lambda list is non-empty, then the condition passed to the handler function is passed to the handler case. The body of that handler case then produces the results that are returned from handler-case.

Any conditions signaled from within a handler case will only be able to invoke handlers established outside the handler-case form that bound it.

A single handler case with name :no-error may be provided. This case will be executed when form returns normally. The values returned by form are passed as arguments to the :no-error case, and results are the values returned by the body of that case.

When there is no :no-error case, if form returns normally, results are the values returned from these forms.

## 5.4.8.3 Macro IGNORE-ERRORS

- (ignore-errors &body body) → result*

  - body – an implicit progn; evaluated.

  - result – arbitrary Lisp data.

Evaluates body in a dynamic environment where a new error handler is established. If that handler is invoked, control is immediately transferred outside the body of with-simple-restart, returning two values: nil and the condition object the handler was invoked with. Otherwise, if the body forms return normally, then results are the values returned from these forms.

**Examples**

```
CL-USER> (handler-bind ((condition (lambda (c) (format t "~&;; ~A~%" c) 24)))
           (signal 'condition)
           42)
;; Condition CONDITION was signaled.
42
```

```
CL-USER> (handler-case (progn (signal 'condition) 42)
           (condition (c) (format t "~&;; ~A~%" c) 24))
;; Condition CONDITION was signaled.
24

CL-USER> (handler-case 42
           (:no-error (x) (format t "~&;; No error: ~A~%" x)))
;; No error: 42
NIL
```

# 5.4.9  Condition types

## 5.4.9.1  Condition Type CONDITION

- Class precedence list: `condition, t`

The base condition type; a supertype for all condition types.

## 5.4.9.2  Condition Type WARNING

- Class precedence list: `warning, condition, t`

The base warning type; a supertype for all warning types.

## 5.4.9.3  Condition Type STYLE-WARNING

- Class precedence list: `style-warning, warning, condition, t`

The warning type representing situations which involve code that is conformant but that is considered to be of poor quality by the Lisp implementation.

## 5.4.9.4  Condition Type SERIOUS-CONDITION

- Class precedence list: `serious-condition, condition, t`

The condition type representing all situations that require handling or interactive programmer intervention. These situations may happen due to programming errors or limitations of software or hardware that prevent the program from continuing execution.

## 5.4.9.5  Condition Type ERROR

- Class precedence list: `error, serious-condition, condition, t`

The condition type representing all erroneous program situations; a supertype for all error types.

## 5.4.9.6  Condition Type SIMPLE-CONDITION

- Class precedence list: `simple-condition, condition, t`
- Argument: format control
  - Type: a format control.
  - Initialization argument: `:format-control`
  - Reader function: `simple-condition-format-control`
- Argument: format arguments
  - Type: a list.
  - Initialization argument: `:format-argument`
  - Default value: `'()`
  - Reader function: `simple-condition-format-arguments`

The condition type representing conditions whose reporting is driven by a format control and format arguments.

## 5.4.9.7  Condition Type SIMPLE-WARNING

- Class precedence list: `simple-warning, simple-condition, warning, condition, t`

The condition type representing warnings whose reporting is driven by a format control and format arguments.

## 5.4.9.8  Condition Type SIMPLE-ERROR

- Class precedence list: `simple-error, simple-condition, error, serious-condition condition, t`

The condition type representing errors whose reporting is driven by a format control and format arguments.

## 5.4.9.9  Condition Type STORAGE-CONDITION

- Class precedence list: `storage-condition, serious-condition, condition, t`

The condition type representing serious conditions related to implementation-, software-, and hardware-dependent limits that affect program execution.

## 5.4.9.10  Condition Type TYPE-ERROR

- Class precedence list: `type-error, error, serious-condition, condition, t`
- Argument: datum
    - Type: arbitrary Lisp datum.
    - Initialization argument: `:datum`
    - Reader function: `type-error-datum`
- Argument: expected type
    - Type: a type designator.
    - Initialization argument: `:expected-type`
    - Reader function: `type-error-expected-type`

The error type representing situations where a Lisp object is not of the expected type.

## 5.4.9.11  Condition Type SIMPLE-TYPE-ERROR

- Class precedence list: `simple-error, simple-condition, type-error, error, serious-condition condition, t`

The error type representing type errors whose reporting is driven by a format control and format arguments.

## 5.4.9.12  Condition Type CONTROL-ERROR

- Class precedence list: control-error, error, serious-condition, condition, t

The error type representing errors resulting from attempts to perform an invalid non-local transfer of control within the program.

## 5.4.9.13  Condition Type PROGRAM-ERROR

- Class precedence list: program-error, error, serious-condition, condition, t

The error type representing errors resulting from attempts to execute Lisp code with invalid syntax.

## 5.4.9.14  Condition Type CELL-ERROR

- Class precedence list: cell-error, error, serious-condition, condition, t
- Argument: name of the offending location
  - Type: arbitrary Lisp data.
  - Initialization argument: :name
  - Reader function: cell-error-name

The error type representing erroneous access to locations.

## 5.4.9.15  Condition Type UNBOUND-VARIABLE

- Class precedence list: unbound-variable, cell-error, error, serious-condition, condition, t

The cell error type representing errors resulting from attempts to reference an unbound variable.

## 5.4.9.16  Condition Type UNDEFINED-FUNCTION

- Class precedence list: undefined-functions, cell-error, error, serious-condition, condition, t

The cell error type representing errors resulting from attempts to reference an undefined function.

## 5.4.9.17  Condition Type UNBOUND-SLOT

- Class precedence list: unbound-slot, cell-error, error, serious-condition, condition, t
- Argument: the instance whose slot is unbound
  - Type: arbitrary Lisp datum.
  - Initialization argument: :instance
  - Reader function: unbound-slot-instance

The cell error type representing errors resulting from attempts to reference an unbound slot of an instance.

## 5.4.9.18  Condition Type STREAM-ERROR

- Class precedence list: stream-error, error, serious-condition, condition, t
- Argument: the offending stream
  - Type: a stream.
  - Initialization argument: :stream
  - Reader function: stream-error-stream

The error type representing errors related to performing I/O on a stream.

## 5.4.9.19  Condition Type END-OF-FILE

- Class precedence list: end-of-file, stream-error, error, serious-condition, condition, t

The stream error type representing errors resulting from attempts to read from streams that have no more data to be read.

## 5.4.9.20  Condition Type PARSE-ERROR

- Class precedence list: parse-error, error, serious-condition, condition, t

The error type representing parsing errors.

## 5.4.9.21  Condition Type READER-ERROR

- Class precedence list: `reader-error`, `parse-error`, `stream-error`, `error`, `serious-condition`, `condition`, `t`

The parse error type representing errors in operation of the Lisp reader.

## 5.4.9.22  Condition Type PACKAGE-ERROR

- Class precedence list: `package-error`, `error`, `serious-condition`, `condition`, `t`
- Argument: the offending package
  - Type: a package designator.
  - Initialization argument: `:package`
  - Reader function: `package-error-package`

The error type representing errors related to package operations.

## 5.4.9.23  Condition Type FILE-ERROR

- Class precedence list: `file-error`, `error`, `serious-condition`, `condition`, `t`
- Argument: the offending pathname
  - Type: a pathname.
  - Initialization argument: `:pathname`
  - Reader function: `file-error-pathname`

The error type representing errors related to operating on files.

## 5.4.9.24  Condition Type PRINT-NOT-READABLE

- Class precedence list: `print-not-readable`, `error`, `serious-condition`, `condition`, `t`
- Argument: the object that is unable to be printed readably
  - Type: arbitrary Lisp datum.
  - Initialization argument: `:object`
  - Reader function: `print-not-readable-object`

The error type representing errors resulting from situations where it is impossible to print an object readably (when *print-readably* is true).

## 5.4.9.25  Condition Type ARITHMETIC-ERROR

- Class precedence list: arithmetic-error, error, serious-condition, condition, t

- Argument: operation

  - Type: a function designator.

  - Initialization argument: :operation

  - Reader function: arithmetic-error-operation

- Argument: operands

  - Type: a list.

  - Initialization argument: :operands

  - Reader function: arithmetic-error-operands

The error type representing errors while performing number arithmetic.

## 5.4.9.26  Condition Type DIVISION-BY-ZERO

- Class precedence list: division-by-zero, arithmetic-error, error, serious-condition, condition, t

The arithmetic error type representing errors resulting from attempts to divide by zero.

In practice, signaled when division by integer zero is attempted or when the IEEE floating point exception "Division by Zero" is signaled.

## 5.4.9.27  Condition Type FLOATING-POINT-INVALID-OPERATION

- Class precedence list: floating-point-invalid-operation, arithmetic-error, error, serious-condition, condition, t

The arithmetic error type representing floating point exceptions related to invalid operations.

In practice, signaled when the IEEE floating point exception "Invalid Operation" is signaled.

## 5.4.9.28  Condition Type FLOATING-POINT-INEXACT

- Class precedence list: `floating-point-inexact, arithmetic-error, error, serious-condition, condition, t`

The arithmetic error type representing floating point exceptions related to inexact result. In practice, signaled when the IEEE floating point exception "Inexact" is signaled.

## 5.4.9.29  Condition Type FLOATING-POINT-UNDERFLOW

- Class precedence list: `floating-point-underflow, arithmetic-error, error, serious-condition, condition, t`

The arithmetic error type representing underflow floating point exceptions.
In practice, signaled when the IEEE floating point exception "Underflow" is signaled.

## 5.4.9.30  Condition Type FLOATING-POINT-OVERFLOW

- Class precedence list: `floating-point-overflow, arithmetic-error, error, serious-condition, condition, t`

The arithmetic error type representing overflow floating point exceptions.
In practice, signaled when the IEEE floating point exception "Overflow" is signaled.

**Examples**

```
CL-USER> (error (make-condition 'division-by-zero :operation '/ :operands '(1 0)))
;; Debugger level 1 entered on DIVISION-BY-ZERO:
;; Attempted to divide by zero: (/ 1 0)
;; Type :HELP for available commands.
[1] Debug> (abort)                                  ; user input here
; Evaluation aborted on DIVISION-BY-ZERO: Attempted to divide by zero: (/ 1 0)
```

# 5.4.10  Debugger invocation

## 5.4.10.1  Variable *BREAK-ON-SIGNALS*

- Value type: a type specifier.

- Initial value: `nil`

Describes a condition type for which signaling forms will enter the debugger via `break` before proceeding with signaling the condition.

## 5.4.10.2  Variable *DEBUGGER-HOOK*

- Value type: `nil` or a function designator for a function of two arguments.

- Initial value: `nil`

When non-`nil`, this function is called before the normal entry to the debugger. This function must accept two arguments: one that is the condition with which the debugger is attempted to be entered and the value of `*debugger-hook*` prior to entering the debugger. (At the time of calling the function, `*debugger-hook*` is bound to `nil` and its value is passed as the second argument to the function.)

## 5.4.10.3  Function BREAK

- `(break &optional format-control &rest format-arguments)` → nil

  - `format-control` – a format control.

  - `format-arguments` – a list of arbitrary Lisp data.

Binds `*debugger-hook*` to `nil`, establishes a `continue` restart, and enters the debugger. If the `continue` restart is invoked, `break` returns `nil`.

The format control and arguments, if provided, are used to report the condition with which the debugger is entered.

## 5.4.10.4  Function INVOKE-DEBUGGER

- `(invoke-debugger condition)` → |

  - `condition` – a condition.

Calls the `*debugger-hook*`, if any. If the hook function does not exist or returns normally, enters the debugger with the provided condition.

**Examples**

```
CL-USER> (let ((*break-on-signals* 'condition))
          (signal 'condition))
;; Debugger level 1 entered on SIMPLE-CONDITION:
;; Condition CONDITION was signaled.
;; BREAK was entered because of *BREAK-ON-SIGNALS* (now rebound to NIL).
```

```
;; Type :HELP for available commands.
[1] Debug> (continue)                                    ; user input here
NIL

CL-USER> (block nil
           (let ((*debugger-hook* (lambda (condition hook)
                                    (declare (ignore condition hook))
                                    (return 42))))
             (invoke-debugger (make-condition 'condition))))
42

CL-USER> (break "Breaking with ~S." 42)
;; Debugger level 1 entered on SIMPLE-CONDITION:
;; Breaking with 42.
;; Type :HELP for available commands.
[1] Debug> (continue)                                    ; user input here
NIL

CL-USER> (invoke-debugger (make-condition 'condition))
;; Debugger level 1 entered on CONDITION:
;; Condition CONDITION was signaled.
;; Type :HELP for available commands.
[1] Debug> (abort)                                       ; user input here
;; Evaluation aborted on CONDITION: Condition CONDITION was signaled.
```

# Index

Printed in the United States
By Bookmasters